Heroes of Hope

By

Primus S. Butler

2012

(previously published in 2009 i Tooele County, Utah)

PRESS

Heroes of Hope
A ranking of 52 people who changed the world by daring to hope
by Primus S. Butler

Printed in the United States of America

ISBN 9781624198427

www.xulonpress.com

Charlie,
I will always
be honored to count
you among my early
readers.

Rino

J. Butler
2017

*D*edicated readers may want to get the C.D. Or even the 2009 version which after Xulon distributes it could become the "souvenir edition."

The book had about eighteen different pages and the study questions, defined words and *glossary-positive mentions*. Heroes of Hope is a text, solely the responsibility of the writer, and I'm grateful for Internet distributors like Xulon who will allow it to reach a wider market. This is, however, a short text which touches many themes and subjects, so I hope this book is beneficial even in its smaller topics of self help and amateur counseling, Americana, the concept of democracy and the U.S. republic and disabilities are also pertinent topics. In the writer's estimation the two main topics are history and religious studies. In all seriousness I'm blessed for every reader I get, and hope and pray for me as I take myself to be a serious writer and intend to do more serious as well as enjoyable material as my career progresses.

(IF YOU @ XULON do this-you may even want to *instead of saying that put the topics in order like)-1. Hope, in history 2. history, American 3. religious studies 4 hope in Christianity 5 self-help, counseling-Biblical perspective 6.Americana 7. democracy-American republic, influence in the world 8. disabilities (I may be the only reader who like to read this feature in some books-but it sometimes comes in handy especially to a writer)*

Heroes of Hope is dedicated to Dr. W. Charles Harris, distinguished professor (emeritus) of Bible and pastoral studies at Central Bible College, one of the greatest institutions of its kind anywhere in the world. My friend and teacher, Dr. Harris has done more than his part to teach the next generation of ministers for three and a half decades. With others, he was responsible for my getting a good enough education to write this and other books which should get better as my readers get more numerous. True to the initial of the Christian name he uses, he was also known for giving "C"s but I got an "A" on every test I remember, from him. I did not, however get "A's" on papers which require good typing and physical presentation I often botched with spelling and typing mistakes. Thank God, that starting with spell check I will have good presentation for this book once the good people at Xulon print it.

I also thank Roger Baker who helped get the names on C.D. form so this could be undertaken as a multiple-dimensions work and Charlie Roberts for his computer work. I thank Brad Rowland and Andy Roberson who helped proofread the document. Thanks to my cousin Jacob DeLeonardis, the book was printed in timely fashion, and two other people who since then helped make it a reality, Dr. Larry Keefauver, a writer I strive to emulate and Scott Treloar at Xulon who made the marketability product understandable for this writer with no business experience.

TOP 52 heroes of Hope where Documented-August 2006-renewed-2012

Aces; Winston Churchill of spades C.S. Lewis Clubs Martin Luther King-hearts AND Ace of of diamonds Norman Vincent Peale

The Kings; Billy Graham is the King of Hearts Dan Quayle K O Diamonds Clarence Thomas CLUBS and Woodrow Wilson Spades

The Queens of hope; Margaret Thatcher spades Helen Keller Diamonds Joan of Arc Hearts Mother Teresa is the Queen of Clubs

Jacks:Pat Boone-Spades Hearts Abe Lincoln Ronald Reagan Diamonds Theodore Roosevelt-Clubs

10s Dr. Laura Schlesinger diamonds Pat Robertson Spades and 10of hearts Alan Keyes AND Billy Fiske is 10 of Clubs

9s Clubs-Orrin Hatch Spades-Zell Miller Hearts Joni Earakson Tada Diamonds-S. I. Hayakawa

8 Spades-Dave Reover Clubs Harry S Truman Hearts David Ben Gurion Diamonds-Rush Limbaugh

7 Spades-Tony Blair Clubs Cardinal O'Connor Hearts William Wilberforce Diamonds-George Marshall

6s Spades-**William Jennings Bryan Clubs** James Dobson **Hearts Ben Kinchlow Diamonds Queen Wilhelmina**

The Fives:Spades Jerry Falwell Clubs-Richard Simmons Hearts Edward Flanagan Diamonds William McKinley

The Fours Spades-Lech Walesa Clubs-Fanny J. Crosby Hearts Christian X AND Diamonds-Douglas Macarthur

Threes-Spades Bob Dole Clubs-Whittaker Chambers Hearts-Nathan Hale Diamonds-Herbert Hoover

The Twos:Spades-Branch Rickey Clubs Condolezza Rice Hearts Florence Nightingale Diamonds-Elizabeth Blackwell

NOTE ON Heroes of Hope The naming each individual relative to a deck of cards is in the hope I can market 3 products-this book, the CD, and the cards with pictures. Since each hero is its own "Chapter" and each chapter a deck of the cards, the book does not have a formal index. The introduction on hope gives it fifty-three "chapters" and I hope you read the after-materials. It will start with The workbook format as quizzes-to give those of you who want a chance to test your memory of what you read. It is followed by an explanation on those who were heroes during exceptional times as well as the Also-rans, near misses, definitions, and glossary.

Table of Contents

                                                      page numbers
Introduction: ON Hope xiii

 1 Winston Churchill-Ace of Spades of Hope 17
 2 C.S. Lewis Ace of Clubs of Hope 23
 3 Martin Luther King, JR Ace of Hearts 28
 4 Norman Vincent Peale Ace of Diamonds 31
 5 Margaret Thatcher 36
 6 Clarence Thomas 43
 7 Dan Quayle 48
 8 Billy Graham 54
 9 Helen Keller 60
10 Woodrow Wilson 63
11 Joan Of Arc 68
12 Mother Teresa 72
13 Abraham Lincoln 76
14 Ronald Reagan 79
15 Theodore Roosevelt 85
16 Pat Boone 90
17 Pat Robertson 97
18 Alan Keyes 105
19 DR Laura Schlesinger 109
20 Billy Fiske 115
21 Joni Earaskson Tada 118
22 S. I. Hayakawa 122
23 Orrin Hatch 128

24 Zell Miller 137
25 Dave Reover 141
26 Harry S Truman 144
27 Tony Blair 151
28 David ben-Gurion 157
29 Rush Limbaugh 162
30 William Jennings Bryan 169
31 John Joseph O'Connor 174
32 William Wilberforce 177
33 Queen Wilhelmina 182
34 Jerry Falwell 186
35 James Dobson 194
36 Ben Kinchlow 200
37 George Marshall 206
38 Edward Flanagan 211
39 Lech Wales 214
40 Richard Simmons 220
41 William McKinley 225
42 Christian, X 230
43 Fanny J. Crosby 235
44 Douglas Macarthur 238
45 Herbert Hoover 246
46 Nathan Hale 251
47 Bob Dole 253
48 Whittaker Chambers 258
49 Branch Rickey 264
50 Florence Nightingale 267
51 Elizabeth Blackwell 271
52 Condolezza Rice 274

Concluding Remarks 281
Study Questions 291
Trivia Questions 297
Matching Questions 301
Second Bonus Feature 311
Third Bonus Feature-W ALSO Rans-and near misses 315
Definitions 319

Glossary 341
Select Bibliography 361

ON Hope

§

I will begin by exploring a definition of hope. While hope may be in need of no introduction and either present or absent, but obvious when there, I will attempt to give a preliminary explanation of what I mean by the term throughout this book. Hope is the concept by which one feels inspired to go on in spite of the circumstances, a knowledge with or without evidence, that whatever doubt or loss may be overwhelming me now, I will have a better tomorrow and much to look forward to in the future. By simply believing things will be better in the long run and those better days are coming, we have proof to see ourselves through. Jean Kerr, *said "Hope is the feeling you have that the feeling you have is not permanent."* It has also been said that hope is the feeling that the situation makes sense regardless of *how it turns out, implying that even if you do not get your "victory" or what you are believing you have a right to hope for, there is reason for hope in the presence of conviction and the overwhelming belief that good will prevail in the end. When we struggle, we can hope whether we are going through the worst nightmare or simply trials of ordinary life.* Whether we can summon friends, or armies, or simply survive, whether we can stand on our own feet, or fall down and need the help of strangers we may never be able to repay. In the absence of evidence, perhaps hope is all we need. Hope can and indeed does change the course of civilization. From **Winston Churchill** admonishing his people And the occupied nations of Europe and China, to "have faith, have hope, deliverance is sure," to **Ronald Reagan** from his boyhood in Illinois to his days as a millionaire actor who knew the truth and wanted to share it with society, succeeding from Moscow, to Berlin, to Denver; to **Lech Walesa** believing that the Communist imposed governments in Poland And Eastern Europe were sure to fall And give way to freedom; to the radical Baptist preacher **Martin Luther King, Jr.** stirring his countrymen Black And White for equality to inevitably act on it; to mild-mannered writers and thinkers like **Norman Vincent Peale** and **S. I. Hayakawa** hoping and planning for success for themselves and their country. That spark within the human heart, the stir of longing for better days with righteousness sure to prevail in our time. Money, power, and even leadership have helped to make the world go around, but only hope can set the world on a right course. From **Billy Graham** knowing the timeless message of the Word of God must be preached in a timely fashion to all nations, to **David Ben Gurion taking** the teenage nation of Israel from Diaspora to their homeland; to **Abraham Lincoln believing** in the right cause for his country and winning it despite dire obstacles; to **Theodore Roosevelt taking** a teenage national and making it the leaders of the world for freedom and righteousness; to **Richard Simmons seeing** the need for an emphasis on fitness and making it a revolution; to Condolezza Rice rising against the odds to become one of the leaders of her country in true **Teddy Roosevelt-like** fashion, people of hope have made great names and caused great changes in the world.

The Bible speaks of the substantiveness (as if seeing and holding) those things hoped for but yet unseen. It has been said that humans can go three minutes without oxygen, forty-eight hours without water, six days without sleep, and up to forty days without food, and science has proven that we can go longer, perhaps an unlimited amount of time without pain avoidance, but we cannot go long, perhaps even not a minute without hope. *That is true given the fact that hope is not necessarily happiness and certainly not a life without problems, but the sense that even with problems And obstacles, there is a better moment yet to come.* Emily Dickinson wrote "hope is the thing with feathers that pierces through the soul And sings the tunes without the words And never stops at all." The common way the word "hopefully" is used implies our natural longing for something better out of something difficult and a belief that it will come. Men and women of the Bible persevered because they had hope. Job said, "Though he slay me, I will hope," (Job 13:15). Interestingly, horses are used in the Bible as a sign of people who do not put their hope in God, and some believe the prevalence of donkeys and mules and oxen in the Bible (even in war) was God's way of making the people know their hope was in Him. Despite the occasional use of horses and chariots, for the most part God's people rode donkeys and camels, quite likely to insure their faith would remain in Him. This assurance of victory through faith gives credence to the Scripture, "the horse is made ready for the day of battle, but victory rests with the Lord." (Proverbs 21:31)

If you believe that the Bible is the Word of God as I do, you have reason to put your hope in the Lord and believe that victory is sure. Psalm 91 is for you if you have trusted in the Lord And believed in the deliverance He promises through Jesus Christ to all who are under His protective care. Psalm 119 speaks of putting your hope in the Word of God And He will not disappoint you as you trust in His promises. "Those who hope in the Lord will renew their strength they will soar on wings like eagles" (Isaiah 40:31). Romans 5:4 said as we struggle in hope for the righteousness of God it will lead to perseverance leading to character, and back to hope, (v.5) as *hope* never disappoints. The apostle Paul goes on to speak of the hope God has given us as evidence of the love he poured into our hearts by the Holy Spirit. God is described as *the God of Hope in Romans 15:13. Our Savior Jesus Christ is called the Hope of Glory in I Colossians 1:27. Most Christians with a layman's understanding of Scripture know two portions on hope, the one commonly called the Love , in I Corinthians 13, which says in verse 7, love always protects, always trusts,, always hopes, always perseveres." I*t goes on to say that as Christians we live in a world with but a poor reflection as a mirror as we look for Him Who is the Object of our Hope and devotion. Even the apostle *Paul* the great pillar of hope and the greatest writer of true Christianity said that he can only know and prophesy in part, but when the perfection of God's own presence comes to us *He will be made fully known.* He closed by saying that these three remain, faith, hope, And love And the greatest is love. These were later designated the cardinal (or basic) truths of Christianity. The other well known Scripture is Hebrews 11 in which the writer describes those who persevered in faith and were rewarded because of their hope in God. Against the strongest obstacles, they overcame and either preached or inherited the salvation of those with a belief in the promised Messiah. They are pillars of faith and examples to us as the heroes in this series are for us in our time And future generations. The last theological point is that Christ's return (told in *I Thessalonians 4:16-20) is called the Blessed Hope. In Titus 2:13, God is called the God of Hope and he also gives us one of the greatest theological evidences that Jesus is One with the Father. As Christians,* therefore we have double reason to hope, greater things in this life with Jesus as our Lord and Constant Companion, but more importantly we have the Blessed Hope of being caught up with the Lord Jesus and specifying eternity with Him in Heaven where we will always rejoice in a place no words can explain.

Finally, I cannot overemphasize that Hope is not the absence of worry struggle, or obstacles, as only in dealing with these things as problems with perspective solutions, can one hope for better. The first twenty-four suicide prevention line in America was *Robert Schuller's* Tower of Hope. T*he people in this series all had major problems to overcome and did it by hope, by winning over adversity, solving those problems or substantially redressing them. They are heroes of hope for strength in the midst of problems. Remember, that history is His Story, and there is only One He Who will be ultimately the Author and Completer of history the One Who in His time,* will come and set up perfect life. He is the Example as the Author of History the One Who will bring it to its triumphant conclusion. With these hopeful thoughts in mind, I refer you to fifty-two men and women (*more exactly forty-one men and eleven women*) who dared to hope and so changed the course of nations and the world for the better.

1

Winston Spencer Leonard Churchill (1874-1965)

Ace of Spades of Hope

*W*inston Churchill was born at Blenheim Palace, London, in 1874 the son of Lord Randolph Churchill a longtime member of British parliament and Mary Gerome Churchill an American-born daughter of a wall street millionaire. With the combined greatness of the English-speaking people, he rose to become the man many called the last lion. As the last ferocious, regal, raging but ultimately loving victorious warrior of a generation of leaders, Winston Churchill is the greatest hero of hope in recent recorded history.

A man of many talents and various contradictions, Churchill grew up in a home of conservative values with an alcoholic father and a mother who turned to her constant love affairs with prominent European men, albeit only after her husband contracted a sexually transmitted disease. In spite of going to the best schools money could buy, young Winston was under-motivated and until his late teens had little desire to learn much besides English literature and history and the classics. Raised on the English virtues of solitude and Christian temperance, Winston laughed long, cried hard, prayed in public, and always wore his emotions on his front collar both in good times and bad. A veteran of two battle campaigns he opted out of military combat in his early twenties to pursue a career as an embedded journalist during the Boer War. Though it was actually illegal he pursued the captors of British soldiers and was himself taken prisoner by South African 'rebels' (known as Afrikaners or Boers for the Dutch word for "farmer)." He heroically escaped prison only to be caught in the midst of gunfire aimed at escapees which he inevitably survived, returning to Britain around 1902 Interestingly, he became good friends with one of the South African officers, Jan *Smuts,* who went on to be one of the co-founders of the U.N. (and sometime president of South Africa who became *the only non-resident of the U.K. to serve in his wartime cabinet)* and Winston always joked he was the only leader of a former British colony who always came in the front door to see him.

Though his last taste of combat had been sixteen years ago, the British people never forgot that this eminent statesman started his adult life as a cavalry officer, and so commanders gave in to his requests in between service in cabinets during *The Great War* to let him lead a low-level outfit to serve in trench warfare in France. His approximately seven *months of service in the World War fulfilled a dream for him to be a man of action as well as words and leadership (a-three-pronged key to success)* and in *all* his service for the British Crown/Empire he was decorated with fourteen metals. *He led* the light artillery/cavalry unit for roughly seven months. In the years after his last taste of combat he became a prominent member of the British Labor government eventually 'crossing the line' of Parliament to work in the Liberal government of David Lloyd George. Under both prime ministers, Winston served as first lord of the admiralty, making sure the British and their allies had sufficient ammunition on the land on the sea to defeat the Central powers, primarily Germany, Austria-Hungary, and Turkey. His most noteworthy accomplishment was his help in modernizing the use of tanks for the first time in history military tanks (as well as airplanes) as they became used as an effective weapon of combat helping the British Empire and the other Allies, mainly France and Belgium and from 1917 on America along with the entente Italy, Japan, and Greece, win the bloodiest war in history, then known simply as 'the Great War.' From 1914, when the German Kaiser refused to back down and the overrunning of the to-then perpetually neutral Belgium, became cause for war, the United Kingdom partook in the Triple Alliance with France and Russia and led the *Entente*-Italy, Japan Belgium, (and later Greece) in the bloodiest war then on record and to them simply called *'The Great War."* In 1917 when the Americans entered the war the USA and U.K. were comrades-in-arms for the first time and led the war effort along with the French. Significantly, his other major event of early middle-age was switching to the Conservative party, this time permanently, a *paradigm* for which he once said 'everyone under thirty should be a liberal or you may think he has no heart, anyone over thirty who is not a Conservative must have no brain.' At the age of thirty-six Winston married the young Mary Clementine with whom he lived happily the rest of his *fifty-five years*.

From the mid-30s when Adolf Hitler consolidated power as an absolute dictator throughout Germany, Churchill was the first and loudest voice to tell Britain and the rest of the English-speaking world not to trust the madman but to do everything in our power to resist Nazi Germany freeing her people and preventing Hitler and his gang from gaining more power. That along with his absolute stance against giving up the glorious overseas empire, particularly India and the sub-continent, which had largely been ruled by the United Kingdom for three centuries (though officially as an empire since 1876) made Winston Churchill stand alone, the voice of one crying out in the wilderness preparing the way for freedom in a world half mad, the other half running scared. Though a member of parliament, best-selling author, and internationally known spokesmen for millions of Britons, including his prime minister *Neville Chamberlain* and others within the British parliament, the outspoken sexagenarian was an embarrassment. Chamberlain and the rest of the world watched in antipathy as Hitler strong armed into Austria and consolidated his hold over neighboring Czechoslovakia, until September 1,1939 when Nazi Germany invaded Poland and her ally, Britain pledged to protect the independence of Poland (though then unable to defend a pre-conquered state-as it or France or perhaps even Czechoslovakia could have prevented six years earlier) honored the pledge to fight to protect the independence of Poland, and with several other European nations, plunged into a second war with Germany in twenty-five years. The only non-English-speaking ally to maintain a standing army and navy at the time, France also declared war on Nazi Germany immediately, but it was defeated within a few months. *Chamberlain* stayed on during the first days of the war, asking Churchill to come back on as first lord of the admiralty. Within a few months the former prime minister disgraced, stepped down, with his life in shambles, and King *George* VI invited Churchill, at age 64, to head the government as prime minister.

From the fall of France in May of 1940 until the final surrender in 1945, *no one in any country* could compare to Churchill as a beacon of hope to the free world. Due to his brave hearted, staunch and ultimately profound heroic leadership the Free world, particularly that of the English-speaking people, but also European, Asian, and Latin American democracies survived the complete onslaught of the Axis Powers, Nazi Germany, imperial Japan, and Fascist Italy. First with French General *Charles De Gaulle, and the few* brave Frenchmen who remained after the fall of France, he along with the dominions, reassured France and more than half a dozen occupied European nations, that Britain, though leading the battle alone, would defeat the enemy and rescue them. *As Churchill had long expected the world's greatest (although then not always most internationally active) democracy-the United States of America got involved in the war, in 1941, although sadly it took the attack on Pearl Harbor by Japan, to bring us in. From this point on,* along with U.S. President *Franklin D. Roosevelt, General Eisenhower,* and to a lesser degree Soviet dictator Josef Stalin, Churchill's leadership of the Allies brought about the complete fall of those three criminal governments and the recovery of peace and righteousness through the sword. Though defeated for reelection in *1945,* Churchill attended the first United Nations meeting in San Francisco as the primary representative of the United Kingdom. For the next six years he was the Conservatives leader in Parliament, also spending much time writing the memoirs of the war.

Along with leading the Conservatives as the "second statesman" of the time and writing wartime memoirs, he achieved very necessary accomplishments by rallying British, American, and other democratic allies to withstand the Soviet Union and her Communist satellites throughout the world. On March 5, 1946 he drew the lines with an immortal speech at *Westminster College* in Fulton, Missouri in association with U.S. President **Harry Truman,** enunciating the truths about freedom and anticommunism even before the famous *Truman doctrine, on March 5,1946.*

When Clement Attlee's government fell, Churchill, then seventy-five years old, regained the reins of power as prime minister of Great Britain. He and his fellow Conservatives had previously conceded to the independence of India. Also during this time Churchill mourned the death of Britain's much loved King and participated in the coronation of his daughter *Elizabeth, II,* who remains sovereign of Britain to this day. By bowing to her, a woman one-third his age, he set the precedent of bowing to an institution far older than anyone, and helped keep the United Kingdom, as such, with the determination to last longer and adhere to its ideals. Possibly the most lasting hallmark of Churchill's two decades in the international limelight is the supremacy of the *transatlantic relationship. Every* prime minister since has kept the tradition of standing with America as the Kingdom's dearest friend and ally. While he set the tone, that influenced America, a far greater country, it mainly insured that all great Britons (and to a lesser degree Canadians) can live as "half American, half European, and purely British," just like the great Sir Winston. This is certainly not to say that Britons have no identity of their own, quite the contrary, that the two major English speaking countries have shared a cultural identity that was originally British and has so impacted both sides of the Atlantic, as well as Europe, that a truly great Briton has characteristics of both European and American qualities that have contributed to the English speaking world what nobody as much as Churchill has done to make him great in the modern sense. The culture that is Britain, having indescribably influenced American culture, is today its own while retaining great characteristics of both American and European culture, to form its own third way just as the U.S. as the robust leader of the Twentieth and Twenty-First centuries has been influenced by Britain and combined with her to influence the small, but great next door neighbor of the U.S. in a way no one else could. Churchill was arguably the first (along with his deputy and friend Beaverbrook*) to see the indefatigable Maple leaf* rising as a medium to extraordinary power, and potential third partner of the English-speaking world. He loved his trips both to the U.S. and Canada, and encouraged the nation of about twenty million, that became the fourth largest navy in the world, and with it, and with its American and British immediate family, helped to save the world from barbarous dictators. Winston Churchill was knighted by Queen Elizabeth, April 24, 1953. He retired from Parliament in 1963, having been there nearly fifty years (with one brief interruption) and being a leader for thirty-eight, though in the last several years he more often than not made it to the Westminster building with the aid of a wheelchair.

Courageous and versatile, even as a former leader, Winston Churchill never left public service. He served his country and the free world for seventy years of adult life, completing his monumental five volume tomes, *The History of the English-speaking people, to go along with his war memoirs.* For them he was awarded the Nobel Prize for literature. His biographies include at least nine books about his experiences, more than half of them a running commentary on his leadership in World War II. Also a personal favorite was his book about his ancestor, the Duke of *Marlborough. In* 1963 he became only the second person in history to be awarded honorary American citizenship. Taking philosophy handed down from one of his predecessors *Benjamin Disraeli,* this ace hero of hope became one of the first and greatest Zionists in the modern world and helped campaign for the establishment of the independent state of Israel which was recognized as a nation in 1948. The greatest quotation to hang a the end of the card on the greatest hero of hope modern history produced, comes from his grandson, Winston Churchill, III 'this was the friend and ally that convinced the tortured nations of occupied Europe that their day of liberation would surely dawn, this was the historian whose writings fill fifty volumes, the builder who laid 10,000 bricks, the artist who filled 500 canvases, what a man, what a life, what a debt owed by all the world to one.'

2

Hero Of Hope
C.(live) S.(taples) 'Jack' Lewis
1898-1963

Ace of hearts OF HOPE

B orn in Belfast, Northern Ireland to Anglo-Irish Protestants Clive staples Lewis never liked his given name and was known as Jack from an early age. Losing his mother at an early age made him sour and often questioning of the faith in which he was raised. Nonetheless his conservative British education gave him full reason to fight with his countrymen in World War I during which he was wounded on a battlefield in France. Thankfully for the world, and particularly the Church of the Lord Jesus Christ, Lewis did not meet the fate of his comrade in arms Paddy Moore who died on the battlefield just weeks after Jack was wounded. Honoring a promise to look after each other's' dependents, Jack spent the remainder of his life from college on as the surrogate son to his much loved, if overly demanding, mother Janie "Minto" Moore, who became the mother Jack got to know. Also of the utmost importance to him throughout his life were Janie's daughter Maureen and Jack's brother Warren "Warnie" Lewis, himself a professor at Oxford and scholar of Eighteenth Century French culture and literature. In spite of his early doubts about Christianity, Jack went to Oxford National Church college of literature, where he began a lifelong reputation as a scholar specializing in the Classics of Sixteenth and Seventeenth Century British literature, he would eventually be one of the most learned men on the topic. A wise man, Lewis wrote his first novel *Boxen* when he was thirteen and by his twenties completed two books of poetry and short stories.

Though a lecturer and private tutor at Oxford, Lewis was hired on a contingency basis to teach only poetry and the classics without saying anything to undermine the Church of England's religious teaching, while he himself struggled with his theological beliefs. Throughout his twenties and early thirties his religion could easily be termed as fluctuating between atheism, agnosticism, and neo-paganism. After long discussions with college cohorts including J.R.R. *Tolkien* and reading many books of literature and philosophy including the Bible, Lewis became a devout Christian at the age of thirty-six. These could be termed his wilderness years, though Churchill was in the wilderness, knowing what was right and trying to convince hundreds of millions of people The right, Lewis was in The wilderness trying to figure out what was The truth. His finest piece of writing during his wilderness years was D*ymer* a lyrical poem of the clay of a *Beowulf* or *Paradise Lost*. His first post-conversion book is *The Pilgrim's Regress,* though often overlooked it is one of the most ingenious books about the struggle to live the Christian life ever written.

Like **Churchill**, World War II made C.S.. Lewis' reputation overwhelming and immortal throughout the English-speaking world. The intellectual and spiritual giant, C.S Lewis would study Catholicism like his friend *Tolkein* but eventually reject it to embrace the Protestant branch of Christianity. He wrote of Christianity as the theology of simply Jesus and the clear message of the Bible and did not favor any particular denomination in his speeches radio addresses, and writings..

Unlike **Churchill** Jack Lewis did not believe that such a reputation could be won and maintained thought political victories or conservative principles as ingenious and at times necessary as they may be. For Lewis hope rested with a soul *knowing* its *ultimate place* in the *universe* before its *Creator.* Not a dogmatic theologian or a 'churchy' prophet, Lewis became a Christian while undergoing a lifelong case-study which he previously believed would prove all religion false. While studying "pagan religions" particularly Hinduism he learned that what man has believed for centuries has ultimately amounted to a battle of intellectual and spiritual wits, between good and evil, hope and futility, and ultimately life and death. Like the ancient Greeks, Romans, and other ancient pagans, the Hindus were correct in believing that life was a daily struggle for physical and spiritual enlightenment and one could ultimately triumph by mastering oneself and submitting it under a perfect will. Where The classical pagans went wrong was in believing that such a submission to spiritual enlightenment under a perfect will, could be attained in the absence of a supremely Divinely Creator Who created the concepts of "good," and "evil," "Hope" and "fear," "Submission" and "Morality," and therefore holds the key to immortality and retribution. Only a Divine, all-powerful, all knowing, intelligent, enlightened and good Supreme Being could bring about both earthly enlightenment and eternal salvation. Studying all The philosophies that have taken shape in prominent societies, Lewis concluded that only the Truths taught *by and about the* Man, Jesus Christ, the Enlightened Teacher from Israel, can bring a man to intellectual and moral enlightenment in this life and eternal salvation in the next. *By studying that only He can be the ultimate Source of both life and immortality, Lewis helped to popularize the concepts (though its been said for two thousand years but perhaps never so eloquently) that people are making a grave and illogical philosophical error if they repeat the common concept that Jesus* was a great man and good moral teacher but not God. *If he claimed to be God, and His claim was false, he would be neither a great man, nor a good moral teacher; therefore we must accept that he was either a liar or a lunatic, or else bow down and call him Lord, reality, intelligent philosophy or logic, and Jesus' own words about Himself, did not leave any other options open. This same Jesus, proving by His life, death, and Resurrection that He is God from eternity,* is The only Savior who can give hope and eternal life to every fallen mortal.

He thoroughly explained his beliefs in *Mere Christianity* a three-part series taken from his radio speeches during the war. They provide some of The greatest philosophical arguments for the Christian faith in modern times. *His other theology books very readable to both Christians and sincere seekers of truth include The Problem of Pain, Miracles, The Weight of Glory, and The Abolition of Man.*

In 1952 C.S. Lewis first met the 'abrasive New Yorker' Joy Davidman Gresham, a Jewish-American converted Christian poet going through a divorce. At first confused and arguably leery, Jack agreed to marry her in a civil ceremony for the sake of giving her sons David and Douglas h. Gresham permanent British citizenship and thus taking them away from their alcoholic father. Within just over a year Lewis fell completely in love with the volatile outspoken, though ultimately lovable 'bundle of joy.' Tragically he learned she had cancer and was diagnosed with a condition treatable only in a limited sense. at first leery of making his vows religious and even consummating the marriage A sacramental wedding was performed and Jack and Joy were man and wife both in spiritual as well as legal facets. Despite the doctors' doubts, tithe Lord lengthened her life and Jack and Joy had three years and four months to share one of the greatest love miracles in modern history. During this time he wrote some of his greatest literature, R*eflections on the Psalms, Letters to Children, Till We Have faces, and The Business of Heaven. In may of 1960* Joy Lewis was taken into the arms of the Heavenly Father she loved. C.S.. Lewis never stopped grieving. A man of faith and hope he never gave up, and in the three years God gave him to continue, he wrote four more books including *Letters to Malcolm Chiefly on Prayer and A Grief Observed. On November 22, 1963 Jack Lewis went home to the father of Hope for whom he had been one of the most intelligent, persistent, faithful, dutiful, and productive servants.*

In addition to Renaissance literature and theology for the common person, C.S. Lewis was a major contributor to two other literary genres, for the English -speaking world, children's literature and science fiction. In the former, for his *Chronicles of Narnia* series about Aslan, the savior of the parallel world who is seen in Narnia by the Penvise children. In the latter he wrote of the world of Paralenda the 'deep magic' of both British and Parelendan truth most ingeniously displayed in T*hat Hideous Strength.* Though a hero to millions of Britons and Americans throughout World War Two and the aftermath in which Lewis lived, he was largely seen as an anachronism or an unapproachable gray-haired scholar, and only his Narnia series and *Screwtape reached classic* status within his lifetime. He never fully recovered from Joy's death, regaining the grip on life and positive thinking that were his anchor in his early to midlife years as a Christian, instead he made every day a time of grief for her, so perhaps years or even decades of his productivity may have been snatched away. Since his death the name and literature of C. S.. Lewis has gotten a second wind in Europe and even more so in the United States, where he has millions of fans, and has developed somewhat a cult following, for fans, dozens of whom have written books, movies, plays, and host literary events and clubs about both the ingenious literature and the mysterious but marvelous life of the most hopeful communicator of Christianity in modern times.

3

Martin Luther King, Jr.
Rated 3 (1929-1968)

ACE of Clubs of Hope

§

orn the son of a preacher, January 15, 1929 in Atlanta, Martin Luther King, Jr. *never tired of a desire to preach. He* always had a firm belief in preaching the Evangelical Gospel and mixed that highest duty, with the belief in doing what was best for all mankind. He was a firm believer in The ability and responsibility of men and women, especially springing from a church setting, to be "*the conscience of the nation" and change the world.* A son of The South, he got his first Northern exposure shortly after World War II, attending colleges in Boston and Philadelphia. After college he forewent opportunities to pastor up North, first returning to Dexter Avenue Baptist Church where he was associate pastor to his father. The following Year he took his own pulpit as pastor of Ebenezer Baptist Church in Birmingham, Alabama.

Beginning his career as a pastor and scholar overly educated for a primarily rural pulpit, but the Lord knew what He was doing and he used King's scholarly knowledge of the Bible and popular culture. In 1955 at the age of twenty-nine King helped to organize the Montgomery Bus Boycotter along with Rosa Parks. Within months he became a household name throughout the USA, Europe,

India, Africa, and most of the world. Without the force of government, he persuaded the state of Alabama to change their policies on segregation. The following year he launched the Southern Christian Leadership Council. Though many Black and White *viewed him as fanatical, he was awarded the Nobel Peace Prize, The fifth American to win The award.* Throughout his lifetime *he quoted* many sources including the Founding Fathers, Aristotle, Edward Bellamy, *St. Thomas Aquinas,* **Abraham Lincoln,** *and Fredrick Douglass.* His favorite sources, however, remained the Bible, followed by *Gandhi, followed by Henry David Thoreau.* Martin Luther Kings' books and sermons were a source of inspiration and new knowledge and they brought a source of hope to African-Americans a new knowledge to millions of whites particularly Jewish, Catholic, and poor rural Southerners. He was certainly not immune from persecution throughout his life, arteriole at least a dozen times for violations of minor statues and for a brief time was watched by the FBI and suspected of un-American activity. *Often called an eclectic* rather than primarily a preacher of The Gospel, King made it clear his main objective was to preach The Gospel of Jesus *Christ, by word, precept, and example. Since Civil Rights for all of God's creatures are part of the message of both the Bible and the American Constitution, he believed he was acting in consistency with his calling.* He also preached against Communism and as surprising as it may be to some of today's media structure (especially incorrectly taking Dr. King for a liberal icon), he spoke out against extremes in media saying the media should be less violent and television and movies should adopt a code by which sex, violence, and other evils were toned down especially for kids, ironically in an era when very few evils had yet crept in*to media.*

During his eight year period in the limelight, Martin Luther King changed the world for democracy. In 1968 he was gunned down by an armed man named James Earl Ray. His faithful wife Coretta and friends like Dr. *Ralph Abernathy* continued his work when he was gone. Within a decade Martin Luther King, Jr. was honored with a place in history that is without equal among African-Americans. Placed on commemorative stamps and given statues in Washington D.C. and honored with many streets (my current home in Salt Lake

29

City, which is about 2.4% African-American has a Martin Luther King Boulevard), he is especially the namesake of many streets and buildings and an object of renown throughout the South. Martin Luther King became the first African-American to win the respect and philosophical endorsement of American society at large. In 1975 President *Gerald Ford* proposed celebrating Martin Luther King's birthday as a national holiday, and though it was debated in many states and at the federal level, in 1987 January 15 (or the third Monday in January) became a federal holiday Martin Luther King Day, signed in to law by **Ronald Reagan,** only the fifth federal holiday to honor a person's birthday and the third to honor an American citizen, the first American so honored since **Abraham Lincoln**. One of the greatest American heroes of all time, greatly misunderstood during his lifetime, today it is considered un-American to say a word against him, and he stands with *Washington* and **Lincoln** as the symbol of the American dream, a man born in a humble rural situation rising to conquer all adversity by Christian values and American principles.

4

Norman Vincent Peale (1898-1995)

Ace of Spades OF Hope

§

*N*orman Vincent Peale was born in Cincinnati at the turn of the Twentieth Century. His father, both an ordained Methodist minister and a medical doctor taught him the beliefs of the conservative Wesleyan Methodists and the Republican Party. He earned three college degrees eventually getting his doctorate. Early after college he went to work for the *Findlay Morning Republican as a reporter.* While highly intelligent and glad to be working for a newspaper, he early on got a call that he would be more effective in ministry. With the Findlay *Republican* and later in the Army Reserves during World War I, Peale made alliances that were to last a lifetime, getting his feet wet in the pulpit, which created a burden to preach and he went to seminary, eventually becoming a great speaker about the love of God Norman Vincent Peale was not at first comfortable around people like his father had always been. He was in the Army Reserves in World War I and while not serving overseas it gave him a military philosophy that lasted over six decades and influenced Presidents and generals.

Though he was Midwestern to the core, since 1924 he had been ministering in Methodist churches in New York, and by 1934 when he took his new pulpit, he relocated there permanently *an*d became accepted as a New Yorker even by New Yorkers. He had the opportunity to take a struggling but promising church, and with his positive thinking philosophy built it into one of The largest in New York. A Methodist, he was hired to preach in a church that was historically Dutch Reformed and was ordained by that fellowship. Clearly a conservative and *Evangelical* in *his own preaching* he parted company with his Evangelical brethren on a few matters. A lifelong participant in the Masonic order, he was such an ardent supporter of the work of **Helen Keller**, he agreed to write the forward for her spiritual autobiography though it was largely written to further the religious philosophy of a "prophet" of universalsim.

As a preacher, author, speaker, statesman, and moral psychology advocate, Norman Vincent Peale has few rivals in American history. Even before his all-time classic *The Power of Positive Thinking* was published in 1951, he had already written over twenty books. Some of them were merely booklets and extensions of sermons, far less popular than now (so he helped to pioneer it) others full length books, while the Twentieth and Twenty-First Century concept of the bestseller was not popular until the 1950s. His two monumental works that would take most a lifetime were established by his middle years, first *Guidepost* a monthly journal of positive primarily Christian tidbits from home and hearth. The other, the first of its kind anywhere in the world was the Blanton/Peale Institute for positive living. Along with psychologist *"Smiley" Blanton,* his lifelong friend and collaborator they set up a mental health institute to turn people on to the power of positive thinking through spiritual principles. In 1934 he became pastor of Marble Hill Collegiate Church, a role he held for *fifty-four* years. His greatest bestsellers are compared to other great American positive thinkers like *Dale Carnegie* who spoke at his pulpit. He spoke in front of church pulpits, Rotary clubs, lawyers' conventions, labor unions, before Presidents, doctors, astronomers, authors, and blue-collar workers delivering over 20,000 speeches and sermons throughout his long life. He knew every President of the U.S. from **Theodore Roosevelt** through George Herbert Walker *Bush*. He influenced five generations of Americans from the one that fought in World War One (his own) through the end of the Cold War.

During World War II, he was one of the country's stalwarts, especially in the New York area (which by extension includes much of the East Coast). His philosophy to help rally America was simple, but like at other times ingenious, and though he stayed home to rally The troops, he successfully convinced himself and many others it was of benefit to the nation, and he would be one of America's top patriots in future wars, he helped rally Americans to the truth of giving peace a chance by supporting our troops.

Peale's legacy as a statesman in addition to a preacher, author, and positive speaker is cemented by his relations with Presidents and military figures. He knew sixteen Presidents in his ninety-five years and was particularly close to Dwight D. Eisenhower, Richard Nixon, and **Ronald Reagan** who shared many of his beliefs. In 1960 he got both good and bad publicity for participating (as the most famous conferee) in a conference on raising up a godly man to succeed *Eisenhower* in the White House, which the media took as an all-too clear reference to keeping the White House Protestant, not letting John F. Kennedy, a Catholic win the election. When Kennedy did win, however, he became friends with him and met with him several times. A staunch Republican from his boyhood days in the heartland, Peale could be happy with a Democrat in the White House, like his friends Franklin *Roosevelt* and **Harry Truman**, but he seemed to have more issues with Democrats like the latter's firing of the stalwart **Douglas MacArthur**. Nonetheless Norman Vincent Peale was an American's American and he ministered to Presidents, servicemen, and leaders regardless their views.

He wrote more than forty books, preached and spoke in at least three dozen countries, and was a spiritual adviser to troops in Vietnam. He traveled millions of miles in his lifetime counseling people in Singapore, Cincinnati, Chicago, Cleveland, New York, Nairobi, India, Israel, Latin America, Louisiana, London, and Lisbon through five decades of pulpit ministry. *Though known and honored as much for his presence as a national and international statesman as for his church work, he was obviously held in high esteem there, from 1969-1970* he served as president of the *Reformed Church in America* and for four years was president of the Protestant Council of the City of New York-an alliance of eighteen hundred churches.

On **March 26, 1984** he was awarded the **Presidential Medal of Freedom, the highest award the president can give a civilian. In so honoring him, as the first Protestant minister who made his name primarily on that basis to be so honored in Washington, Reagan wrote:**

With a deep understanding of human behavior and an appreciation for God's role in our lives, Dr. Norman Vincent Peale helped originate a philosophy of happiness. . . Few Americans have contributed so much to the personal happiness of their fellow citizens as Dr. Norman Vincent Peale. He had also performed the *wedding of Dwight D. Eisenhower's grandson* David *to Richard Nixon's daughter* Julie. *At eighty-six, he was still being honored and speaking to Presidents and other world leaders and continued writing books to the age of ninety-two.* His wife threw him a very special ninetieth birthday party at the Waldorf Astoria Hotel and President **Reagan** who *was* meeting with Gorbachev *participated via video. Other participants included* Donald Trump *as a main funder and Art Linkletter.*

Even in his nineties he remained still interested, enthusiastic, and concerned about human affairs. A few years later *he thanked God he got to live to celebrate the worldwide collapse of Communism.* It was about this time he wrote the monumental but relatively brief autobiography, *This Incredible Century*, in my estimation his most important and well-written book, which reads *as both a commentary on his own life and the Twentieth Century, two stories of triumph from the ordinary to the extraordinary.* By the time he died in 1993, Peale could say he had seen America at her best and worst, in sickness and in health, in good times and bad and he always loved her and worked to advance her causes. In 1993 he was found dead by his wife, Ruth, herself an American icon, and he is and will always be remembered as one of the greatest legacies of hope, faith, writing, excellence, and the American ideals for centuries to come. Norman Vincent Peale's example of faith and the love of God will always be remembered. His philosophy of life and his ability to enjoy and influence so much of it for so many decades **was simple; think positive, forget your age, remember it is just a number and thrive at any age, always see yourself in good health and pray with**

continuous affirmation of love. Love God and love people, hate no one, think the thoughts Jesus taught, try to practice your Christianity at all times, go to bed early and rise early, always put complete trust in the Lord, *eat moderately, and never use tobacco or alcohol.*

5

Margaret Thatcher
(1925-Present)

Queen of Diamonds

*B*ritain's greatest Prime Minister since World War II can be credited as a major winner in the *Cold War*. She was born in 1925 to a working class family but early taught the values of statesmanship and the nobility of all work as conservative (or Tory if you like) principles. An early devotee of **C.S. Lewis**, she became a staunch Methodist mainly by studying the works of one of the Church of England's proudest theologians. With a career in public service going back almost three decades and having served in the cabinet of Prime Minister Edward Heath, in the mid-seventies she found herself the Leader of the Opposition in British Parliament, the highest office a woman had held in British Parliament.

Like many of the American obstacles, the Britain of the 1970s was a place of Twentieth Century excesses and entitlements not known to free people since the 1920s. While their parents' generation (into which Margaret was born) had won World War II, the generation now owning their first family size vehicles and homes were able to live the affluent lifestyle of their parents that they rejected, largely because of their parents' values and especially their parents' money. Like **Ronald Reagan**, much of her life, Margaret Thatcher had been running against the Twentieth Century. In 1979 the Labor government led by John Callahan was defeated for a major vote in Parliament and as Leader of the Opposition; Thatcher led her party in the election. Callahan was the first Prime minister since *Clement Attlee* to be defeated for an election for incumbency at the polls following a humiliating defeat in Parliament, like Jimmy Carter at the same time (The first incumbent President to lose an election since **Herbert Hoover),** the United Kingdom, like America was ready to see some changes for which they would have been unprepared at other times. Margaret Thatcher and her Conservative Party won a fairly close election but in the big cities especially in England she won nearly 60% of the vote. The first woman elected leader of a large, modernized democracy was ready to lead Parliament to some full scale changes not seen since World War II. At the time she took office Britain was the third largest exporting country in the world (behind the U.S. and Germany) and the fourth richest (also trailing Japan).

Though immensely respectable especially for an island nation smaller than the other three, Thatcher was born into a world where the U.K., the founders of the *Industrial Revolution,* were still the largest exporting nation and owned more collective businesses worldwide than any nation. She made it a starting point to rally her nation to friendly but aggressive competition with America, Germany, and Japan. With 44 seats more than the Labor Party she believed she had a mandate to do it her way. When asked what it was like to be the first woman Prime Minister, she said she doesn't know the alternative, it is the only kind of Prime minister she could be.

Her first weeks in office saw her taken to the Queen where, with her loyal husband, Denis and faithful staff members, she committed to making the Kingdom the best it could be as they prepared for the 1980s. Unlike some thought, she was never a soft touch, within months the longtime legislator, until then known only by British and outside political enthusiasts, was now called "the Iron Lady" in most English-speaking households throughout Europe and the educated world. Within her first several months she passed two groundbreaking measures, the increase in the earned income credit, thus increasing by several percent the amount of income that successful

wage earners could keep of their pay, and the reversal of the Labor
Party's ban on private schools income distribution. The counterpart of the "vouchers" program in America had a long history in
the United Kingdom and though American liberals and some others
despise the idea of paying for Christian schools (and not only one
church as in England minority religious including Catholic, *Pentecostal*, Baptist, Jewish, *Muslim*, and nonsectarian private schools are
also funded) it had a long history in England, albeit interrupted by
almost twenty years of Labor governments, and many other indus-
trialized nations including Japan which is about 1% Christian pay
for religious schools with tax dollars if they educate as well (usually
better) as public schools. Though the early eighties hit a mild recession and a boom of inflation, by mid to late 80s the Thatcher tax
credits and other economic policies led to a surge that in the nineties
became known as the Thatcher boom.

Early in her administration Margaret Thatcher met one of the
worst politician challenges of any Prime Minster. The tiny, American
hemisphere-situated, British- governed, Falkland Islands had been
occupied by their neighbor Argentina, when a military *junta*, taking
over from the government under Evita Peron wanted to plunge into
military adventure to gain the respect of their people. Not knowing
that Britain was willing to fight for the tiny islands, the Argentine
junta military had no idea what they were up against. Like Evita
Peron, Britain was now led by an iron-fisted woman, but unlike
Mrs. Peron, one who stood for democracy and the rights of human
beings, particularly British subjects, about two thousand of whom
would be subject to foreign un-democratic rule. *She was said to (in
private meetings) have compared the situation to Hawaii in the days
of Pearl Harbor* and *junta* Argentina was definitely a Fascist regime.
The Prime Minister immediately informed the junta that the military
must vacate the Falkland Islands and give the British enough time to
engage the people who lived there, thus giving Falklanders a chance
to vote on gradual transfer to their neighbor's jurisdiction. In spite of
the more than generous offer, the Argentine military kept a tight fist
upon the islands to show who was boss in the region and so Thatcher
answered by sending troops in and destroying the invader. Within
two months the Falklands were free of their threat and Britain's

military muscle was flexed like it had not been since World War II, leaving Argentina to look for life after military rule. This short and concise battle made Margaret Thatcher arrive on the world scene as an iron fisted leader who cared about even the Queen's smallest and most vulnerable subjects. Unlike past experiences where America tended to dominate affairs of the hemisphere themselves or favor the American country (even South American ones) her good friend Ronald **Reagan** was thoroughly behind her and his Administration offered to mediate, while making it clear to the junta any help would go to our English-speaking partner.

Thatcher also had major foreign influence in places as diverse as Hong Kong and Zimbabwe. She helped to see the governmental of Zimbabwe come under majority rule, one-man-one-vote. Though the democracy that came wasn't to the Western world's liking it was an internal affair and Britain did not become directly involved. With Hong Kong, a longtime British protectorate, but very much a free and independent place for its eight million citizens, she tried a more hands-on approach but was rebuffed by the Red Chinese. Though she reiterated Britain's commitment to dissolve the protectorate and hand over the islands to China in 1997, she tried to get a commitment from the Chinese to retain business as usual with independence for Hong Kong's citizens. Though she was not successful in gaining such a commitment, two British governments have since followed her example of a benevolent hands-off policy to Hong Kong with fair results. She met Prime Minister Fitzgerald of Ireland and made a joint Anglo-Irish commitment to peace, a landmark step though it did little to affect the peace process in and around Belfast, Northern Ireland. She had a very good meeting with Prime Minister Fitzgerald, but it did little for the people living in and around Belfast. This was in response to a 1983-84 uprising of violence by the IRA and backlash by "Protestant" terrorists, which killed a number of people. Over two thousand people have died throughout *"Thirty years Troubles", include Thatcher's good friend, World War II hero, then serving as the minister for Northern Ireland, Airey Neave.*

In 1983 she was reelected to a second term, and with an overwhelming margin, it was here she led more for the good of Commonwealth goals and also showed her staunch anti-Communism. While disagreeing with America about policies in Lebanon and Grenada, she made great friends with Americans in the **Reagan** Administration as no British leader has had since **Churchill** with Roosevelt. **Reagan** and Thatcher were kindred spirits in fighting against Communism and after The Berlin Wall came down, **Reagan** quipped in answer to journalists, yes he was instrumental in bringing down the Iron Curtain but he could never have done it without the Iron Lady. **Reagan** and Thatcher are correctly given praise for being the main two people who ended European Communism, along with Pope *John Paul*, II, **Lech Walesa** and others. Her most positive commitment to the **Reagan** Administration and the rest of the free world in defeating Communism was her strong stance with Reagan to build Strategic Defense Initiative (SDI) a nuclear shield that could protect the Western world from a nuclear attack. Although belittled as "Star Wars" by American liberals, and attacked as too costly and ineffective by other European, Canadian, and Japanese allies, Thatcher strongly believed with Reagan, that a nuclear shield could prevent nuclear war and in this case too was proven right. Though the two were uncommon in their belief that Soviet Communism could be defeated within their lifetime, they succeeded amid doubt and **millions of enemies!**

Margaret Thatcher's rapport among her nation, the world, and particularly the Commonwealth of English speaking countries and former English colonies, showed in her visits to Australia, and places as remote as Pakistan and Israel. She was the first to recognize Australia as a regional tiger in her own right and a possible economic giant of the Twenty-First Century. She also saw the initiative in Pakistan and pledged for British help to her becoming a modern democracy. Despite former tension between Britain and Israel her visit there was cordial and she committed her government to a Zionist policy that helped Israel retain its respectability in the region and fight for its continued success at the U.N.

Her popularity was confirmed with a *"hat trick"*, third term election in 1987. In 1990 Margaret Thatcher became the longest serving Prime Minister since *William Pitt* in the Eighteenth Century. Her government stayed on to stand with *George* Herbert Walker *Bush* and other Western democratic leaders leaders against Saddam Hussein bullying his neighbors in Kuwait. Britain sent troops to Operation Desert Storm to free Kuwait and keep Iraq from becoming a regional bully. In 1991 after almost a full twelve years in office she gave in to her party's requests that she step down and allow one of her brightest Conservative heirs to lead the party. In *John Major, The Conservatives* won a de facto fourth term election, in what was thought to be a sure loser, even as the country was telling her, *"Thanks Mrs. Thatcher, now it's time to give someone else a try,"* they got in with *great British spirit, "Okay, Maggie, that someone, will be the one of your choosing."*

Her knighting on December 9, 1991 was a very important moment, since she was awarded the Legion of Merit, the highest gift of sovereignty, far beyond being a knight or lady of the Round table, only twenty-four living persons can hold it. She officially retired from Parliament in 1992, accepting the ceremonial appointment to the House of Lords. In choosing not to run for her seat from Finchley, it was the first time since 1959 she did not run (and resoundingly win) that seat. She then devoted her full time to speaking and more importantly writing her memoirs. The first installment, *The Downing Street Years*, are an indispensable work of insight on the ins and outs of history from one of the events' greatest influences, **Churchillian in scope.** Her second edition *The Path to Power*, is equally recommended. In 2002, she wrote *Statecraft* which examines the new post-Cold War realities of the world. Tremendously, from her seventy-six-year-old mind she speaks of the achievement of America, winning the Cold War, giving principal credit to **Ronald Reagan.** The dynamics of other former Commu*nist satellite stats are discussed in depth, and as at other times in her career she spoke prophetically, saying there will be no peace in Iraq until Saddam and his regime are toppled. She also traveled extensively participating in the dedication of the **Reagan** Library in Los Angeles and touring America like never before. The three prime ministers in this book are admired, among their reasons, for their love for America, **Churchill** was just as American as British through birth and commitment, **Blair** came to love America during his service, and in the case of Lady Thatcher it became her spiritual home during and after her premiership. Though her speeches in*

North America commanded fees, she accepted no pay for speaking in Britain, *or in* Russia, China, Hong Kong, South Africa, or anywhere else where she is speaking "politically" and therefore wants to be free to speak her mind without constraints.

Though conversations between the monarch and prime ministers are strictly confidential, Mrs. Thatcher found her majesty *Elizabeth, II* to have a firm grasp on the issues of the day. She helped Margaret remain in office so long because she and the Queen were kindred spirits politically and personally. In 2003 she suffered the loss of her dear husband Denis. In 2004 she delivered a eulogy at the funeral of **Ronald Reagan,** making her the first foreign head-of government, in fact the first non-American, to ever speak at the funeral of an American President. In a world that had been losing hope to laziness, entitlement, and Hippie culture, a Europe confused by Communism and the ongoing threat of war, and an *England* and *British Commonwealth unsure* of its *place in the world* and its *future status* as a *great power*, the *Iron Lady*, Margaret Thatcher, *became one of the clearest examples of hope in recent times!*

6

Clarence Thomas
(1948-Present)

King of Clubs OF Hope

*B*orn a poor son of the South in 1948, a black child who, along Ruth is brother was unable to be sufficiently protected by his single mother he went to live with his grandparents who adopted him as their son. At first restless and less than scholarly by his college years he was a law student and was expecting great things. His deep Southern roots were ingrained in him as he went to study at the University of Georgia from which he graduated law school and passed the bar exam. In the early seventies he worked in civil rights legislation though he refused to be stereotyped as a "lawyer to the black man." Part of both his high school and college were spent in Catholic education and while had not been raised Catholic he eventually partook in baptism and Communion. At first embracing the liberal causes of the majority of African-American civil rights leaders, two things set him apart, his Catholic upbringing and his iron-willed belief in what Edmund Burke termed 'natural law." From Catholicism he had devoted himself to a staunch anti-Communism, knowing that even bigots, acting within the American system of democracy and free enterprise as fearful and harmful as they may be, were not the scariest Eurocentric viewpoint that could hurt Blacks and other

Americans. Like many of the era he knew that Communism, that Western heresy if there ever was one, had the potential to make all Americans slaves to an evil system that was already bringing horror to Europe. Only through a system with respect for law ultimately rooted in the Divine Being, could a democracy be governed to thrive. As a believer in "natural law" or in other words the common law, as imposed by God in His revelation, both creation (natural revelation) and Scripture (Special revelation) could one truly enforce governing principles. Though this is not often talked about in America especially in legal or academic circles, the fact remains it was what the Founding Fathers, both *Evangelical* Christians and deists (one Catholic) had in mind when the wrote the Constitution and because of that the rights of man to his freedom and equal protection under the law, particular in matters of safety, religion, pursuit of happiness, and property, are ours' not because of any government, but because they were given by God and government is merely an institution-1TcivlA1rcgnsd active guarantee of those freedoms.

This emphasis on natural law and its inevitable strict *Constitutionalism* made him different from the overwhelming majority of politically active Blacks. Though he was a lawyer, not a politician, by the mid-seventies he threw in his lot with the Republican Party. He worked with some of the biggest names in Washington D.C. including *Antonin Scalia,* for whom he worked. In 1985, only 37-years-old he was appointed by President **Ronald Reagan** to chair the EEOC. Only the third director of this largely informational branch of government that seeks to end discrimination based on race, gender, religion, or other protected categories. More than any former EEOC director, Clarence Thomas worked to make The mostly informational section of government relevant to The daily lives of people, particularly those in groups that were likely to be discriminated against. He presented the oral arguments in *Clark V. Vinson,* which allowed it to be easier to sue employers for harassment or other acts of discrimination, establishing the phrase *hostile environment*. He was a visiting professor and traveled all over the country giving lectures and touring colleges, and was equally accepted as a speaker at religious schools like Oral Roberts University as Georgetown. In 1988 **President Reagan** appointed him to the Washington D.C. Third Municipal Court. Within a year he was so distinguished in that body that he was moved up to the Second Court of Appeals, making him the youngest ever to serve on that bench and easily the most conservative. At forty years old and on the second highest court in the land, even if Clarence Thomas had retired or somehow had to end his public service he would have been one of the most distinguished Americans, but living mostly in obscurity. Ironically as the obscure, young, handsome, conservative, confident, and energetic Judge Thomas, he was able to be confirmed to federal potions three times, sailing through Senate nominations easily. Contrary to popular belief most justices have no bench service when appointed to higher courts, *Potter Stewart* had been deputy mayor of Cleveland, Earl Warren had been governor of California and candidate for Vice-President, Chief Justice William *Rehnquist* and Justices Stevens, Bryer, and Souter had never served a day on a bench before being appointed to the Supreme Court. Fortunately Thomas' Black detractors picked up on this and its implied racist dimension when they were making excuses why Thomas should not serve on the High Court. Despite his youth, he had far more judicial experience than most Supreme Court justices and nominees who are often nominated for political experience rather than judicial prowess.

In 1992 at age forty-four he was a surprising nominee of President George Herbert Walker Bush to replace the outgoing Justice Thurgood Marshall as associate justice of the U.S. Supreme Court. As expected he had many detractors on the left who despised his political views and sought to defeat his nomination. At first, however, the NAACP and other Civil Rights groups enthusiastically supported his nomination. Since his detractors could not defeat him on his record which was virtually impeccable, they cooked up a maniacal scheme, "digging up" a woman with whom Thomas had worked in law in Oklahoma and at the EEOC. Anita Hill came to testify. Aided by Senate Republicans, led by Utah's **Orrin Hatch**, Pennsylvania's Arlen *Specter*, Missouri's *John Danforth*, and South Carolina's *Strom Thurmond*, Thomas was defended by the very people who had been labeled insensitive to the plight of Black America. Danforth was his close friend, they had worked together in

Missouri, and he was instrumental in recommending Thomas for the nomination. Remarkably the old-fashioned Southerner, Thurmond pushed for and sincerely came to love this Black American married to a white woman.

Thomas later said that his mistake was not in the way he spoke to Miss Hill, but hiring her in the first place, not so much because of her legal and other on-the-job performance, but due to her ultra-liberal stances, she was not philosophically qualified to serve such a highly conservative jurist in a Republican Administration, yet he was good enough to give her that and several other jobs. His detractors were largely unable to argue against his career and when Anita Hill was not a prudent issue to debate they focused on his opposition to abortion, racial preferences, and the use of federal funds to silence religious debate particularly when it came to government funding of religious schools. While not denying his record on these issues, he refused to engage in debate over legal matters that may come up before the Court during his tenure. Following the debate, the Senate voted completely along partisan lines, to confirm Clarence Thomas 52-48. He then became the second African-American and the youngest jurist to serve on the court.

In almost two decades on the Supreme Court, Thomas has sided with the conservatives, most notably *Rehnquist and Scalia*. He had previously clerked for *Scalia* when both were new to Washington and considers the veteran jurist his mentor. He also became good friends with **Rush Limbaugh** and officiated at his third wedding. One of the most conservative justices ever, he was a staunch opponent of the Clinton Administration's funding for abortion and military experiments, but a supporter of welfare reform and free trade, he sided with the conservatives almost 100%. Though considered to be heavily ideological by both his fans and his many detractors, *Linda Chavez, a conservative commentator and sometime advisor who worked with him in President **Reagan's** EEOC said he was then more of a "down to business" type, not an ideologue. Though often accused of "making religion the issue", in spite of his later pro-Christian stances,* he admits that in his earlier days in the Missouri Justice Department he used to tease John Ashcroft for his commitment to faith. Since President *Bush* took office Thomas sides with his Administration almost completely. He has as expected, been a strict Costitutionalist and argued for the absence of federal law except where it is necessary to protect people or protect the support of established precedents.

Though at first not wanted to do much speech making unlike most nationally known jurists, in 1998 he was invited to address the American Bar Association. In a heartfelt speech he told the predominantly Black audience that in spite of how many feel about him, he will not have his beliefs, he refuses to have his beliefs assigned to him nor will he allow himself to be an intellectual slave. He went on to say that in this day and age affirmative action is bad for Blacks because it looks like "begging the man" for benefits Black men and women can get on their own if they tirelessly work to climb to the top. While many label it simplistic, it has worked for millions of Americans of all races, and Clarence Thomas is a shining example. This Black American, from the poor side of town, betrayed by his father, and committed to the care of others, by a financially unstable mother, became a hero of hope by believing that there is hope in the Lord Jesus Christ and in working hard to follow his dreams from the first day of school till the day you are able to reach the top.

Like many Supreme Court justices his biography is sketchy and its hard to tell what he believes and how he lives, but in thirteen years on the national scene he has established himself as one of the greatest Americans ever committed to America and the defense of our Constitution. During the course of this writing, he too published his first full-length book, *My Grandfather's Son, which clears up some* of the questions. At first seen as the likely replacement to be the fifteenth Chief Justice of the U.S., *Bush* chose not to have another ugly battle and let the newly named *John Roberts* serve in that capacity. Thomas is the father of two and although he attended a very conservative Episcopal church in Washington for many years, one source says he has reconverted to Catholicism.

7

Dan Quayle
(1947-Present)

King of Diamonds of Hope

§

J ohn Danforth Quayle was born in Indiana in 1946 the son of a well-to-do entrepreneurial family who nonetheless grew up as down to earth Midwesterners. He attended public schools in upper-middle-class suburbs, was raised by lawyers, grew up in church, with golf, fishing, and the Republican Party as pillars of his young life. It was not surprising that in 1964 he entered law school, graduating with honors and passing the Indiana bar exam. The following year he married Marilyn Tucker and the two went on to have three children Ben, Corrine, and Tucker. Throughout his life he has always been called "Dan", attended public schools and the state university, and while a member of Congress as at other times always lived on his present salary. Though his grandfather was rich, the family believed everyone should make it on their own.

He and Marilyn started a law form largely committed to helping independent businesses in the early seventies. In 1976 at the age of twenty-nine he unseated a long-term Democratic incumbent from his district to become a member of the House of Representatives. He was only the second youngest (under thirty) congressman elected in the Twentieth Century. The people of Indiana loved his folksy down-to earth sense of humor, his young smile, and his vindication of their family values which were evident in the way he interacted with his wife and children. It was therefore not surprising that in 1980 at the age of 33 he was elevated to U.S. Senate again unseating a popular incumbent. Through eight years as a senator he largely worked on military issues serving on defense and space exploration commit- tees. In 1986 he authored the Job Partnership Training Act with a very unlikely ally, Massachusetts Senator Ted Kennedy but he tow helped to provide jobs for thousands of young people, especially in te inner-city. He was one of the **Reagan** Administration's most stal- wart Senate supporters and could be counted on to help insure the buildup of military defenses particularly SDI passed the Senate and was on the table for the President's passing. In addition he sought to end federal funding for abortion ad increase the quality of public schools by decreasing federal regulation. A supply-side economist, he was a firm advocate of *Reaganomics* believing that helping big businesses fuel the economy would benefit middle and lower class workers by providing more jobs and stimulating the economy.

In 1988 then Vice-President *Bush* shocked the political world nominating Dan Quayle to run for Vice-President.. While Quayle was a fairly experienced loyal Republican who had never lost an elec- tion, the forty-one-year-old was not well-known outside of Indiana and had never run on a national platform. Many older and more experienced contenders had entered the national scene including **Bob Dole**, **Pat Robertson**, Pete Dupont, Jack *Kemp*, Pat *Buchanan*, and *Howard Baker*, and other veterans like South Carolina's Strom *Thurmond* and Illinois Governor *Jim Thompson* were hoping to be rewarded for their long and loyal service with elevation to the second highest spot in the country. While people often joke about the job of Vice-President, it may be one rarely sought but it is cer- tainly never turned down and past Vice-Presidents like Martin Van Burren, Hannibal Hamlin, **Theodore Roosevelt**, *Calvin Coolidge*, Richard *Nixon*, Lyndon *Johnson*, Spiro *Agnew* and *Gerald Ford* have given the office a new look of leadership potential. Some Vice- Presidents are true leaders while others are mere spokesmen and representatives. After years of being Vice-President himself, *George H. W. Bush* wanted someone he could depend on, and as a staunch conservative, a *Baby Boomer,* a Midwesterner a great campaigner and speech maker, Dan Quayle brought a positive balance to The ticket. He was a new face with no negative baggage, which was just what the nominee ordered. Though a surprise choice, unknown to 98.7% of the electorate outside Indiana, he deflected attention from the top of the ticket.

In debating the Democratic nominee, Lloyd Bentzen, he proved witty, sharp, and poised if lacking in experience. Though he became The butt of many jokes within less than a week, The Democratic nominee for V.P., running for number two, with Massachusetts governor Michael Dukakis, even The Vice Presidential nominee at first was able to say that his credentials were impressive, even remarkable for a man his age. *In groundbreaking events both for the media questioner as well as candidates, the media sharply played up his alleged lack of experience, which had not been an issue four years earlier for* Geraldine Ferraro or for Jack Kennedy who ran and won the Presidency at basically the same age, with just two years more experience than Quayle had. *When Quayle countered his questioner with these facts,* Lloyd Bentsen made the infamous (and unnecessarily personal assertion) "You're no, Jack Kennedy," (I'd say he's a much better all-around man) but Quayle threw it right back in the Texan's face. From that point on, debates were changed to forbid candidates from addressing each other. In spite of the polls and the then dominant culture of the media, the *Bush*/Quayle team won an impressive thirty-one state victory.

Living in the Vice-President's mansion with his supportive wife Marilyn, Dan Quayle began to embark on one other biggest challenges a human being can know. The job of Vice-President is misunderstood largely because by Constitution it is so narrowly defined. The only two functions given to Vice-President are presiding over Senate (*a mostly ceremonial role) he or she is chief legislator, as The President is chief executive* and to step in if the President dies or resigns which has happened seven times in our history. A number of Vice-Presidents have risen to The challenge of becoming President themselves either by the President's death **Teddy Roosevelt,** *Lyndon Johnson, and Gerald Ford* made strong showings; while others ran their own national campaigns later on, (Nixon and Bush are our recent examples). The role can be prestigious and challenging or it can be honorary and ceremonial. By Constitution it simply requires a healthy body ready to step in if the President is incapacitated and requires a Yes-man making him as involved or un-involved as the President wants him. *President Bush* had every intention of using Quayle's many talents and as a leadership asset to his Presidential team, and in the four years they spent together Bush and Quayle became what Quayle believed to be as close as any President/Vice-President team in our history. Dan Quayle was named head of the Space Program and ex officio chairman of *NASA* in which he raised money for the stated purpose of putting human beings on Mars by 2020. He traveled the world meeting foreign dignitaries in places like Iraq, Nicaragua, Panama, and The Philippines. In 1989 when the Philippines came under attack by terrorists and its elected president, Cory Aquino had difficulty controlling the military, it was Quayle who went and gave the proper talks and support needed to keep the island nation democratic. In 1990 Quayle was a key part of the team to decide to involve the U.S. in the coalition to free Kuwait and stop the Iraqi advance in what became Operation Desert Storm. In his four years as Vice-President, Dan Quayle proved a prolific speaker, a voice of reason and hope for both the nation and the conservative administration.

Throughout the Bush Administration, Quayle was a key participant in all matters of foreign and domestic policy, and he made no secret of The fact he was running for President in 1996, a plan thwarted when the incumbents were surprised by a loss to challenger Bill Clinton in a three-way race with Ross Perot. Having been out of the national spotlight for four years Dan Quayle would not be the front-runner in 1996. He did, however, continue a lucrative law practice and write two books in the interim *Standing Firm* one of the greatest political memoirs to date, and The *American Family: Discovering The Values that Make Us Strong. Most recently he wrote Worth Fighting For, a great conservative book.* He endorsed **Bob Dole** at the Republican National Convention and campaigned for him and other Republicans in Indiana. In 2000 he ran a brief campaign for the Presidency which fizzled in Iowa and he chose to go back to private citizenship, though he still occasionally writes and comments on national policy when asked.

Some may find the man I just described fairly impressive among Americans and perhaps even stellar in legal and intellectual accomplishments, but hardly worth a place, let alone such a high one, on a list of the most hopeful public figures to attain heroic premonition. Dan Quayle, however began his ride on the national spotlight a marked man, because while thousands of *Baby Boomers* had achieved prominence in many fields, he was the first member of the Baby Boom Generation, the people who grew up in the '60s and came of age during The *Civil Rights* struggles and the Vietnam War, The first to grow up with television, to be nominated on a national ticket. While coming into the spotlight with a generation of leaders who included, Bill Clinton, Al Gore, Ross Perot, Richard Gerhardt, Joe Biden, Hillary Clinton, and Jerry Brown, more than any of them, Dan Quayle represented his state, his party, and his generation, with the energy, integrity, and dedication that as the leaders of today Baby Boomers want to be recognized on, Quayle was insulted by the media and attacked by a liberal establishment that saw conservatism as the domain of the old and mocked the religious, patriotic, and homegrown values of this young American hero. They even distorted his military record, while he did not go overseas to Vietnam, he did **volunteer for service, when he could have easily gotten a deferment as a legal student. Unlike Clinton, Perot, Nixon, and other national figures, both successful and less so (Alan Keyes springs to mind) the forty-fifth Vice-President had a gift,** perhaps unparalleled *in my lifetime, for doing his job and letting every vile insult, no matter how unfair, just roll off his back with never a care for what his enemies thought. Dan* Quayle is so great, like his autobiography's title he is, like **Clarence Thomas,** one of America's greatest examples of *standing firm, and while like many Americans I wanted to see him surging ahead to the Presidency, he* has pretty much accepted that it will probably never happen. It's still good to think about what a Quayle Presidency would be, how good it would be for America. At any rate Dan Quayle was the first American to represent the Boomer generation in a national election, and with the qualities he showed, unlike the first Baby Boomer President,

Dan Quayle will always be remembered as a great example of what an American, a husband, a father, a Christian and a national leader should be.

8

William Franklin "Billy" Graham 1918-Present

King of Hearts

§

*B*illy Graham was born in Park Road, North Carolina, just
outside Charlotte during the final weeks of World War I. A
country boy from a family with wavering religious faith, his grandfather swore and drank but his parents were largely church-going
Christians. He experienced a life he admirably describes as down
on the farm. Like other Southerners of his time he grew up under
tense race relations, but he knew a lot of Blacks and some Hispanics
who worked with his family on the farm, and though arguably a
less-than-excellent way to relate to "minorities" as subordinates, it
laid the groundwork for his racially tolerant future which embraced
all peoples. In his early years he went to church sporadically but
when he was almost seventeen he was coaxed into going to a revival
with a friend. That night Billy's life changed forever as he came forward to commit his life to Jesus Christ after hearing the preaching
of Dr. Mordecai Ham. Billy credits Dr. Ham as a sort of mentor
although the relationship was brief, he felt called to preach and
largely emulated Ham's style in his early years. He played basketball and once made the newspaper as a star on his high school team.
After feeling the call to preach he immediately began working as a

door-to-d salesman to raise money to go to college and in 1937 he enrolled at Bob Jones University. Then the most prestigious Christian college in the South (it remains reputable today although it has changed much) Graham had difficulty fitting in and transferred to Florida Bible College a Presbyterian-based school largely staffed with professors from mainline denominations but with an Evangelical flavor. He was rigidly disciplined in academics and devoured many books both spiritual and scholastic. He earned degrees in both theology and anthropology and eventually his post-graduate degree from Wheaton College in Illinois. He was twenty-one when he went there, it was his first time North of the Mason-Dixon Line.

Billy Graham's turn to the Christian faith and subsequent embracing of conservative education and speaking made him prepare to become one of the greatest servants of God for a new era. With the outbreak of war he seriously considered leaving college to serve his country and was offered a possible chance to work as a chaplain in Europe if he completed his masters degree first. Billy Graham served in the Army Reserves during the war and briefly worked on a base in the Army chaplaincy program. In early 1944, though still affiliated with the Army chaplaincy program he was hired as pastor few the Southern Baptist church in Western Springs, Illinois which to this day remains the only church Billy Graham ever pastored. He met Ruth, a missionary kid who grew up in China and Korea, while both were attending Florida Bible Institute. They married in 1943 and have been a blissful couple for sixty-five years! She has born him five children. This period in is life also saw him tilt toward the Baptist tradition though eh had been raised Presbyterian as had Ruth, who retains her membership in the American Presbyterian fellowship to this day. From the Western Springs church he began his first broadcast ministries on radio and for over sixty years Billy Graham has had a radio ministry. He was then offered a job with the fledging ministry Youth for Christ and he became its first full-time evangelist, with the endorsement of the chaplaincy program. who felt he had a better chance to better the spiritual well-being of more in that ministry. For the next five years Billy Graham ministered primarily to youth. It was there he struck up a friendship with Grady Wilson and the two were friends and traveling companions until Grady's death in 1987.

By 1949 Billy Graham clearly had a global ministry. He was first appointed president of Northwest Schools of Minnesota with YFC a position he held for three years and spent half the time traveling. By the age of thirty-one he had preached a series of campaigns in Britain and other European countries. With other YFC evangelists he was invited to meet President **Truman** at the White House. The thirty-year old preacher and his buddies, after first counseling the President on the spiritual needs of the nation, made his first public blunder. As reporters cornered him about the meeting he immediately began telling everything he could remember, not realizing he was violating White House protocol. Years later he visited the former President at his home shortly before **Truman** died, and the Missourian forgave him, admitting he had never been properly briefed.

Billy and his team held a series of campaigns in Atlanta, Florida, and in England and Ireland in.1948-9 and in a special series in Modesto, California. Billy and his staff had the turning point when they set together and signed a pledge uphold each other accountable for certain rules. The *Modesto Manifesto* changed them not so much in practice but in the way they related to others, most notably Billy and his friends agreed never to be alone with a woman who was not his wife. The LA Crusade of 1949 made Billy Graham a national figure, and he followed it up by globally ministering in Asia, touring Japan, Korea, Hong Kong, Singapore, the South Pacific, Australia, and New Zealand withe Gospel message. He met **Winston Churchill** and **C.S. Lewis** in Britain. He had branched out of Youth for Christ and launched his own Billy Graham Evangelistic Association, headquartered in Minneapolis. His ministry has raised more money and preached to more people than any association in history. In the fifties he also helped lay the groundwork for *World Vision,* a benevolence ministry that raises money for needy people in poorer parts of the world, with Bob Pierce who was World Vision's president for four decades. In the mid-nineties when Pierce died, Graham's; son *Franklin Graham* (William Franklin. Graham, IV) became president of World Vision. Billy's skills also shine as an author with *Peace with God* which has sold over four million copies, and he had written, ministered on radio and television, and helped to start four worldwide organizations including *Christianity Today* which remains the most popular *Evangelical* periodical geared toward a predominantly lay audience.

Doors opened for the Billy Graham ministry team in the sixties to places as diverse as South Africa, Ethiopia, India, and even behind the Iron Curtain in Hungary and other Communist countries. His South African crusade was unprecedented for being completely integrated even in the land of *apartheid*, he refused to preach to racially separate audiences. He also forged a relationship **Martin Luther King** and the two held services together in several Florida churches. He ministered as a spiritual leader to Richard *Nixon* and John F. Kennedy who faced each other in the 1960 election. Though clearly behind *Nixon*, he was nonpartisan and when Kennedy became President he golfed with him and joined him whenever possible. He maintained close ties to Nixon and also to Vice-President *Lyndon Johnson* who became President when Kennedy was tragically gunned down in 1963. Graham and *Johnson*, a couple of Southerners, both Baptists, hit it off very well and were great friends throughout the years, especially while Johnson was President. Lyndon Johnson even encouraged Billy to take time away from preaching and run for President, promising to get him nominated as the Democratic nominee, but Graham said he would never enter politics, the Lord called him to preach, and that is all he will ever do.

In 1968 he was clearly close to *Nixon* in his second run for the Presidency and while never officially making a political endorsement, he stuck by him, even through President *Nixon's* crises. Billy also ministered to President Ford, played golf, and counseled him to pardon Nixon. A close friend as well as spiritual advisor, Graham participated in both the *Johnson* and *Nixon* funerals delivering the closing prayer at the former and the main sermon at the latter. The middle years saw the Graham team branch into movies in addition to broadcast radio and television and he formed Billy Gram Films which has made at least a dozen movies most notably *Joni, The Hiding Place, Two a Penny, A Cry from a Mountain,* and *Road to Redemption.*

In the seventies and eighties he made at least three visits behind the Iron Curtain to Hungary, Poland, and Russia, preaching the Gospel in hostile territory and influencing members of the nations for Christ, in one case of Hungary even influencing the nation itself. Another key ministry partner was the Gospel singer Ethel Waters who attended crusades and sang. In the eighties he went.to East Germany and Czechoslovakia and in 1984 his long anticipated visit to Moscow itself was extended. A spiritual leader and committed anti-Communist, Billy encouraged Jewish emigration to Israel and a relaxation of dictatorship, influencing the world for the anti-Communist message along with heroes of hope like Margaret **Thatcher** and Lech **Walesa.** In all of his travels, however, the crux of his message remained the same, you must be born-again through faith in Jesus Christ, the salvation He offers by His death, shed blood, and Resurrection, repentantly giving your life to Him. In the late '80s he toured China making it into a part of the world even more impenetrable than Iron Curtain. All this was done with mutual advising and boundaries coordinated thought the White House and Graham was a friend and advisor to **Presidents Reagan**, Bush and Clinton who also advised him on technical things like protocol that a preacher is less adept at knowing. In 1994 he was invited to meet with Kim Il Sung in North Korea the most Communist and (with the possible exception of Iran) most anti-American nation on earth, but he was as always a cordial and spiritually enriching guest. In 1983 he was given the Presidential Medal of Freedom by **Ronald Reagan**, the first Protestant minister so rewarded and in 1995 the Congressional Gold Star (the 114th recipient) the first was *George Washington.* In 1993 he met Pope *John Paul, II* at the Vatican. When the Soviet Union came down he met with *Boris Yeltsin* in Moscow as the two were there to dedicate one of the first Christian schools sanctioned since the demise of Russian Communism.

Through more than three quarters of a century Billy Graham, with his stalwart wife *Ruth*, has ministered to millions and been personal friends with hundreds. Some have been Presidents and royalty, others have been prisoners and gangsters, most served Jesus Christ, some have been dictators, others have turned away from the Gospel after long lives of faith. In his literally thousands of evangelistic crusades, more than thirty million inquirers have come forward to pray with his staff and more than any other person connected with the Evangelical world, the name of Billy Graham stands out as the spiritual leader of Protestant Christianity in the Twentieth Century. The only clergyman to receive both the Presidential Medal of Freedom and the Congressional Gold star. the only person to make *Good Housekeeping and Gallup poll* list of most admired Americans thirty times, the only one to speak as an acceptable orthodox voice for virtually all Bible-believing Protestants, Billy Graham's greatest honor is th**at he has served Jesus Christ according to His will and when He finally takes him home, the Lord will say** *Well done, thou good and faithful servant.* **His legacy also includes at least** twenty grandchildren and great-grandchildren, a good many of them in ministry. *Ruth Bell Graham went home to be with Jesus in 2008 and the shocked Billy grieved but proceeded to continue a writing ministry, having written or revised at least four books since turning eight-six.* **An ordinary man, Billy Graham set out about seventy years ago to do the will of God, and with a select few like** *John Wesley, D. L. Moody, Charles Finny,* **and C.S. Lewis** he can say he has done extraordinary things by the power and with the blessings of God.

9

Helen Keller
(1876-1967)

Queen of Diamonds OF HOPE

§

*H*elen Adams Keller was born in an affluent Alabama family in the late nineteenth century. At first an ordinary child she sufferer an early routine illness that do to the available medicine of the day left her blind and deaf. While she could speak her young vocal abilities never developed into adulthood and she briefly lost her ability to smell and taste though that was restored in childhood. At first she became a terror around the house, throwing everything around while her indulgent parents simply put up with it feeling to blame for her situation. Gradually, however, they found a private tutor for her in Anne Macy Sullivan who not only taught Helen but molded her bringing out a genius potential that was both present in her and brilliantly developed by her teacher. By the time she was in her early twenties she was an accomplished poet, who without seeing or hearing, spoke several languages, and wrote voraciously on political and international affairs. She attended Radcliffe College one of the few women to attend what was then a women's' college at a time when less than 3% of all American women studied after high school. She became the first blind woman and the first blind/Deaf person anywhere in the world to earn a college degree.

Throughout the 1920s and 30s Helen Keller embarked on a national and somewhat international series of meetings. Like **Billy Graham**, she had a message the world needed to hear and was willing to leave her comfort zone and go to earth's ends to tell her story. From fundraising for the blind, to the rights of prisoners and others arrested, to a need for social change (which eventually bordered on Socialism) Helen Keller spoke boldly on topics of interest in the world. At first she was a strong supporter of **Woodrow Wilson** whom she thought would extend equal rights to women and open the doors for social engineering to benefit the poor and most needy Americans. Though never officially assigned to any of his task forces, she spoke for many of his programs and met with him and other leaders throughout the U.S. When the U.S. got involved in World War I she refused to support the President, and said that our democracy was in serious danger if we went to Europe to help imperialist nations win out over others. While she did not protest the war, she supported professional protesters and even raised funds for them when possible. The red scare and its subsequent crackdown on crime saw her proclaim a loud message on both sides of the Atlantic about the rights of free speech. She toured Britain, Italy, Sweden, Germany, and eventually went to the Soviet Union and met with Lenin, calling him a worthwhile if transitional leader into a more tolerant era of equality. She also toured Australia, Japan, and India, filling stadiums, raising funds, and making worldwide friends who touted her friend both to nations and individuals. She of course was not without her enemies as well and some of the criticism bordered on the absurd. The one legitimate criticism at this stage, however, was that while she was a champion of individual free speech, she paid little attention to the voices of the majority in her own country and seemed to think policy should be dictated by the opinions of a minority of rich liberals who shared her views.

By the late thirties Helen Keller was a millionaire but with even more determination to spread her message. She developed a faith, Swedenborginianism, a mystical sect, rarely heard of even in its native Sweden, but Helen Keller was easily its most proficient spokesperson and she gained converts in the United States And Europe. She also preached in Baha'i congregations speaking of tolerance and inclusion in religion. When World War II hit, however, she did not preach open tolerance of all views and became openly 100% behind the U.S. and other allies in total annihilation of the imperialist governments of Japan and Nazi Germany and their allies. She worked to raise funds and help our Allies and visited thousands of American servicemen in hospitals. While she supported the Soviet Union as a war ally, her idealism about Communism was long over, and she denounced Stalin as a hypocritical murderer. After the war she toured the war torn capitals throughout Japan, Italy, Germany, and Eastern Europe and where **Billy Graham** and others could not go, she had an open door for her secular message. During her lifetime Helen Keller helped to establish at least twenty schools and hospitals in Europe and Asia. A final tour to Australia at the age of seventy-five proved her traveling days over and she remained home, largely committed to the care of others for her last years. Beating the odds as she had done expertly throughout her life, Helen Keller lived almost a hundred years and continued to write and comment on world and personal affairs in her last quarter century.

In her lifetime Helen Keller wrote nine books, spoke in over ten thousand gatherings, served on boards of at least three national organizations, and influenced Presidents and kings. She was a patriotic American who criticized her government when she saw fit, a universalist who condemned many crimes and criminals, a Socialist who made millions of dollars, a writer who could not see, a commentator who could not hear, an actress who could not speak in an articulate voice, a teacher who never got credentialed in her own country, a student who mastered language, literature, and philosophy, a Disabled woman who achieved more than ninety-nine point nine percent of American men! More than anything else Helen Keller is a testimony to the human spirit a determined woman who shows Disabled and others that achievement can be won by anyone who expects it accepts his or her purpose in life, has high goals, and never gives up until they are achieved. Though she never married, by her books and speeches she taught the world about the needs of people with disabilities and that overwhelmingly we have the same needs and wants as others, and the same ability and desire for social acceptance, relational and sexual fulfillment, and financial stability.

10

Woodrow Wilson (1856-1924)

King of Spades of Hope

*B*orn in the dark days of Southern outcry against Northern interference, *AKA War of Northern Aggression,* a son of the South though his father had migrated from Ohio and his mother had emigrated from Scotland. Woodrow Wilson was born to British Presbyterian stock in Virginia. He was a preacher's kid who received his education at home, though his father was a learned doctor of ministry and education, young Woodrow had difficulty reading. At age thirteen he was reading everything he could get his hands on, but largely forgot most of what he read unless he said it. A supreme example of various kinds of learning, what many would even term learning disabilities, he was an auditory learner, clearly able to think with the left side of his brain and remember what he heard far more than what he saw. Using fledgling recording instruments available to his day, he became a lifelong student, eventually studying at Princeton and earning postgraduate degrees in education and a doctorate in political science. Some say he had dyslexia, which had yet to be diagnosed, but more likely he had neurological impairments that made his reading suffer and his left brain work better. He remains the first and only President to have an earned doctorate.

In the 1880s he embarked on a career as a college professor and writer of textbooks first working at Wesleyan University as a history teacher and debate coach, he also was an assistant football coach (one few two Presidents to have that job). He later returned to his alma mater, Princeton to teach and in 1903 became the president of Princeton, the first layman to hold that job. Though still a son of the South in every sense, living in New Jersey for educational reasons saw him enter New Jersey politics and in 1910 he was a surprise nominee for governor and won the election. As a tough man of study which often takes more energy than physical pursuits, he was a stalwart governor and in jurist two years, accomplished things the state had failed to accomplish for years. In 1912 he became a surprise compromise candidate for President of the United States, the Democrats needing a respectable and well-spoken governor who was unknown to the electorate and brought no negative baggage as they were facing two strong Republican challenges, incumbent President William Howard Taft (the endorsed party candidate) and former President **Theodore Roosevelt** running as a Progressive (or Bull Mouse Party) for an unprecedented third term.

Like at Princeton and in the Trenton governor's mansion, Woodrow Wilson was a leader of the United States with optimism, conviction, energy, and wit. No President since **Abraham Lincoln** had been so adept at telling humorous and insightful stories in ways that would d spellbind audiences and communicate the need to further his agenda. Ironically he held very strong political views against **Theodore Roosevelt**, though he did not dislike him personally. It was **Roosevelt** who as President expanded the role of the U.S. in world affairs and while TR and his mentor slain President McKinley set us to inherit an empire, it was Wilson, who even more than Taft, Roosevelt's; immediate predecessor, expanded the role of the U.S. in foreign affairs. For the first six years of his Presidency that role was limited to inter-hemisphere affairs endorsing and helping numerous political factions in Cuba, the Dominican Republic, and other Latin American and Caribbean countries. Ironically the one place where it failed to work was our border neighbor, Mexico, who had at least four revolutions during his term including the murder of several American citizens by Poncho Villa, an act Wilson was unable to avenge. By 1914 the great European powers were at war with Germany battling in Belgium and France and the Central Powers, primarily Austria, Hungary, and Turkey at war to keep their empires while Britain, France, Russia, and the other Allied Powers fought to contain them and expand their own influence. At first Wilson committed to benign neutrality but a series of events culminated in the German sinking of the USS *Listinania*. A few months later, a telegram German Foreign Minister Zimmerman sent to Mexico invited the Mexicans to join them if America ever fought for the Allies and Germany would reinstate large American holdings to Mexico.

Wilson was reelected over a strong Republican challenge by *Charles Evans Hughes* in 1916, and committed the country to continue peace not victory. In April of 1917, however he sought a deceleration of war and within weeks Americans were in Europe fighting to defeat the Germans and help the British and French win the World War. Successful beyond our wildest dreams, America, just twenty years before (and throughout most of Wilson's life) a rural republic of one horse towns and a few large cities, had become the leaders in international affairs. When Wilson sailed to Versailles, France to work out the pace agreements in November of 1918 along with the heads of the other five major Allies, he was credited as being the man who made the world safe for democracy. Over a million French and other Europeans lined the streets to see him as he walked thought the streets of France along with the other delegates. There was no doubt that "Wilson the just" was the leader of the campaign and recognized by American, British, French, Russian, Belgian, Italian, Japanese, Greek, and most of the "free" world as the undisputed leader of the world, the foundation of Pax *Americana who would usher* in an era of world peace. Ironically the very religious Wilson was a *Post Millennialist (or believer in post-millenarianism)* and believed that man had to make world peace and rule for a thousand years of Christian justice as a prerequisite to Jesus coming back. He led the meetings calling for a League of Nations and most Americans and Europeans listened. Ironically, Wilson became a victim of his own success, the Republicans needed staunch opposition to avoid being a minority party since ti was the Democrats who got most of the credit for the great victories. In Henry Cabot Lodge, Sr., Republicans successfully found the leader that divided Americans and made it difficult for Wilson to maintain American leadership. When back in the States touring the West to promote his message, the sixty-two-year old President suffered a stroke and was bedridden for a number of weeks. Though incapacitated for a time, Wilson bounced back to lead the party and the nation to the end, even hoping to be offered a third term.

Instead he was out of office when his term expired, the Republicans led by Warren G. Harding won the Presidency in 1920 and Wilson's views were largely ignored by Congress and his successor. Remaining a great memory in the American mindset Woodrow Wilson was a character unrivaled as an international peacemaker until *Richard Nixon* and a charismatic media presence before **Reagan,** though he lived pre-television. He died in Washington D. C. four years later, largely living the life of a private citizen at the age of sixty-eight and was mourned by a nation who loved him but was divided about his legacy.

Woodrow Wilson was a hero of hope because he had hope for a better day for America and the world and did everything in hi power to strive to see that day come. While he loathed the thought of war having grown up in the days of the Civil War, he cringed at the thought Americans fighting overseas but committed our troops knowing Americas' national interests were at stake. While being the single most leader of the most horrible war recorded by man at the time, Wilson hoped for a brighter future and campaigned in the American spirit of unity and victory, on both sides of the Atlantic, to see peace inaugurated. Again, like a quintessential American, when he lost the second war, the battle for public opinion, he took it like a man, kept a stiff upper lip, and returned to private life. Twenty-one years later another American President, Franklin D., *Roosevelt*, a student of Wilson who had served in his Naval Department, implemented many of Wilson's policies to help form the United Nations to keep America, Europe, Asia and the world from having any further such conflicts. From beyond the grave, Wilson's' old friends and supporters who remained could remember the hope this hero of hope inspired to bring the world to peace, with largely American principles, and though it has not been achieved, it has remained the goal of every American and all the Presidents since have built on Wilson's points of world peace. Personally, he was a hopeful and loving man, loyal to his wife, both the mother of his children who died, and his second, his children, his students, his friends, and his supporters, striving to serve God with a clear conscience and do the best for his family and his country.

11

Joan Of Arc
(1412-1431)

Queen of Clubs of Hope

❦

A little peasant girl, from a simple French village who knew neither prosperity nor peace, the French-speaking girl whom the English speaking world would come to know as Joan of Arc was born in 1412 to devout Catholic parents. Joan D'ark was born in Jeremy, a French village on April 6, 1412. The village was still half in France and half Anglo-Burgundun duchy under the British partition of the Hundred Years War. At the age of thirteen she first began hearing what she called voices from God and His saints. While she has been canonized by the Catholic Church for her devotion to God and faith, no pope or Protestant leaders have ever said that believing the authenticity of her message or their divine source is a required matter for faith or practice. That said, as a thinking man I cannot fail to believe that the voices and revelations Joan of Arc received from God were as real as the words we hear from the President, pulpit, professor, and Perkins' waitress. An uneducated, but very wise, lower middle-class girl not even at the age of majority, influenced and changed the course of European history through military victory, thwarting the most powerful army in the known world on a relatively minor mission to regain a relatively small piece of land.

That that could be done is a testimony to a divine source that Joan of Arc was led and chosen by God and that He guided her with the French soldiers under her to win a spectacular victory for Christianity and propose God's purposes for Western civilization.

She was seventeen when she stood up in front of the titular King of her French region and encouraged him to reclaim his throne. At first hesitant, and unable to see her divine mission, Charles eventually committed to reclaiming his throne with her help. Unbelievably within two years, he would be restored to his throne, France would enjoy more territory over the Northern half of their kingdom than they had had in seven decades, and the world's most powerful Army would be defeated by a teenage girl. Furthermore she was both strait-laced and witty, she never smoked, drank, or swore, nor did she allow those behavior sin her soldiers, but she was also giddy, laughed a lot and played kids' games with the other girls all the way until a few weeks before she confronted the King.

Within just one year, Joan of Arc led the French soldiers to the Duchy to Bergundun where the French won the most significant military victory of a war that actually lasted more than 100 years. Obviously the ramifications are hard to understand for our day while both Britain and France were solidly Christian and followed the same Pope in name, both claimed they were holding the hope of Christian civilization, while his recognized leaders of Christendom were more than nine hundred miles to the East and were taken over by Muslim Turks in the same century. Joan was a true Christian influence, unlike most of both "sacred and secular" leaders of her day, was seen by her weeping over the death of English soldiers particularly when they went with sin on their souls. In one instance she cradled a dying English soldier in her arms while vainly sending a wounded French officer to get a priest to be with the man for his last moments. May 7, 1429 was the great day of victory ruin the city of Orleans and residents that city celebrate suit to this day for the vindication of their culture and place nm world history. Ironically after winning back Orleans, the key to Northern France which the British had taken, and then driving the British back to Agincourt,she allowed British prisoners to leave Agincort on Sunday, committed to making it a day free of bloodshed, thereby cutting off what could have been a greater French victory over the whole of the Norther Gallic region. She celebrated the victory with the troops and participated in the coronation of Charles July 17, 1429. By that summer England also recognized his sovereignty over France, though they continued to recognize their king as being over portions of Northern France. The following day she was captured by English forces.

Again this reality is understandable only in light of the philosophy of the Middle Ages. The English having just surrendered and been beaten by the army led by Joan, still saw fit to punish her, a woman for leading men and claiming to have heard from God. Her trial would be set up by both English and French ecclesiastical authorities and judged mostly on religious charges. Joan pleaded categorically not guilty to all of the charges but herself began to have some doubts. If she were God's chosen vessel, why was He now allowing fer to suffer this torment? And if God had used her to win such a significant victory why did He not protect her so she could be there to lead others? Unfortunately these questions will never be answered, at least not this side of eternity.. At first she was persuaded to recant her former statements in exchange for a promise she would not be killed. To one question, however, she pleaded innocence, a fairly typical medieval response. That was whether she was in God's grace, she said she did not know, seeing it as a trap and that only God can ultimately judge how the condition of one's soul stands. The English saw it as a confession of guilt, at least feelings of guilt for her wearing men's' clothing and usurping authority that God rightly gives to kings, not mere women. Taking over the trial, the English eventually condemned her for her refusal to recant a divine source for her voices and insisting that God's favor was part of the victory. In this some have called Joan of Arc the first great Protestant before Protestantism. In a sense she was more purely Catholic and more purely Protestant than any great Christian of her age, being given the wisdom to think for herself with solely divine guidance, being given a wisdom greater than the Pope or any Cannon of doctrinal seals could give, she stood on her principals. The other great question that must be asked is why did the French particularly King Charles a very devout Christian, not intercede on behalf of the woman who had won their war and restored him to his throne. Again only a medieval understanding of authority can help us, he was very grateful for her involvement with Joan, but believed that the Church authorities had originally forced her recantation were greater than any human or national crown and her life was now in God's hands needing no such intervention from the mortal king.

Joan of Arc was of course executed by burning with English and French soldiers. Shortly before she died she asked to hold a cross in her hand and like Jesus she prayed for her assailants. Her last word was "Jesus" and like those who orchestrated our Lord's ultimate Sacrifice, an English soldier said "We are doomed, we have burned a saint." *In addition to her status as a great hero for Catholics and Protestants, and military people throughout the ages, Joan of Arc became a legal example as a defendant, since her case is unique for its time for having minutes recorded including legal questioning, answers, and testimony-quite likely the most ancient trial of history so recorded.*

Eventually the Roman Catholic Church did *cannonize* her and she has been revered as the patron saint of France one of the great historical figures of Western civilization. **Winston Churchill** in writing the great history of the English speaking people wrote of her as a Christian saint of undaunted courage and was able to praise her for her victory, though she was fighting his ancestors. Her influence and importance as a Christian, as a saint, as a woman, as a French person, and as a European are reinforced by her treatment by the great writers George Bernard Shaw in Britain and *Mark Twain* in America. But for me, paradoxically enough, what is even more remarkable is that she was mentioned along with other prominent woman in the theme song of *Maude*, one of the most controversial and radical TV shows in history. That Norman Lear, **the pioneer of secular humanistic television, would allow audiences to hear this Christian's name announced after which it was said** *with the Lord to guide her* **before watching his offerings of liberal indoctrination speaks volumes to the broad and universal appeal of the m**essage and eternally significant life of this martyred nineteen-year-old girl.

12

Abraham Lincoln
(1809-1865)

Jack of Hearts of Hope

§

*B*orn in a log cabin in Kentucky in 1809 Abraham Lincoln was a humble child of the American Midwest raised on Bible stories and tales of great Americans particularly George Washington, Thomas Jefferson, and Benjamin Franklin. He came of age in an America largely rural and still heavily British influenced, received his education at home, and grew up mainly in Indiana and later in Illinois. By his mid-twenties he was a lawyer and began embarking on a political career. He was elected to the Illinois legislature and by 1846 became a representative in the U.S. Congress. Ironically Lincoln lost several elections including the first in which he was engaged in 1836. Though a legislator in Springfield for the better part of two decades, he proposed little legislation and spent most of his time practicing law, largely defending poor and often oppressed clients, and riding back and forth from Springfield to his district. He did nothing in Illinois to make him stand out as a great leader. His one shining moment in this early part of his career came in 1846 when the thirty-five year-old was elected a United States congressman. Lincoln went to Washington for the first time as a Whig, all but appointed by his securely Whig district and he acccpted the nomination as a compromise having recently committed to serving one term in exchange for letting two friends in legislature also take a turn.

A decade later Lincoln ran his first campaign for United States Senate. No longer a Whig, he was now, like many disgruntled members of the more federal but socially conservative party, disgruntled and became an early supporter of the Republican Party. Having embraced its original standard-bearer, former California governor John Fremont, Lincoln seemed born to be the leader of the Republicans. He was, however, seen as one of their more moderate members, staunchly anti-slavery, but committed to voting with his constituents, who wanted to abolish slavery without going to war or otherwise alienating the South. Furthermore as the major anti-slavery party of the day, Lincoln saw the need to unite all anti-slavery interests, including the abolitionists, Freesoilers, who were prospectors of the West, staunchly opposed to slavery but wanting peaceful co-existence in the territories, moderate Midwesterners, and even pro-Union Democrats and those from the border states.

While his task of unity was monumental, he rose to the challenge with a series of speeches debating Stephen Douglas in various venues throughout Illinois. The relatively conservative state was expected to elect Lincoln to Congress, the Kentucky-born Unionist and anti-slavery Republican over the Illinois-born Democrat with Southern sentiment. The brilliant debates became a model for newspaper men of their day and a standard for issues talks and candidate contests for a century and a half. Ironically Douglas won a close election to U.S. Senate in what some would say was an act of God. If Lincoln had been elected to Senate in 1858 he would most likely have become one of thirty-eight Union voices (thirty-nine counting Andrew Johnson) who sat and debated issues, while a lesser man sat in the White House trying to deal with the national crisis. Instead Douglas went to Senate while the Lord was preparing Abraham Lincoln for his monumental role two years later.

In 1860 Abraham Lincoln was nominated as the first Republican to be on the ballot in all states in the Union. The country divided, voted on completely regional lines, with most of the states where slavery was illegal going for Lincoln including the new free states of Kansas, Nebraska California, and Oregon, while all the Southern states voted for his opponent. The Southern states of the Cotton Belt not one vote went to Lincoln. President Abraham Lincoln stepped into a role never before filled nor since. He was the first President to preside over the succession of a part of a country built on democracy and this at war with itself until allegedly democratic principles controlling both sides. So much can be said about the Civil War, but Lincoln's role in it proved there was hope. Abraham Lincoln ingeniously proved himself a hero of hope, choosing the most able men to advise and to fight and to lead the war, most brilliantly Ulysses S. Grant who won the final battles for the Union and brought about the screened of the South. After the great but mutually bloody victory at Gettysburg, Pennsylvania Lincoln gave the address that became one of the most popular speeches ever recorded. That day he wrote the Emancipation Proclamation which promised freedom to all slaves in the rebellious states. On January 1, 1863 after a rousing speech Lincoln gave to inform the nation of the new law, Union soldiers, many of whom had joined the Army as liberators, became freedom fighters, going into the Southern states in rebellion, with the famous battle cry (from the **Battle Hymn** by Julia Warde Howe) as Christ died to make men holy we will die to make men free. The bloodiest war in American history was over within seventeen months after hundreds of thousands of deaths on both sides and a literal brothers' war with Americans fighting in units literally made up of brothers against brothers, fathers against sons, grandfathers, against grandsons, uncles against nephews.

In 1864 Lincoln was resoundingly reelected to a second term, this time winning a majority of popular votes over pro-Union Democrat and former general George B. McClellan. All was not happy as just weeks after the election his youngest and most beloved son Tad died. It was the third time the Lincolns had lost a child but the other two died in infancy. More than ever before Lincoln turned to the Lord Jesus Christ to give him hope. Ironically Lincoln was one of the few Presidents who was never a member of a particular denomination though clearly Protestant, his mother had been Presbyterian and his father Methodist and records dispute whether he was ever baptized. He was however, one of our most Christian Presidents and his speeches are full of quotes and paraphrases from Scripture and references to faith both Old and New Testaments. Clearly a hero of hope, Lincoln presided over the end of the war. When Robert E. Lee came to Washington to officially sign the papers ending the war, Lincoln asked the White House orchestra to play "Dixie," causing **Winston Churchill** to say more than half a century later that the American Civil War was the last one fought by gentlemen. The Republican Party still claims him as their standard bearer calling itself the party of Lincoln, his home sates Illinois is the land of Lincoln and more towns, counties, and companies are named after Abraham Lincoln than any other American. He is enshrined in the folklore of America with February 12 being a holiday and the observance prompting state dinners and Republican Party dinners and events. His face is on the five dollar bill and enshrined on Mount Rushmore as a Americanization unity.

Just like Jesus, the hero of Hope Americana died on Good Friday being the target of an illegal conspiracy that put a bullet through him in April 15, 1865. Ironically he seemed to know he was not going to live long having recently told his extraordinary wife Mary and Union commanders in the South to make sure Blacks got the right to vote immediately (something he previously said he had no intention to do) so that the freed slaves would have political clout in the area where their former oppressors would most likely take charge. Ironically he was the man of American unity, though he presided over the bloodiest war in our history while within months of his death the largely political disunity saw few people killed but domestic squabbling under three less capable executives that led to wounds between North and South that would not be healed for a generation. Abraham Lincoln, the greatest leader America ever had, was the hero of war, but more importantly the unifier, and hero of hope.

13

Mother Teresa
(1924-1997)

Queen of Hearts of Hope

*T*his authentic hero of hope rose from truly hopeless circumstances to bring hope to millions around the world. Interestingly though Eastern European from Albania, a country of mixed
religious and ethnic claims, she is a prototype for an American success story, a medieval Catholic heroine like Joan of Arc, an Asian
ascetic Mother Teresa settled in India where she eventually became
a citizen. Though seen as a poor woman of hope for the hopeless,
Mother Teresa managed to summon the eyes and ears of the world
to the plight of the people among whom she works so that her message could be known the world over. Known for her quiet strength,
simple and direct speaking one-on-one, and her prayerfulness,
Mother Teresa's administrative skills formed an organization that
has reached 106 couturiers and boasts over 4000 nuns and 40,000
lay workers in her employ, planting schools, hospitals, children's
homes; and the like throughout India, Europe, and all over the world.

She was born in 1924. Very early on she heard the calling of God
and became a missionary to India. She founded the Sisters of Charity
an organization that would bring food, medicine, understanding, and
the Gospel message to millions the world over. As a fledgling min-

istry it made its mark in India and within a generation on millions of Catholics and others throughout the world. Universally recognized as a leader she was honored by millions of Protestants and others who did not share her theology or embrace her commitment to universal population and condemnation of abortion.

By 1959 she had settled in India and began her work amongst poor of that country. Based in Calcutta she has become the embodiment of both local and worldwide philanthropy. While promoting the Roman Catholic theologian views of Christianity she has become the defining figure of Christian missions of modern times and has brought thousands of Hindus and Muslims to make professions of faith in Jesus Christ.

Like her predecessors *Francis of Assisi*, Ignatius Loyola, and St. *Benedict*, Mother Teresa is a *rigorous* personally disciplined woman who refuses to waste minutes and while having taken the vow of poverty, her organization takes in millions they put to good use by the dollar. In all her missions and outstations thought the world the Sisters of Charity, and their volunteers get up early and adhere to a very structured day of prayer, discipleship, and outreach. Mother Teresa personally spent about three to four hours in prayer every morning before meeting her resident sisters for prayer usually during the first hour of daylight.

The sign on the door of her order offices in Calcutta says "he that loveth correction loveth knowledge." Talked about thought the 1980s and '90s as a living saint, she was in fact beautified (nominated for sainthood) within weeks after her death and in 97 was canonized by the Roman Catholic Church in record time. Like hundreds who lived under the papacy of *John Paul*, II she was given the ultimate honor for one of her faith, to be made a subject of veneration and hope for centuries after her death. She received a knighting from Queen Elizabeth in India and the 1980 Nobel Peace Prize. She has been honored with at least nineteen different medals of greatness by various nations including India and America, becoming the third non-American to win the Presidential Medal of Freedom and having **Ronald Reagan** bestow honorary American citizenship on her, also the third time the honor was given to a foreigner. Though apolitical throughout her life, she had less success in convincing later Presidents and Prime ministers the wrongness of their policies. Her good friend and supporter Indian Prime Minister Indira Gandhi enacted an illegal forced sterilization law that was overturned by Indian courts. At a dinner given in her honor at the White House in 1995 she preached against her favorite target, abortion and though there was overwhelming applause from the crowd only one table where as seated the President Bill Clinton and his wife and his Vice-President and his wife, only four people did not cheer. The tragic scene caused Pennsylvanian Bob *Casey* a pro-life Roman Catholic Democrat to say what a tragedy politics is when you can be forced by a commitment to your beliefs and special interests not to cheer one of the most remarkable women to ever live. Though her death in 1997 was overshadowed by the death of Princess Diana the same week, it is Mother Teresa who will be remembered by historians, theologians, and psychologists as an example of hope. Like Saints *Francis* and *Benedict* she will be remembered for the foundation of an order, a system of discipline, peace, and philanthropy modeled on the Master Himself by which bodies and souls are fed, helped, and saved through the Word of God.

14

Ronald Reagan
(1911-2004)

Jack of Clubs of Hope

*R*onald Wilson Reagan was born in Tampico, Illinois on February 6, 1911, a kind of dream making American story very much unlike the America of his day and unlike anything America had achieved before. He grew up with a father who worked as an itinerant cobbler and moved around often, settling in Dixon but moving at least three times within the tone. During World War One he grew up in the Presidency of Woodrow Wilson and early on was given the nickname "Dutch" which stuck with for life. His father was a lovable alcoholic his mother a very devout Christian of the Disciples few Christ and she raised Ronald to be a devout Christian, a Bible-believer, panda proclaimer of his faith, lessons he Hellespont pr life. Reagan became a lifeguard in his teenage years and saved over a hundred people from drowning. In 1929 he enrolled in Eureka College in Iowa eventually earning a bachelor's degree in economics and sociology. In 1933 he became a local sport announcer for the Chicago Cubs farm system and eventually did Cub games through telegraph. In 1935 he won a contest for being the best local sports announcer and was given a chance to go to Hollywood to be screened for films.

In 1936 Ronald Reagan began making movies, first largely ste-
reotypic and many of which are not even on video. He was in what
were then termed "B" movies, the first showing in usually double-
featured films. By 1939 he was seen as "the Erroll Flynn of the
B-movies" and would be comparable to being the Michael J. Fox or
even Leonardo DiCaprio of his era. In 1940 he played a relatively
minor role in *Knute Rockne: All American* the very poignant story
of an American football legend and how he revolutionized the game
for consumption in American colleges. By playing George Gipp, a
defensive lineman plagued by health problems, he showed he could
act at serious roles and was signed to a multi-million dollar contract
by MGM. In 1941 he starred in *King's Row* and also went on to
make *Bedtime for Bonzo, The Santa Fe Trail,* and at least twenty
more movies. In 1941 war came and Reagan immediately volunteered for combat as he had already been in the Army Air Corps
Reserves. Unable to make it as a pilot due to vision challenges, the
Army thought he would be better suited by making war films fueling
the patriotism of Americans and also worked as a decoder, gathering
intelligence work from Germany. An early marriage to actress Jane
Wyman ended in divorce but produced two great kids Maureen and
Michael. In 1952 he married Nancy Davis, the love of his life and
they were blissfully married for fifty-two years. In 1953 he became
president few the Screen Actors Guild and though voted out the following term he again became the union's president in the late fifties
during the Hollywood walk out and took the major studios through
their first strike negotiating contracts with minimum guidelines for
movie and television actors that have been in place for five decades
and changed the course of the entertainment industry. He was host
of General Electric Theater and raised funds for that organization.

In the fifties he got his first taste of political fever. As a working
class Midwesterner, Reagan had grown up a Democrat and cast his
first four ballots for Franklin Delano Roosevelt. In the fifties, however, he supported Eisenhower and struck up a friendship with Vice
President Nixon. Not until 1956, however, did he switch his party
affiliation to Republican. His father-in-law Loyal Davis introduced
him to Senator *Barry Goldwater* and Reagan campaigned to help
him win the Republican nomination. Reagan gave a speech to the

Republican National Convention in August nominating Goldwater for President and millions of dollars poured in for the candidate following what later became known as *the speech.* When Goldwater lost in a landslide to President Lyndon Baines Johnson, millions of Americans believed there was nothing wrong with Goldwater's philosophy but it was his delivery and the baggage he carried and that Ronald Reagan was really the man who should carry the same values to the White House. At first Reagan laughed about it saying he was an actor and union man with no ambition or design on elective office. After much coaxing, however, and nationwide petitions in 1965 Reagan agreed to be a candidate for governor of California. Winning the election in a landslide over Pat Brown, Reagan allowed himself to be taken lightly by the governor and then capitalized on his mistake one that will be always be associated with Brown but was followed by many others. As governor Reagan became one of the most adept governors in the nation, enforcing the law in race riots, giving magnificent speeches (then all written by him) cutting taxes and welfare rolls, putting millions to work, while increasing the grants to needy recipients. In 1970 he was reelected governor and emerged as a potential candidate for the Presidency in 1968. He did not campaign for the Presidency then, while allowing himself to be nominated by some California delegations, he threw his support behind Nixon.

From 1974-1980 he was seen as leading a group of ultra-conservative Republicans. He became a very popular radio talk-show host, and in 1976 made a run for the Presidency, this time challenging the incumbent President Gerald Ford. He maintained under normal circumstances he wouldn't challenge the incumbent of his party but since Ford was appointed not elected the competition would strengthen the party and challenge both men and voters on the issues. Ford won the nomination and though Reagan campaigned for him, he went on to lose a very close election to Jimmy Carter. *Michael Reagan* and others believe it was nothing short of miraculous that he was kept out of the Oval Office in 76, a miracle God had ordained to bring an end to European Communism in His own time, letting Reagan come at just the right time, when Pope *John Paul*, II, Lech **Walesa, Margaret Thatcher**, *Vaclav Havel,* and Helmut *Kohl* were also in place and on board with him to affect events in the Soviet Union.

Of course Reagan became President in 1981 after winning in a landslide over the incumbent a feat not equaled since 1932. At first considered a lightweight actor by his enemies, Ronald Reagan became the greatest President in the technological age. So much can be said about the Reagan Administration that my survey her will suffice it to say he was a man of hope who set out to give Americans a little more hope than they had four years and ended up revitalizing a nation, the Western world, and hundreds of millions throughout the world with the message of American values that had first brought hope in the Revolutionary era. Like no President since **Abraham Lincoln** he believed that America was meant to be the last best hope on earth and he successfully saved the world for democracy. In the eight years of the Reagan Presidency taxes were cut, the economy was revitalized, jobs were created, our military expanded, American hope was revitalized and the Soviet Union was defeated. When he took office in January coif 1981 the Soviet Union had superior military weapons and was in a postilion to win a war against any nation in the world including the U.S.

Within five years Reagan built up a defense system that made the Soviet Union know they could no longer get away with military adventurousness because they had met their match, in fact they met their better, and it was not going to allow them to get away with anything. Every American is taught about World War II, and wars in Korea, Vietnam, Operation Desert Storm, and Operation Iraqi Freedom. Interestingly few American know about and some have never even heard of the war that had the most direct impact on the Western hemisphere and more impact on modern times than all the others. When Soviet and Cuban Communists exported their revolution to the tiny island of Grenada in 1983, Reagan sent troops of Americans and other hemisphere troops under the auspices of the Organization of American States. Within a weekend the tiny island which was to become The Soviet Union's second domino in their attempt to stack the thirty-four of the Western nations of **the hemisphere, was knocked down and within a weekend Reagan insured the Evil Empire we would never again play domi-**

noes, we would *knock down* all theirs **and** keep **them** from ever playing dominoes again. **Interestingly Reagan quipped that the Communists were trying to steal Christmas by taking over the world's eggnog supply and he would stop anyone who tired to ste**al Christmas. That simple, humorous and dead right attitude led Ronald Reagan to be the leader of the free world who eventually saved over three hundred million Europeans and others from living under Communism.

Along with **Margaret Thatcher,** the Western world won the tremendous victory, the Soviet Union was defeated the Berlin Wall came down, and Europe was purged from the scourge of the most evil and violent philosophy in history. By believing in the principles of the Bible, the American Constitution and the ability of people to succeed through faith and godly principles, Ronald Reagan became the leader of peace and hope who will be forever remembered Ironically he had what someone once described as the two most difficult jobs a human being could ever have, President of the United States and announcer for the Chicago Cubs. These two jobs, though unrelated, are more difficult than any other and only one man could have done both in one lifetime. Reagan let every American believe again for The first time in decades that America's best days were ahead of her. The election of George Herbert W B as the 41st President in 1988 vindicated the Reagan principles as only four times before did a retiring President succeed in handing over the office to his hand-picked Vice-President. Like other former Presidents he gave speeches throughout the nation and other nations and when he visited Eastern Europe, though hated by many in his own country, tens of thousands of Poles, East Germans, Lithuanians, Latvians, Ukrainians, Romanians and others had pictures few him in their homes, and welcomed him as the man from West who liberated the East and fought for their children to live in freedom. His last speech in 1994 he announced he has Alzheimer's disease and a few weeks after that Republicans won their largest Congressional victory in forty years, partly due to nostalgic memories of voters remembering their beloved leader though out of office for six years. Despite declining health, Reagan lived to the age of ninety-three dying in 2004. His death marked the passing to new life of the most dynamic Christian since **Joan of Arc, that one man, born once in a thousand years who just like Jesus,** *speaks to God on behalf of his people, speaks to his people as The voice from God, and spoke through God as the voice of authority for his people, thus filling the roles of prophet, priest, and king.*

15

Theodore Roosevelt (1858-1919)

Jack of Clubs

*T*he leader of the Rough Riders was born in Hyde Park New York in 1858 to an aristocratic New York family. He grew up among wealthy elite people and he himself became a mover in society *very early in life being interested in everything from hunting to conservation, business and literature, horseback riding, barefoot running, swimming, and his favorite interest of all politics. In 1880 at age twenty-two with a degree from Harvard he married a woman named Alice Lee.* Asthma plagued his youth and even into adulthood he had frequent asthma attacks, though millions are shocked to learn that one of our most rugged Presidents, the quintessential example of what it is like to be an American (along long with Ernest *Hemingway* and *John Wayne*), was an American with a disability. In 1884 Alice gave birth to their child *Theodore, Jr. (known as Ted Roosevelt-who became an **icon** and World War II hero)* but she tragically died as a result of the delivery. As a different, albeit very American way of dealing with it, he took a job as a marshal in the fledgling territory of North Dakota capturing several outlaws. He worked as a cowboy and Western lawman for a year and a half, a good preparation for his political future. Later *in the 1880s he*

became New York City police commissioner, a job he held a little under two years but like other expert work in his career, he cleaned up the city and particularly corruption among local officials in near miraculous fashion. He had been a reserve officer in the U.S. Navy and though like **Churchill** he saw his true calling in government leadership *not "soldiering", he was a once-and-for-all warrior ready to don the uniform when his country beckoned.* In 1891 Teddy remarried Edith Kermit with whom he had five children. Again, like **Churchill** he fulfilled the three-pronged stations of success, man of war, man of letters, and man of leadership.

As the decade progressed and he reached the tough but tender age of thirty-seven he became a statewide figure, being elected police commissioner of the state. Again he brought optimism and energy to a job *badly in need, in a little less than three years reforming much there before being appointed assistant* secretary of the Navy under **William McKinley.** In 1898 he led the Rough riders in the "splendid little war" to revitalize the hemisphere, he helped democracy sprout in Cuba and Puerto Rico. He then dispatched *Commodore Peary* to fight in the Philippines, releasing the stranglehold on the last of Spain's international holdings. The most prominent figure of the Spanish-American War then became governor of New York.

In 1900 **McKinley** chose him to run for Vice-President though he had less than two years elective experience as higher than a legislator. The **McKinley-**Roosevelt ticket won what was then the largest landslide in American history. Less than a Year later, **President McKinley** was assassinated, and after grieving, Roosevelt rose to The occasion governing as a strong leader in his own right. It was the age of the *bully pulpit* and more than anyone else, he popularized the concept that the President is not just chief executive and commander-in-Chief of Armed Forces, but a moral example to all Americans, using his office to get his priorities out and direct the American free market of ideas. While he was not the first President to do so, he expanded it to an art from, unbelievably so, since most Presidents in the past who used a bully pulpit were wartime or expansionist leaders, even some of the more capable chief executives like *Grover Cleveland* left their personal judgments a mystery to their fellow citizens and governed with their heads never their hearts. Theodore Roosevelt set new examples for governing with a full head and a huge heart giving the old adage "speak softly, carry a big stick" an American maxim status. Even the term "bully pulpit" was coined from Roosevelt's frequent use of the expression "bully for you", usually used to tease those with whom he disagreed.

In 1904 Roosevelt ran for a term in his own right and became the first Vice-President to do so after having been thrust into the office. It is remarkable for us to think of incumbent Presidents losing elections, but ironically at the time ascending to the Presidency on the death of a President was not a very respected feat and the four Presidents to do so (Tyler, Fillmore Andrew Johnson and Chester A. Arthur) were weak leaders. Roosevelt as a strong leader set a precedent later followed by Calvin *Coolidge*, **Harry Truman**, and Lyndon *Johnson*, governing as a strong leader, mandated to lead, because the people did elect him on a national ticket and for these men it paid handsomely. Theodore Roosevelt supported our natural resources preserving millions of acres in the West as national forests and parks to be maintained by the government. Teddy Roosevelt was only forty-six at the time and had almost four years of experience behind him as President, amazing when we consider that most leaders are over fifty and the process of maturing in adulthood, which most people would say begins around twenty, increases somewhat at thirty, and considerably at forty, still a quite pedagogical decade. He worked with the *"muckrakers"* another term he put into the language, to get rid of corruption in numerous industries and enforce fair standards of labor. He sent troops to quiet rebellions and in some cases even support a specific faction in various wars in the hemisphere including the Dominican Republic, Cuba, Venezuela, and various places in the hemisphere. In 1908 he won the Nobel Peace Prize for negotiating a peace treaty between Russia and Japan. This was the first time America was seen as the leader of the free world, and the only one that could act as the father figure and lovingly guide and discipline arguing brothers. It was no accident then, that Roosevelt, as the man who elevated America from one of Europe (namely England's) many children to the patriarchal leaders of the world, that his face is enshrined on *Mount* Rushmore as the symbol of American advancement.

Though he could have easily won a third term and some said he was entitled since he did not serve two complete terms, he chose not to run in 1908 and supported William Howard Taft. In 1912, however, he got angry at Taft for some of his policies and ran against him, actually defeating the incumbent President, while both men went down to defeat at the hands of **Woodrow Wilson**. Roosevelt remained an elder statesman, wrote many books, and debated against some of Wilson's policies. In 1916 he supported a strong Republican challenger, Charles Evans *Hughes,* but he was defeated by Wilson. When America became involved in World War I Roosevelt offered to command troops but was denied because of his age and years away from the military. All of his sons served in the war including *Quentin* who died on the Western Front. He suffered the tragedy with quiet dignity and said he was proud and glad that all of his sons were able to give service to our country. He said it was sad that *Quentin* died, it would have been worse if he had never gone. Though he did all for the honor of his country, he was sad for many reasons, among others he said, was that he missed the honor Quentin got, dying for his country. Theodore Roosevelt, however, as his sister Corrine pointed out, lived for his country every day. With strong reason to campaign for President in 1920, he appeared to be a shoe-in since neither party had a Presidential leader. Tragically, he died of *an embolism in the coronary artery in 1919. Had he lived, he probably would have been our first three-term President,* and set policy in North America and Europe that would have lasted long after his lifetime. The other sad reality is that medical science could have easily prevented his death, just over a decade later.

A man of hope and vision Theodore Roosevelt stands as one of America's greatest Presidents. The only leader in peace to be "canonized" as a leader of America, Teddy Roosevelt is enshrined on Mount Rushmore as the symbol of American advancement. Like *Jefferson* for law and **Lincoln** for unity, Theodore Roosevelt became a symbol of America growing from in **Winston Churchill's** words "the rural republic of **Lincoln** and Lee" to the most powerful nation in the world, a fledgling confederation of states becoming the great colossus of the New world with the traditions of the old forging ties to start a still newer and greater present-day reality. All the greatness of America taking a place, not only among the nations but becoming their leader, and unlike Egypt, Rome, Greece, France, and other past world leaders, a leader for righteousness goes back to The Presidency of Theodore Roosevelt. In addition, he began the tradition of using The Presidency for pep talks, as needed and every President, most famously his relative, FDR, borrowed that tradition. Two other achievements, for which he rarely gets sufficient credit are launching the first bi-racial and international coalition after The Civil War, bringing the sons of Union veterans together with the sons of Confederate veterans, and paving the way for Black equality by setting a moral tone with his friendship with the Black educator *Booker T. Washington.*

16

Pat Boone
(1934-Present)

Jack of Spades of hope

*A*rguably the hero of conservative Christians with the greatest longevity in the limelight, albeit well past his heyday, Pat Boone was born June 1, 1934 in Jacksonville, Florida. His farming parents raised *him in Florida and Tennessee, eventually becoming affluent, but when he became a celebrity as a singer it was a whole new lifestyle. He is a direct descendant of legendary Kentucky pioneer* Daniel Boone-and his parents were devout members of the Church of Christ, raising him on strong values of the neighborhood Christian family man.

In the 1950s he was the clean-cut performer who appeared on The Ed Sullivan Show, before *Elvis* and the Beatles. Though he was always clean-cut, he competed with *Elvis* to be the number one rock-n-roll star, and some years he even outsold him. He was the undisputedly the second biggest solo performer of the 1950s and he built a good relationship with Elvis, at times they appeared together. From 1957-1960 he hosted The *Pat Boone Chevy Showroom,*a variety show similar to Ed Sullivan, but with the distinction of being (quite possibly the first) performer to host such a show and therefore a man of Hollywood's inside. Since his show was sponsored by GM/Chevy he did lots of promotions in Michigan and came to spend a fairly good portion of his life there-so when Michael More was filming *Roger and Me,* his first "mainstream documentary" he and *Anita Bryant* were both there, and had lived there enough to know the state and become "naive targets." His Gospel dimension was present then, in 1957 he released the record (when they were still called and looked like records) *Hymns We Love.* He built relationships with all the top performers, Black and White at the time, and his friends also included Nat King Cole, Fats Domino, *Little Richard* and Carl Perkins. *Love Letters* in the *Sand* made him a hit with the primarily white audiences that dominated music halls recorded for early TV-and as I demonstrate, he continued such hits to expand his career and his audience. For most of his adult life he has lived in Michigan and/or Beverly Hills, California.

Like Elvis, Boone decided to take Hollywood by storm. Appearing in his first starring role in *April Love,* in which he sang The song of that name, it remains his most defining song. He also starred in *Mardi Gras and The State Fair, which* included his only on screen kiss. Even in the sixties he refused roles that compromised his faith, including a chance to star with Marilyn Monroe in a role that implied fornication. He later appeared in heavily religious films, *the Cross and The Switchblade, (in which he played Assemblies of God minister David Wilkerson), the Greatest Story ever Told, and as the voice of t*he animated series *Music Machine. In 1960 he married Shirley NE* Foley and they have blissfully married since. Though he got most of his radio and record sales as a "secular" rock musician he was the standard force in Gospel music and has helped scores of Gospel musicians break into the pop music world. *He has sold over forty-five million albums and CDs, and in the late '90s he was ranked ninth among the greatest rock stars of the Twentieth Century. His transition to television was as mandatory as it was risky, with TV taking the day in the sixties, his variety show was likable but not competitive. With regaining vitality in his spiritual journey, his marriage and family life, and beginning successful as a writer,* Pat Boone proved too likable and too spiritually successful for his own good, much like Elvis, a pop icon and movie star who had no where left to go but down. Unlike *Elvis,* however, Boone had a vital marriage, a great relationship with the Lord Jesus Christ, and other interests that kept him from taking solace in bad habits. He wrote his spiritual autobiography *A New Song* in which he described his conversion-**because even people from Christian families must convert because Jesus cannot accept any stepchildren or grandchildren-all must be begotten and become His children.** It became a best-seller and he since has written at least a dozen spiritual self-help books. *Unlike most performers he is highly educated, boasting a degree from Columbia as while he was a youthful performer, he did not expect to be able to do it as a career, and was studying teaching. His education has come in handy in making him one of the most intelligent and likable persuasive spokesmen for Christian morality. He is still unfailingly mentioned with* Elvis and Buddy Holly and Bobby Darin as The founding pioneers of rock-n-roll and his record sales are second to any living performer after *Stevie Wonder*. Pat Boone has done all of this while retaining his commitment to Jesus Christ and remaining outspoken about his faith.

He has spoken in churches and conventions both sacred and secular and encouraged millions for Christian values. Though he has friends and acquaintances in the Christian and political world, including Michigander Gerald Ford for whom he campaigned for President, he has also been friends and one-time next-door-neighbors to The Ozzy Ozbornes. *His delight in shaking hands and giving autographs led the clean-cut performer T become the subject of a joke in the 1960s-if you leave a party drunk, shake hands with Pat Boone, and your right side will sober up. To his friends outside the Christian community, he continues to communicate a loving, respectable, consistent Christian witness.*

In the seventies he used his knowledge and talent as a serious basketball fan, he was briefly one of the owners of the competitive professional league, ABA, the American Basketball Association he owned Oakland's team. He has released more than fifty tapes and videos including "Pat Boone's America" and others that reminisce of a more positive age. *For My Country celebrates patriotism, Thank You Billy **Graham**-celebrates the man who became the most noted evangelist of our time, and he has won numerous awards in both Christian and secular communities, the former of which have* *taken his "Let ME Live" as a pro-life anthem, the truth that an unborn baby is a child fighting to continue his life, is a truth for us to acknowledge. His Pat Boone Fifty Year Anniversary included numerous hits from his decades in music.* In less flattering nostalgia he appeared in Michael More's *Roger and Me* filmed in the town where both the fat Fascist More and the quiet conservative Christian Boone lived. More interviewed Boone with a video crew present and asked him and Anita Bryant to sing some things including the Michigan state song, without ever telling them it would be used to make his anti-Christian and largely slanderous "documentary." In a counter joke in 1997 he parodied himself by singing heavy metal songs and appearing on Paul Crouch's TV show wearing all black and dressed in (largely imitation) punk style. The choices like *Paradise City were conspicuous among heavy metal listeners (so I've been told I'm not a fan of the genre) for having no compromising anti-Christian messages.* It *was condemned by many in the Christian community some of whom do not understand or accept crossover styles of entertainment,* including owners of the station on which he appeared and future copies of *"In a Metal Mood" the CD that includes (all established)* songs like *Paradise City,* had a disclaimer that Boone was using *it as a parody* of himself. For *the* same purpose he appeared in the *"Gump"* video with *Weird Al Yankovich* in *a* hilarious parody of the story.

While never apologizing for his faith and in fact being up front about it as any celebrity in recent times, he is not a overzealous ranting and raving Christian, but a quiet conservative, ready to give a hand, take a neighbor take a neighbor on a car ride to dinner, or invite him to church. A friend to most everyone who meets him, it is amazing how he has become *both a punch line for a joke, as well as its best Hollywood deliverer, as well as one of the most serious stage presences when he needs to be. Such sentiment about a man* who had dozens of top ten hits in the heyday of rock-and--roll and was friends with *Elvis* and Buddy Holly, speaks volumes about his example of the sober lifestyle amid a world of excess. Since he often spoke in churches and youth conventions about pledging oneself to sexual abstinence before marriage and then total faithfulness to your partner in marriage, a Republican appointed scientist and writer famously said *as Anita Bryant is to homosexuality Pat Boone is to premarital sex leading to a joke that if you want to know if anyone is gay all you have to do is start praising Anita Bryant's singing abilities and then you will know if by whether the person goes off against her, and if you want to know if someone is fornicating start praising Pat Boone's singing and you can tell from their reaction.* The success of Pat Boone in communicating this message to strengthen the Christian and be a light for the unbeliever is a profound witness, a testimony of a true Christian for the one true faith.

By the late seventies he also became known for his work with Easter Seals, raising money for people with disabilities. Sadly by the early eighties few people wanted to hear of such an open faith in entertainment and he was ostracized f all but the Christian media. He did however, serve on the Board of Directors at Praise the Lord Ministries and has hosted a TV show on and off for Trinity Broadcasting Network. In the 1990s his career hit another spot of vitality when he became the pitchman for The Phonics Game and other products designed to teach children and when need be adults, how to read by the rules of phonics. He made his rounds on talk shows and increased the popularity of promoting phonics, as sadly many adults never learned the rules and therefore, many adults both educated and uneducated read slower and less effectively than they should. *Having previously championed products he rarely used, he made sure not to repeat that mistake, and took the phonics promotions as his own "crusade" teaching the reality to educate with the reading rules.* While other campaigns in which he has been involved have seen mixed rates of success the Phonics games and books from materials he promoted have largely been adopted in most public school by the 1990s. In 1988 he headed up the California branch of **Pat Robertson's** Presidential campaign, trying to get Christian media figures involved, to little success. He has also appeared in episodes of *Seventh Heaven*.

Some may be surprised I would include this "washed up" musician and phonics promoter in such a list let alone include him so high. Despite his plainness and quiet Southern demeanor, Pat Boone is perhaps the only living American who can be termed the last American hero, the bridge between Elvis and Ronald Reagan (many would include John Wayne) who like Pope *John Paul*, II was never afraid of his critics and largely outlived all of them. Like Joe DiMaggio, a quiet, outspoken man who lets success speak for itself, Pat Boone has been an inspiration to millions, proof that one can live his faith publicly without being obnoxious or condemning. Some say he is old news, to be seen at musical revivals and on public service issues-oriented videos, and occasionally coming under fire for some ridiculous statement, which is almost unavoidable for someone with a public career for almost sixty years. His status as a hero does not mean everything he has ever said, every song he ever sung, or ever joke he's told is heroic or upright, and I'm sure he would agree in assessing his mistakes, as anyone with a multi-decade career, be it in broadcasting, entertainment, government service, or any other public outlet. He is still remembered and honored as a man of today. In 2011 he won a lifetime achievement award for support of conservative principles and values by the Conservative Political Acton Committee Conference. His recent critiques of President Obama, however, have been heartfelt and in coming out for gay marriage, the President has made millions who voted for him question why. Boone has said that by pandering to gay rights groups he has largely ignored the larger needs and desires of most Americans and all who value morality and the principles of America should seriously think before voting for the "first gay President." He said that certainly not to question the President's sexual behavior, but as an analogy, since Bill Clinton called himself the first "Black President" one who could (in self-proclaimed rhetoric) help the Black community more than any before him, Boone accuses Obama of being the first to pander to the gay community just so he could tout his own language about being the one who can help the gay community like no one before him. I would love to see Boone become the first Pentecostal President, while highly doubtful at this stage, if he ever does he would be both the oldest man ever to become President (unless of course it happens after someone born before 1934 is elected). He would also be the first teenage President, the *perennial hipster* who can combine (for all of us children thrown overnight into the adult world) the carefree spirit of youth with the mature **Teddy Roosevelt-like** man of action. Either way, Boone is the perennial man of God, the most

95

dynamic lay Christian of the Twentieth Century still alive in the Twenty-First, the greatest spokesman for the Christian *Renaissance* of modern times.

17

Pat Robertson
(1930-Present)

10 of Spades of Hope

*B*orn Marion Gordon Robertson and for some reason nick-named Pat as a child, he grew up the son of a Democratic U.S. senator from Virginia. A very intelligent, and energetic youth, Robertson graduated from law school but was unable to pass The bar exam. He served as a Marine with The U.S. Navy during the Korean War, making him one of two Marines in this series. Though his mother had been an energetic Christian and raised him to be a Christian, Pat saw little need for the Gospel or moral principles until shortly after his military service, he had a conversion experience and became a very committed Christian. In the early sixties he turned to the ministry and bought a local channel in Virginia Beech, broadcasting locally, within weeks he had a full-fledged market. He remained a Democrat most of his life. Eventually he became a successful businessman and not long after his embrace of Christianity his business career took off. His one room studio he bought in The 1960s eventually became The Christian Broadcasting Network (CBN) and later The Family Channel which worked its way up to the sixth largest cable station in national broadcasting. Though having once been a apostate, a friend's witness helped bring him to

Christ, and credits a lifetime of prayers by his friend and his mom. His loyal wife Deedee was at first hesitant but by the mid-sixties she too was a committed Christian and they have been happily married for over forty years raising five strong Christian children.

By the end of the 1960s Pat Robertson was not a household name but definitely was known within the Christian community. At the time most Evangelical Christians especially of the Baptist tradition where Pat had studied and earned his doctorate degree in the early seventies as well as the Pentecostal fellowship in which he later became a part, took seriously the admonition from I Peter 2:9 which in the King James Version says *we are a chosen generation, a royal priesthood, a holy nation a peculiar people who should show forth the praises of Him who has called you out of darkness, into his marvelous light.* In Middle English "peculiar" did not mean strange the way we use it, but more like *set apart, other, the exception, and by extension the exceptional.* Since Evangelical Christians are often slow in translating ancient concepts to The modern principles of their faith (parenthetically many Evangelicals did not switch to The New International Version until The 1990s even though there are many English translations far better than The King James) many Christians emphasized the "peculiar." Because we are a peculiar people many believe Christians should be far different from the world, that the *Christian* should be Christian and the secular secular, and never the twain shoal meet. Pat Robertson was the first highly articulate, educated Christian particularly in the media, to set a major educated Christian challenge to that concept. Like **Pat Boone,** he was able to convince millions of Christians, that yes, we are different, yes we are the exception, and in a supernatural sense the exceptional, that is only half the story.

The big picture for Christians also for Christianity also involves communicating The Gospel in the context in which you live and if that means having better fashion sense, looking as good or better on TV, marketing bands, comedy shows, news, and other TV shows, that is good. He encouraged his listeners and set an example for himself by trying to do better than secular competitors, and make us as Christians show we are much like our non-Christian counterparts, while at The same time we have an attractive and refreshing difference. While we may emulate non-Christians in some ways, we must give them a reason to emulate us, which can never be done by sheltering us in the Church or lying down like ostriches with our intellectual heads in the sand. Unlike other Christian television personalities, most notably Jim Bakker of the PTL Club, made it clear that Christians can be in our culture, even one of the most successful in our culture without emulating The worst elements of The secular world and without compromising with non-Christians in their philosophy or values. Christian TV, music, or and comedy are always a ministry never a mere performance. Unlike Jimmy Swaggert, he emphasized sanctity not spiritual grandiosity, and unlike Bakker he made it clear he was a minister on TV not an entertainer who happened to be a Christian. By hosting his hour long talk show *The 700 Club, which* started in 1971 and still broadcasts daily, Robertson became a kind of Christian Ed Sullivan, *Johnny Carson, and Paul Harvey* in one. Like the apostle *Paul*, he became "all things to all men that I may win some." Though ridiculed by many critics both Christian and secular, Robertson has succeeded in winning many.

By the mid-seventies he began Operation Blessing a humanitarian work that feeds the hungry and provides flood and disaster relief that has helped millions. He has sent thousands of missionaries to various countries and paid enormous sums of money to translate the Bible in over twenty languages. In *1980 he was one of two co-directors of the Washington for Jesus March on the nation's capital, an event drawing hundreds of thousands of Christian advocates, the other director was Bill Bright.* Obviously all this grandeur took a lot of money, and Pat Robertson was very successful at fund raising.

He has also earned much money, unlike most Christian leaders even those with national reputations, Robertson is a multi-millionaire but his 1988 holdings showed him at about $70 million which means he gave away a lot more than he banks for himself. When the show became syndicated throughout the United States, he hired **Ben Kinchlow,** an African-American as his co-host and substitute host. In becoming the Christian Ed McMahon, **Kinchlow** like McMahon has an agreeable and mild disposition but unlike him is a media and philanthropic giant who spent years much of the '80s on the front lines delivering Bibles and other materials into Iron Curtain countries.

He founded Regents University in Virginia Beach one of the largest Christian colleges in the world and the first Pentecostal school to have an accredited law school. His media,ministry and other labor for Christ have seen him venture into stock holding's s in many blankets including South African diamonds mad pother [precious metals for which he has been criticized but which he correctly maintains is all for The good of Christian interests. That sentiment is confirmed by the fact that virtually every year he gives away more money than he keeps. Robertson is a firm believer in building The Kingdom of God which has led to him to support many Christian candidates as well as nationally.

A long time Democrat who supported the *Civil Rights movement* in The 1960s (unlike his senator father) he saw it as The Biblical thing to do, a proper human rights issue for the time and he supported *Lyndon B. Johnson and Hubert H. Humphrey.* In 1976 Robertson cast his first Republican ballot for *Gerald Ford* while maintaining Democratic registration which he changed sometime later. Throughout The eighties he largely supported the policies of The great Christian President, Ronald **Reagan.** As rights for Blacks and other minorities was the largest social issue of the sixties he was on the right side there, and *now rights* of t*he unborn* are the *major human rights* issue, and the Republicans are the party on the right side of that debate today, have been since before the 80s. Unlike many ministries with Christ-centered messages all the time, CBN and The Family Channel had a wide variety of entertainment on the air including Christian soap operas, movies, sit-coms and classic TV reruns and game shows.

In 1988 seeing that all good things must come to an end but that perhaps the next of the Kingdom of God based on faith and family principles, was now being written in America, Pat Robertson decided to run for President in 1988. Many laughed at his political ambitions, saying he was a preacher and talk show host with no experience in government. Like **President Reagan**, Pat was a media entertainer and talk-show host, but unlike the man who ha d just led the great conservative coalition, Robertson was a lifelong student of government with degrees in law and political science. He had more experience as a speaker and a figure on the world stage than any other candidate though Vice-President *George H W Bush* had built his career on being an international presence. He had to deal with other criticisms that would typically have been non-issues for other men. It came out during The debates that his first son was born less than nine months after his marriage and some on the far Left charged he was truing to lead the United States into a theocracy. They said any minister who was running for President could only have at heart, some theological desires on religious jurisdiction for The country. He did (almost definitely see wow.,mdb.com/people/552/000022486/) get his girlfriend "in trouble" and marry her, a common practice in his era. He had also stayed blissfully married to her as husband and father for over thirty years. This of course, also happened before he found his path in Christianity, and we do not usually hold peoples' pasts against them. For instance, prison terms of less than a year, or those that have been expunged, are usually off limits in future political contests. Former Communists or those who admit they have been part of un-American or unpopular organizations in the past, usually have the opportunity to recant that past and it is taken at face value. To charges of theocraticsm, he responded that he believed in the Constitution the First Amendment, and the rights of all Americans to choose their leaders and make their own economic, religious, and family decisions. Yes, he had been an ordained Southern Baptist minister (he resigned his ordination to run for President) but he was purely American and had no desire to force religion on anyone. Many thought his stances against abortion and homosexual rights were theological but he told skeptical audiences that he could wisely demonstrate these stanches made scientific and constitutional sense in addition to the fact that they happened to be Biblical. He maintained that this country's whole foundation was built on Christianity and that if the Founders who wrote the Constitution were alive it would be shocking and sickening news to them that a minister does not have a right to take his place as a citizen and spend part of his life making government policy if he can get elected as a representative of the people.

In fact Robertson did quite well at the beginning winning more votes than any Republican in the straw poll in Washington D.C. and going on to win the Iowa caucuses. The media was harder on him than any other candidate, and then some had the audacity to say if he could not play with the big boys he could not run with them. NBC's Tom Brockaw who did the post-debate coverage used the term "Tel-evangelist" a terrible label which was never called that either by people in their profession or their viewers. That would be comparable to a lawyer running for office being called a "shyster" or a psychologist being called a "shrink." It is true that people in those professions occasionally call themselves that, but that is their perogative to use the pejorative or joking title for their own group, not the place of a newsman to use a negative label. Others spoke of Robertson as getting his "flock" or his "followers activated." Since he was not the pastor of a church he could not be spoken of as having a "flock" in the Christian context and all the TV talk-show hosts I have heard of have "viewers" I have never known any to have followers. Robertson rebounded, saying he did not expect special treatment because he had been a minister, but he asked to be treated as an equal which was not happening.

The media treated a Democratic minister, Jesse Jackson who was also a candidate much softer. While Evangelicals did not come out for him in The kinds of numbers many would expect of a ground-breaking candidacy like his, he did quite well at The beginning winning non-binding primaries in Nevada and South Carolina (meaning the delegates who ultimately became electors were not required to vote for The winner of their respective primary, as opposed to some states where ultimate electors who make The actual decision at The Convention are required to vote for their party's winner in their state). With Bush, **Bob Dole**, *Jack Kemp*, former Delaware governor Pete DuPont and others, he competed in all the debates and looked professional as always, with a perspective air of leadership. Given his almost all-superior intelligence, media savvy skill, and sense of humor, he was such a competent debater, only party lobbyists and the only sometimes-accurate belief that experience makes better prevented him from winning the nomination. In fact, even at this level, sometimes it is experience in life and business that prepares the candidate more than experience in politics, especially when someone has little or no executive experience. He finished second in a controversial Michigan primary, but by Super Tuesday where more than ten states were voting, it became clear Bush would be the nominee, and Robertson dropped out and supported him. Ultimately getting the third highest number of votes in the Republican primary, he was glad to support Bush, giving a rousing speech for him at the 1988 Republican National Convention. Though he lost the election to a resounding victory of *George Bush,* his critics conveniently forget that his electoral performance at the Presidential level was far better than Jerry Brown, Mario Cuomo, Ted Kennedy, *Pat Buchanan,* Jesse Jackson, John Edwards, Wesley Clark, Howard Dean, and Al Shaprton.

Though he chose never to seek elective office again, he has been a force in the Republican Party and continues to see building The Kingdom of God and electing godly candidates to office as two related and inseparable goals. GOP hopefuls court his support, while *John McCain a very* impressive candidate who could have shocked the party and the nation with an upset nomination in 2000, was hurt by hateful speech against him (though written by a speech writer). While McCain who had won New Hampshire and looked impressive in debates with younger and more "media savvy" men was possibly cost the nomination, Robertson did not hold any grudges.

In 1989 Robertson returned to television and his philanthropic and education work. He has built Regents University into one of the most respectable colleges in the South and his Operation Blessing has sent out more missionary and relief workers in the 90s and twenty-first than virtually all American ministries. Though not a force in the Republican party's elective politics anymore, Robertson launched the Christian Coalition that favors no particular religion and while headed up by Florida-born Evangelical *Ralph Reed,* it has included Catholics, Protestants, Mormons, and Jews in an effort to elect pro-family and pro-life candidates. It has gone through at least four changes in leadership while in fact Robertson himself resigned as their ex-officio chairman in 2001. It's legal division is led by Jay Sekulow a Jewish-American who has won seven cases before the Supreme Court and until recently was a registered Democrat.

At some time in the late nineties he sold his holdings in the television station to various companies, the largest of whom goes by Pax TV. and still broadcasts the *700 Club* making it a show that has run for almost four decades, so Pat has had more access to television audiences, than most any living person save a few career newsmen. Though Robertson previously resigned his ordination, in 1999 he was re-ordained this time in a television ceremony by the Southern Baptist president, Assemblies of God Superintendent, and others. ordaining him missionary *to the world*. Despite his critics, that is a very fair assessment of Robertson, a man who has done more to preach an intellectual and humanitarian Gospel based on the teachings of Jesus Christ than any of his peers. He is the author of many books on spiritual and inspirational topics of which my personal favorite is *Bring It On,* in which he answers life's most pondered questions on subjects from theology to terrorism to health. At the age of eighty-one, Pat Robertson maintains that he is in better health today than he was in middle age and exercises and takes better care of himself than in his youth. Robertson and his doctors relate better heart and arterial health than most men in their forties and fifties. In addition to abstaining from alcohol and tobacco which are expected of all Evangelical Christians, Robertson exercises regularly, several hours a day and enjoys brisk walking. He has patented an age-defying shake spoken on the need for vitamins, especially Vitamin C which can revitalize the immune system and make a person stronger, and keeps a Biblical diet with no pork or other "unclean" meats and high in vegetables, antioxidants, and fiber. These decisions pay off as other Evangelical figures and seniors on TV have had bypass surgery and strokes, Robertson and his doctors report better heart health than men in their forties and fifties. A man with a legacy that will continue well into the Twenty-first Century, Pat Robertson is a hero of hope who has been an example to millions like fans and supporters in broadcast media for whom he made Christian broadcasting fun, entertaining, and evangelizing.

18

Alan Keyes
(1950-Present)

10 OF Hearts OF Hope

A three time nominee for Senate and contender for President the Marylander has become one of the most outspoken commentators and contenders for the **Ronald Reagan** legacy since Reagan himself. Like Martin Luther **King** Dr, Alan Keyes can be called an eclectic, a polyglot immersed in culture both American and foreign, while happy with the simple home life. Alan Keyes has largely lived a life for a purpose and added eclectic dimensions to further his purpose. In the movie *City Slickers* a cowboy tells his dude ranch visitors we all have to make our lives worth living for that one thing. In the case of Alan Keyes it has never been hard to find, that one thing is living to defend the Constitution of the U.S. based on faith and godly principles. He has also worked to see The truths of The Founding era transmitted to The modern age, particularly modern education.

Alan Keyes was born August 7, 1950 in New York where his father was an Army sergeant but he grew up in Maryland living near both Baltimore and Washington, D.C. He studied at *Cornell* University and then Harvard where he was roommate to one of the godfathers of conservatism Bill Kristol. *Harvard University awarded him his PhD*. A man of many paradoxes a descendant of slaves, Keyes actually built a career by bolstering the principles of the founding fathers many of whom were slave owners. A loyal Roman Catholic, Keyes often prays in public and vocally voices his faith in terms associated with Evangelical Protestants. A Black American with primary connections to Whites, he married an immigrant from India whom he met when both were in Bombay doing humanitarian to boost India's economy. With his loyal wife Jocelyn Marcel he has raised five children.

Though a Republican as long as he has voiced political interests, he served in India under the auspices of President Carter, working at the Bombay consulate and later the embassy in Zimbabwe, in 1979, within the first months the nation came under Black majority rule. In the early eighties just in his early thirties at the time, he was recruited by President **Ronald Reagan** to work first in the Education Department and later to serve as ambassador to Great Britain. He served in Scotland and then as emissary to the Queen herself becoming the most nationalist presence few the Reagan Administration in Europe. More than any other political figure of the post Reagan conservatives, he embodied the principles **Ronald Reagan** held dear and could have carried on the torch of the Reagan legacy under a more idealistic set of circumstances. By 1988, however he was more prepared for state service and some of the **Reagan** legacy in Europe was suspect, though it has since, been largely vindicated. Keyes ran for a Senate seat from Maryland getting 38% of The vote and again ran in 1990. For The rest of The Twentieth Century he had various jobs including teaching at Ivy League colleges and as a visiting fellow in Italy.

In 1996 Alan Keyes ran for President in a Republican primary that included **Bob Dole**, Pat Buchanan and others. He finished third in the race not winning a single primary though both of the other candidates and the more marginal ones invoked the name of the man whose legacy Keyes had borne in England and in America more than any other Republican of his era. Again in 2000 he made a less impressive showing in a race for President, though competing aggressively in debates with George W. Bush, Steve Forbes, **Orrin Hatch**,and others. Though America is not yet ready to have him

as their President if he won he would have been our most idealistic President since **Lincoln** and the most conversant since **Herbert Hoover,** speaking Italian and French fluently and German and
Spanish passably. Of course he speaks English probably more beau-
tifully than any political figure since **Reagan**, but many see him
as too conservative and dogmatic. There was, however talk of his
being nominated to run for Vice-Prescient with George W. Bush.

In 2004 he ran for a Senate seat from Illinois, changing his registration to the Land of **Lincoln,** having been recruited to run against
Barak Obama who won in a landslide. Most observers thought
Obama would win in a landslide no matter against whom he ran,
since The incumbent was in a sex scandal and former Chicago Bears
coach *Mike Ditka* turned down the opportunity to run. Keyes had
previously criticized Hillary Clinton as a carpetbagger for running
from New York where she had never before lived. He defended his
decision to run for Illinois saying he was drafted to run for a Senate
seat no other Republican seemed to want, and he was recruited as
a team player, and was not doing it to boost his own reputation or
career. While the race took away some of his popularity, he remains
one of America's most distinguished columnists and commentators. He has had an on-off relationship with MSNBC Cable news an
hosted his radio show in various markets since 1988.

At first cold to President George W. Bush whom he found inar-
ticulate and felt could use experience, perhaps as his Vice President,
Keyes has been a staunch supporter of the War on Terror. Of course
his most important issue has been abortion which he rightly maintains kills over a million children every year and has to be driven
out of America just like slavery was. Unlike politicians sworn to
tradition, he refused to congratulate Obama on his victory saying he
would act civil, but would not cozy up to a man who supports the
slaughter of children and special rights for sexual deviants, and other
values that go against The original intent of our Founding Fathers.
Like *John Quincy Adams,* he is an eloquent is an eloquent genius
who will not give up his iron fisted stances even if it costs him his
political career and like Adams, Keyes has been cost elections and
jobs for his moral stances. Alan Keyes is the writer of three books.
A committed member of the Knights of Columbus whose hobbies

include singing opera music, Alan Keyes is a remarkable man who has succeeded but not as much as he may have had he given up some of his moral stances. A true hero of hope, he believes that being a conservative means there are principles in life far more important than winning which a truly moral person will not compromise to win.

A poignant series of events happened since I wrote this when his youngest daughter came out publicly revealing she was gay. Though she was hesitant to talk to reporters it was alleged Keyes disowned her and refused to let her live with him or have anything to do with him. She later confirmed he did stop paying for her education, but said it would be kind of contradictory if he did, since they were on opposite sides and she was publicly working to advance a lifestyle to which he is totally opposed. In answer to a caller to his radio show, Keyes in a nearly tearful moment said he still loves his daughter and she knows she can always have a home with him, he simply had to point out the error of her ways and try to lead her back to a better life in Christ, which she has apparently never embraced. This incident reveals both the stern moralist Alan Keyes as well as his loving communicative nature are very much alive and functioning in his personal as well as professional life.

19

Dr. Laura Schlessinger (1947-Present)

10 of Diamonds OF HOPE

*B*orn Laura Schlessinger in Brooklyn in 1947, the woman who would go on to revitalize radio psychology in the 1990s and twenty-first century ironically started out in a life she identifies as poor roll idles. She was from "a faithless marriage" her father a non-practicing Jew her mother a non-practicing Catholic and she pretty much grew up a secularist. Early on in life she entered college first at New York City College earning degrees in anatomy and marriage and family counseling. A first marriage failed and she faults herself for both marital troubles and her lack of early child raising, largely because at the time, she was a liberal feminist. When she began as a therapist she was in private practice and a teacher, though she did get to host some radio shows filling in for the late-night host in New York. For over twenty years she hosted talk radio programs on moral health in New York and later California, but did not have a coherent moral philosophy until she found her path with conservative (and for a time Orthodox) Judaism. In the 1980s she settled down, marrying Dr. Lou Bishop to whom she has been married since, making her legal name Dr Laura Bishop. In 1987 she gave birth to Derek

Bishop and then became vocal about her lifelong calling *being her kid's mom.*

As the product of a faithless marriage Dr. Laura had occasionally gone to church and celebrated Christmas and Easter which were her sole exposure to Christianity by her mother an Italian immigrant, who had never really been a practicing Catholic. Her father a non-practicing Jew celebrated Passover and the High holidays but taught no religious faith to her daughter. It was some time in the nineties when Derek was watching a TV show on the Holocaust when Laura affirmed that she (and therefore her son) were Jewish though she was not in the Orthodox fellowship by birth or choice. Though not considered Jewish by the believers in the Law, she knew she would have been Jewish enough to be taken by the Nazis if she were in occupied Europe and if for no other reason, that should identify her with her people and she and Derek began attending synagogue. In 1996 the family began attending synagogue and she, her son, and husband converted in 1997 eventually finding an Orthodox synagogue and converting to the Orthodox faith. Throughout the nineties and Twenty-First Century she had her critics among largely secular Jews who were embarrassed and did not want her moral example to be associated with the Jewish people. Unlike them, Dr. Laura is a true Jew, observing the kosher *requirements* regarding clean meats, keeping *Shabbot,* and dedicating her life to keeping the holiness requirements of God in the Torah. Though some have said that undermines the variety of the Jewish life, in truth no one can truly be Jewish without *rigorously* striving to keep the Law and practice a godly lifestyle, and while Jewish culture may include secular as well as religious lifestyles, the religion itself, by definition of any religion must have one set of laws and be practiced by those who would claim to keep it.

After her conversion to Orthodox Judaism, Dr. Laura became second only to **Rush Limbaugh** as the most listened to talk-show host in radio. To this day she is still the second most listened to radio presence and while largely ignoring the shock jocks she has bested in the ratings, she became informally of course, "America's favorite rabbi." In the 1990s she had a controversy, when she took herself off a radio station which had her on after Howard Stern. Stern, who also considers himself Jewish, though competently secular, called her all sorts of names and rallied his listeners against poor Derek's mother. Many of his listeners attacked the poor mother, and a few radicals even called in with personal attacks at then twelve-year-old Derek to get at her. Schlesinger is largely supportive of all radio media that has carried her or allowed her airtime to advertise which is shown by the fact hat I have listened to her extensively in San Francisco, Chicago, and Salt Lake City and in every city she promotes the lesser talents like *Glenn Beck*, Gary Meyer, and her one equal or better in the business, **Rush Limbaugh.**

She also gave *Tammy Bruce*, an LA-based radio host an opportunity, salvaging the career of the talented, yet otherwise overlooked youthful host, for whom she wrote the foreword to her *the New Though Police*. The author of *The Ten Stupid Things Men do to Mess Up Their Lives, the TST Women Do to Mess up their Lives, The Ten Commandments: Relevance of God's Law in Everyday Life (with Rabbi Stephen Vogel), Parenthood by Proxy, Proper Care and Feeding of Husbands, and Bad Childhood God Life as well as* at least four books for children; Laura has been a bestselling author and a pacesetter for later psychologists with moral principles including *Dr. Phil.* In 2001 she got her own TV show and talked about moral health on the air for the year the show lasted not making the transition as successfully as others. After 9-11 she came under fire for saying that our military has made more problems than it has solved by becoming a jobs program especially for women who are not prepared for combat. She is an implicit Republican, having never campaigned for a candidate, she supports the conservative values and restraint of government to which the GOP has long been faithful, while encouraging her listeners to vote true to their convictions and whenever possible influence both political parties for the best.

Dr. Laura had long been a supporter of all human beings and has encouraged people to treat people of all races, religions, disabilities, and even sexuality equally. Her main audience has been Christians both Evangelical and pro-life Roman Catholics (and has also included a good many Mormons and Jews). A disproportionate number of people who called her show were homosexual or have had homosexual temptations and she largely encouraged people to act with same moral behavior whether gay, straight, or searching for adult identity. If anything this stance hurt her among her Christian listeners, while over 85% of Christians are civil to homosexuals just like everybody else, there is always that portion of misdirected Christians(like those who condemned **Pat Boone**) says "why were talking to those homosexuals as if they were normal people," or "how could you have a conversation without telling them they were the most vile of sinners and needed to repent immediately to get away from hellfire!" Just as an aside here I'm very embarrassed to have those Christians on my side, and want those of you not in my camp who are reading this to feel assured, the overwhelming majority of us are nothing like that! For the most part however, Christians and Jews liked her messages. As with most highly religious Christian or Jewish people who speak in public, most of her opposition came from secularists, but many of them liked her message just The same as they found it challenging and morally beneficial. Schlesinger had also supported PFLAG (Parents and Friends of Lesbians and Gays) an organization that while not necessarily being pro-homosexual lifestyle encourages people not to reject their gay friends and relatives but instead to affirm their dignity as human beings and help their struggle to reach an identity with which they grow into healthy adults. Eventually however, her moderate condemnations of the homosexual actions and her shift to encouraging homosexuals to seek solace religion, made her more enemies then friends among "political gays."

Her critics most harshly criticized her because by telling homosexuals to seek solace in the religion in which they were born (and/or raised), the fact remains that in spite of much public support for getting churches and synagogues in addition to schools to change their beliefs on the issue, most of the religions that large numbers of Americans practice, including Catholicism, Missouri Synod Lutheran, Baptist, Evangelical Free, Pentecostal, the L.D.S. Church, Presbyterians, Christian and Missionary Alliance, in addition to Orthodox Jews all encourage the penitent and/*or counselees, t*o stay away from the homosexual practice and either adjust to heterosexual relationships or simply abstain from sex. While encouraging people to get counseling and then be the best they can be, whatever their sexual preference may be, she took a firm stance against gay marriage, gay adoptions, and giving any other special rights to sexual minorities, saying that only heterosexuality can properly mold society and raise children that will become healthy and productive adults. While these views are shared by the overwhelming majority of Americans, and even among those who favor gay marriage or gay adoptions, with the exception of the far Left, almost anyone would regard these views mainstream and wise, some in the homosexual community condemned Dr. Laura as a hatemonger and a homophobe. One leader of the Jewish community even accused her of antisemitism saying being Jewish, and therefore a minority means one must defend the rights of all minorities. This is very well discussed in Tammy *Bruce's* first book which I recommend. Her stance on homosexuality as well as her strong stances against certain concepts of feminism, caused her to lose some of a perspective audience, and may have been why her TV show only lasted a year. It got her lots of enemies, some of whom tried to attack her, and she needed security in public speeches around that time. She did however, retain her audience and remain the second most listened to host for most of the first decade of the Twenty-First Century.

Dr. Laura has long been health conscious having earned a black belt in martial arts and she also enjoys biking and has endorsed proper heart health and breast cancer prevention through early detection. Her other major hobby is para-sailing which she does almost every day. She rarely appears outside the LA area being committed to motherhood as her primary career, a couple of her few public speeches were boycotted by homosexual activists and she had to cancel the public celebrations of her 54th and 55th birthdays for fear of homosexual activists threating participants' safety. She has appeared more often outside California since her son has been an adult, but usually one day engagements only. Like **Pat Boone** and Anita *Bryant*, she has never been afraid of losing her audience, sponsors, or money making opportunities and has hence had an extremely large following among Americans who love all people, place faith and priority on their families, and put the Lord first. She and Lou are very proud of their son Private Derek Bishop volunteering to fight in the war on terrorism and in 2006 he became

Deployed Paratrooper Bishop in Iraq. More than any of her several careers, she has been proven a success in her most important career, motherhood, and Derek will be an example to the country among the great many other parts of her legacy. In 2010, *she took herself off live radio for necessary freedom issues, having since been streamlined so her radio show can be heard only on the computer.*

20

William "Billy" Fiske
1911-1940

10 of Clubs OF HOPE

A very interesting although rarely known or spoken of athlete
and soldier, William "Billy" Fiske was born to an upper-class
family Brooklyn in 1911. He grew up going to the best schools in
both America and Europe studding abroad in England for one year.
He took an early interest in sports and by his teenage years was one
of the best bobsledders in the Untied Sates. In 1926 he was the you
jest member of the U.S. Olympic team and won a gold medal as
a snow skier becoming the youngest person to win a gold medal,
in modern times. Intestinally the four man bobsledding team theta
competed in the 26 Olympics had one teammate go on to be famous
as an actor and another become a pioneer surgeon. Fiske himself co-
produced and acted in movies in The thirties putting up some of the
money from his parents' treasure chest. Billy Fiske became famous
for being a moral hero of hope and a pilot and soldier. He also won a
gold medal in the Olympics in 1932 and twice won the Swiss invita-
tional four man bobsled race with his team setting a new recored the
fist time. To this day he is the gingersnap person ever to win a gold
medley in international, completion though he is only a few months
ahead of Michelle Kwan.

When Nazi Germany expanded its military might asserting itself in Czechoslovakia and then taking over Poland most Americans opposed meddling in the affairs of Europe. The youthful visionary, Fiske knew this was not a war like the centuries old conflicts of Eruption but a new manifestation of a demonic philosophy waged by a tyrannical leader with an opportunity to dominate the industrial and technological age. Seeing the war as having immediate ramifications for everyone in Theobald and particularly every American who were at least in theory,the moral leaders of the world, he knew every great American must due to his part to oppose the rise of Nazi Germany no matter what our government said or did. Sadly enough this twenty-five year old was the only American to take this idealistic and dead-right stance as every country in the world sent athletes to Berlin to celebrate the Nazi Olympics. Sadly German Jews were persecuted and some committed suicide during the Games.

Having already had an aristocratic education that like many refined minds on both sides of the Atlantic, Billy was mainly American but almost equally British, Fiske returned to London in 1938 to work for a British company. There he married a countess and relative of British and German royalty. After Nazi Germany expanded its military dominion, he did what few did and proved a true hero of hope. Though an America citizen, the visionary young Fiske knew every American should oppose Germany, immediately he joined the British Army becoming, along with Ted *Roosevelt*, Jr. one of the first Americans to fight in World War II. He became a pilot and led a major bombing raid during the Battle for Britain. Shot down over London, Fiske made it to his feet and miraculously made it to a treatment station, dying of wounds he sustained in the battle two months later. Had it been forty years later he probably could have been kept alive and quite possibly gone on to a career in American or British politics or any of various fields. He became the first American to die in World War II. Though having come to a tragic end at a very young age Billy Fiske was mourned as a national hero on two continents. American and British flags draped over his casket and his headstone in London reads "Here lies Billy Fiske the American who died so England might live." The Billy Fiske Award is still given for the best four-man bobsledding teams. Rarely discussed and almost never listed on things like the greatest Americans, it's time for everyone in the English-speaking world to learn about this hero of hope.

21

Joni Earakson Tada (1949-Present)

9 of Hearts of HOPE

*O*ne of the most versatile and talented Christian spokespeople of our day Joni Earakson Tada has been unable to walk stand, move her arms, or feel anything above the neck since she was eighteen. The author of more than twenty books and painter of hundreds of canvases and pictures she has never known independence in a medical sense but is more financially secure and independent than 99.9% of American adults. Born a "normal" child to an upper-class Christian family in Maryland, Joni (pronounced Johnny" was)named that by her father who wanted a son and named her younger sister Jay. She grew up popular, nominally Christian, a good student, dating handsome guys, and living the life of a popular East Coast high school student. Shortly after high school graduation, on July 15, 1967 the eighteen-year-old Joni hit a rock while swimming with her family and was rushed to the hospital. She and her family was shocked to know that she had survived a broken neck and while doctors would do all they could to cure her she was paralyzed from the neck down and likely to reaming a quadriplegic for life. Eventually Joni began attending daily physic,therapy session in which she regained some limited use of her hands. She still cannot grasp things with either hand nor can hold anything of weight in either hand. She had been a lover of art and drawing before her accident and was told afterwards she could continue to draw. Confused about this, she was educated, that like the blind, one writes and draws with the brain, no the hand and an immobile woman can draw just as well as a walking one. Adjusting to the use of mouth to hold the paintbrush she has drawn many paintings and by now become a top seller of plaintiveness also took up the art of writing with her autobiography *Joni* and with the generous help of Billy Graham her book was able to become a bestseller and in 1970 Joni herself starred in the movie *Joni* financed by **Billy Graham** Ministries. Reliving her own suffering and subsequent rebuilding of her life Joni Earakson by the age of thirty-one the movie got noticed in "mainstream media" and shown in churches as a crowning example of God's Providence and power.

In the early seventies she published *A Step Further* in which she talked about her desire to serve the Lord any way He desires and if He chooses, to be healed. Some of the more *Calvinistic* among her friends and spiritual leaders encouraged her to work for the Lord but not seek healing as the time for miracles had passed. Other Christians particularly of the *Pentecostal* stripe, encouraged her to seek healing and the Lord will perform the miracle to make her walk and millions will come to Christ after seeing this public figure walk out of her wheelchair. A careful study of Scriptures and books and writings on the matter from the Centuries gave her a balanced view. No the time for miracles has not passed, yes God is still a miracle working God, but notwithstanding some extremists only God can decide where, when, and how He chooses to work a miracle. After being prayed for by several and attending meetings both Pentecostal and Calvinistic, speaking in churches and private schools of virtually every variety, Joni came to accept a modified understanding that Yes, God does heal but in her case at this particular time He was and is choosing to use her as an American with a disability and she should not expect or public ally ask for a miracle to get her out of her chair. Instead she has asked for and received the blessing of the Lord every day to carry on her work and be the best Joni Earakson she can be. Her friend and spiritual mentor Steve Estes was instrumental in bringing her to this place, he was on board with her before her accident and throughout her recovery, her ascendancy as a public figure and has remained her friend for four decades of success. Somewhere along the way she married a less exciting man named Ken Tada, with whom she has lived happily for many years. Joni Earakson Tada is a paragon of Christianity, but as noted before she preaches the Christ-centered theology of the Bible, Jesus Crucified, Resurrected, ascended and coming back with life and liberty for all who believe and does not *push any particular doctrine* or association. She got her support first from **Graham** and then from millions of book byers and art buyers and other supporters, that can be found among Baptists, Nazarenes, Presbyterians, Catholics, Pentecostals and others; and while she is clearly not Pentecostal, she is a clear example of what **C.S. Lewis** called *mere Christianity.* I did not even think about it until now, but although I have been following her career for over twenty years, I'm not even sure with what particular denomination she belongs or attends. Although rigidly maintaining the Joni Earakson Tada Ministries as a private, non=political and therefore tax exempt entity she was part of the committee of advisors to President Reagan when they were working on the Americans with Disabilities Acta and later appointed to President G. H W Bush' committee on the Disabled. Along with *Stevie Wonder* and Dr. *Stephen Hawking* she is among our country's and the world's most well known Disabled achievers and like them and like *Bill Cosby* and others have done for race she has helped to foster a culture of abilities blindness. Just as in the eighties and later *millions watched Bill Cosby* and did not consciously think they were watching a Black man and his kids.

Notwithstanding racial myth peddlers like Spike Lee and Snoop Dogg, most Black Americans who succeeded as doctors, lawyers, teachers, entertainers, writers, and fathers and husbands did so without screaming *Black is beautiful* or *down with eh white man* every other sentence. Because of Bill Cosby, and others some profiled on this series including Martin Luther **King**, Jr.,Clarence **Thomas** and **Alan Keyes,** most Americans have a colorblind lifestyle and do not think twice about their heroes, friends, and in many cases dates or family members being Black (or of a different race).

The same has held true to a smaller degree for the Disabled in the Twentieth and Twenty First centuries. Not every time one picks up a Stevie Wonder CD does he think of listening to a blind performer. More people in the English speaking world have bought Stephen Hawking's *A Brief History of Time* than any other scholarly work after the Bible and Shakespeare, and I' don't thin k anyone ever went into a bookstore and said "Give me that book by that Disabled English physicist." Because Joni's ministries have crossed the boundaries of all lines and ministered to various people, one can read her books, listen to her radio show, and hear her speak, without making The conscious connection they are listening to a person with a disability. Society has made not quite a 180 degree turn, but perhaps come 153 degrees around with regard to African-Americans in my lifetime, and while still not quite there in regards to Americans with disabilities, perhaps we may be only a few short years away from it. If any living person will be the key to that success, we can look on Joni Earakson Tada as the hero of hope, The perspective **King or** *Bill Cosby of her and* our people.

22

S.I. Hayakawa

9 of Diamonds

*orn in 1907 in British Colombia his family eventually settled in Manitoba where he attended college Samuel *Ichiye Hayakawa, the son of Japanese immigrants w*ould go on to be a standard scholar and pacesetter f higher education. Though he spent most of his life A A D SIH would champion the Republican and what some would say far Right principles of **Ronald Reagan a**s governor of California and be eventually rewarded with a Senate seat. A man who took civil Rights seriously as an immigrant and longtime supporter of equal rights he later come under fire as one who would deny rights by this who sought to ignore the Constitution and re-mold it into a model for Twentieth Century Socialism.

An ingenious scholar he entered the University of Manitoba at age seventeen, and earned his bachelor's degree in English there. He went on to earn two other degrees, being awarded a doctorate in English and American literature from the University of Wisconsin. His first teaching job was there, where he taught Wisconsin students lecturing and serving as assistant professor of English, and in the forties he was hired by the University of Chicago. He took up residency in that great city, remaining until 1955 where he lectured and taught English, became a married man, and a distinguished writer. His monumental textbook, *Language in Thought and Action* was already being used in Midwestern colleges, when his parents' country bombed his country, and brought both to a war. A staunch supporter of his country, (though unable to become a citizen until 1954), Hayakawa wrote pro-America articles, encouraging fellow Americans INCD Those of Japanese descent to fight for the right cause (though he was unable to enlist). During the war years, he was also a contributor to the **Defender,** a newsletter that promoted Black interests. In the mid-fifties he and Margaret settled in California. He was the father of three, including a seriously mentally disabled son, who was a joy to the family. He had written at least five books which became standard college texts, and hundreds of articles, to mixed reviews, largely works that encouraged moderation in language, and warned how language can be manipulated by demagogues like the Fascists, Nazis, and Communists, who used it to mislead their people. His books and articles touched such issues as psychology, and (Liberally artistic) rhetoric and though he did not use a computer until well into late middle-age he became a pioneer of *"meta-messaging"* the process of a brief but fully equipped document, which many would say help to create email. He also spoke about television becoming a powerful pacesetter for language, and he first famously called *TV* "the *electronic babysitter.*"

Early in 1968 the president of San Francisco College resigned and rather than put up a stink, two other interim presidents resigned rather than attempt to quell protectors. Seeing a need to continue education rather than making a California college a joint for loud agitators, **Ronald Reagan** got personally involved and asked Hayakawa to become president of San Fr. College. Now remember he was an author and lifelong professor, a lecturer who talked fast and quiet, a humble Japanese-Canadian who came of age at a time when **Herbert Hoover** *was* President a middle-*aged lecturer* with no administrative experience who even talked to his own kids like they were pals and equals. Hayakawa did what any hero of hope would do in his situation he took the call from Ronald Reagan and said if this is the kind of college president you want this is the kind you are going to get, funny hat and all. The following week, Thanksgiving week when the protectors were loudly bad-mouthing America, President Johnson, President-Elect Nixon, our troops in Vietnam, the death of

Dr. King and *Robert F. Kennedy* neither of whom approved of what they were doing, the 5'2" Hayakawa was escorted onto the campus by security and put on the stage in front of hundreds of protesters most of whom had never heard of him. The few in the academic circles who did know of him thought the sixty-two-year-old would be a soft touch and the protesters would continue to make all the noise until Governor **Reagan** decided to call in the Guard. Instead, *he jumped off the stage, to the sound truck, where the protesters were making noise, and pulled out all the cords of the mobile truck. By this* symbolic *act he told the agitators to either find somewhere else to agitate or else go to jail where they belonged! With this symbolic gesture, the aging educator earned the nickname "the samurai in Tam-o-shantern"* (A reference to his trademark ancient Scottish hat) *and ignited a spark with The Silent Majority, tens of millions of Americans, who like him, wished they could pull out the cords and silence anyone who spoke with anti-American rhetoric!* Though new to media attention, in The California poll taken just weeks later, to know how Californians felt while entering the new year, the survey said *Ronald Reagan was* the most admired person *in* California and *S I Hayakawa was #2. For six* years, he led San Francisco State College, as its name indicates, a relatively small place *for local* students, to become one of The best colleges on the West Coast. While taking a moral stance for American values, he established the first Black studies department in California. He insured the voices of the protesters would be demoted to dull roar. Notwithstanding even the governor, he eventually had The National Guard called in to arrest the outside agitators. In 1976 he announced his intention to run for U.S. Senate. Winning in a landslide, *over* incumbent Democrat John V. Tunney, he became the first Asian from the mainland elected a U.S. senator and one of the few Canadian-born Americans to serve in the body.

Entering the Senate with no political experience outside college, the very educated Dr. Hayakawa went to Washington along with a stellar freshman class that included **Orrin Hatch** *and Paul Laxalt.* His first year he was on three Senate committees, including The Finance Committee, which he found very irresponsible of The U.S. Senate because he never controlled any financial commodities in his life, including the home, his wife Margaret handles all the finances. He gave a stellar speech against expanding The New Deal measures to states by federal mandate, saying Congress has no right to impose such measures, the only way they can be accepted by a majority of Americans is if the majority, either people or states vote to amend the Constitution from a capitalistic framework to a Socialistic one. *Educated observers know the vast majority of Americans would never vote for that. He also took up measures that opposed busing to school by federal mandate,* selling the Panama Canal, *and* perhaps most controversially of all, he was *in favor of* treating the international crisis with Iran-the taking of hostages from the American embassy in Tehran (in 1979) as an act of war by one country against another, and therefore, at least informally, we were at war with Iran. In 1981 he proposed a Constitutional *amendment* to make English the *official language* of the United States. As a conservative, like **Reagan** *and millions of Americans, like me, he came from the school of thought that generally believed less laws were better than more, so a Constitutional amendment for anything, would be the exception, not the rule. With the influx of immigrants from non-English speaking countries, and decades of educational participation by bilingual and multilingual educators, many of whom never took up the supreme objective of making their students fluent in English, this was a law, even an amendment whose time had come. His simple, yet profound speech said "Bilingualism for the individual is fine, but not for the country." As a prince of the post-sixties conservative movement, he got its king* **Ronald Reagan** behind the amendment. The amendment failed and though largely correct, I would have voted the same way as he with all these laws I highlighted, his ideas were mostly ignored and therefore his one Senate term was relatively uneventful.

One issue however, on which Hayakawa staked his own reputation and career, had a mixed approval during his tenure, but today has come back into vogue with the *silent majority of Americans,* this is the issue of making English the *official language of* the United States and the sole standard for education. During his lifetime only three states adopted measures that would make English the official language of their states, within a decade of his death, the largest state (and the1 with t most immigrants California) had adopted such measures, with Utah becoming the twenty-fifth state to make English the language of public schools. As Hayakawa and millions of others know only someone proficient in English can be truly successful here, and they have also proved America is a fertile field for anyone to succeed if they speak the language well and follow the traditions and general framework of American values. *After failing to see the "English only laws" adopted federally as a legislator, he started a lobbying group in 1983,* U S English, *dedicated to an English language* **amendment.** *Throughout his lifetime, Hayakawa had much like* **Quayle** *and* **Keyes** **and** Barry *Goldwater,* an obsession with being right, and not caring what anyone thought about him, and for that reason he was proud to be a one-term senator. *Like* **Churchill in the '30s and Reagan in The '70s,** *he was a lonely voice crying out in the wilderness, though dead right, unlike those men he did not live (and still from 2007-2012) we have still not lived to fully see this profundity* vindicated. His native Canada, began learning too late, that only a nation, state, or province, with one language understood by everyone can truly be a great people.

*He ser*ved on two unofficial advisory task forces in his golden years, for Presidents **Reagan** and Bush, and before he died California legislators finally took his truthful reminisces on English education seriously. Remarkably, it has worked for Americans from Germany, The Netherlands, Poland, Korea, Spain, Portugal, and Japan (most remarkably of all-the *Nessi*-Japanese for second-born were the most quickly assimilated non-English speaking group, boasting four U.S. congressmen by 1980, only thirty-five years after they arrived in large numbers). All of these came to America, learned the language and succeeded in owning a portion of the American dream. Perhaps legislators largely from Western and conjoining states (like Kansas, Kentucky, and Tennessee) listened because they are citizen-lawmakers not usually beholden to special interests. More recently, *Vietnamese, Cuban, Cambodian, East Indian, Caribbean, and West African* **immigrants have done the same, in the case of Vietnamese immigrants not merely succeeding in business but** becoming the standard for it in at least three major cities (as the Cuban-Americans are in Miami). Interestingly, **this leaves our**

neighbor to the South as the only major country **for** people **to come in and try to own a portion without speaking our** language **and** becoming American. S.I. Hayakawa, hero of hope, proved that Americans from anywhere can do it and that English must be taught everywhere if the Twenty-First Century is to see *all* Mexican-Americans (because *millions a*lready have) be*come* American and have equality of opportunity to succeed and thrive in America. His contributions to *rhetoric* are not in doubt even by those who strongly disagreed with his politics, he is perhaps the greatest rhetorician the English-speaking world ever produced. He died in 1992 at the age of eighty-five. His status a great rhetorician is unquestioned even by his enemies, he is even mentioned in a *Stevie Wonder song, The* **Black Man (from the album Songs in the Key of Life) about** *racial* **inclusiveness** and multicultural America, and throughout his life he was a serious jazz music fan. Hayakawa was a secret American with a disability, a narcoleptic, so since his death we have learned he overcame in more ways than we know to become one of the most extraordinary Americans who ever lived.

23

Orrin Hatch
(1934-Present)

9 of Clubs

§

*B*orn in Pennsylvania to "expatriated" Utahns Orrin Grant Hatch rose from a country lawyer to become one of the Senate's best stars and a candidate for federal office and serious contender to lead the American dream. The son of devout Mormons (officially The church of Jesus Christ of Latter-day Saints, and usually known by The abbreviation, LDS), he was taught from childhood the values of God, family, country, and the intrinsic value of human life. An adopted son of Pennsylvania, with deep Utah roots, Orrin early learned the lessons of both great states. He played basketball in high school and was known for his musical talents. He took a job as a janitor to save money and pay for college, In 1952 he entered Brigham Young University in Provo, Utah, then a fledgling school forming its reputation today most likely The most prestigious school anywhere directly supported by a church. For no reason other than alphabetical seating he sat next to Elaine Hansen in an astronomy class, and the two fell in love. They planned to marry, but not before Orrin returned from his mission. Assigned to the Great Lakes Mission, Orrin and his companion spent two years preaching LDS theology in Ohio, Indiana, and Michigan.

After two years at BYU and two on his mission, Orrin Hatch returned to Pittsburgh and worked construction, meeting Elaine's family in 1956. *Orrin* thus graduated to true Utahn by marrying her. He earned degrees from BYU and The University of Pittsburgh passing the Pennsylvania bar exam. He eventually practiced law in Salt Lake and several other counties.

In 1976 he was first elected to The U.S. Senate winning a Majority in spite of the post-Watergate jinx and the election of Jimmy Carter. Like Carter, Hatch was from the political wilderness in 1976, both heavily religious but the similarities ended there, much like another young man who began his political career then, **Dan Quayle.** Still a fairly young man, Hatch beat a popular incumbent, and as a young man it was always easy to show himself a true conservative, often a need in Utah for Democrats, as Republicans tend to run a little to The left of themselves, Orrin, especially because of his staunch anti-communism never did at this time, by his own conservative self, he handily defeated Frank Moss. Though he did student body politics, this was the first time he ran for a political office, and young men usually do not start out chasing The U.S. Senate. Hatch endorsed **Reagan** for his primary campaign and though against incumbent President Gerald Ford. Hatch's victory was a remarkable with 54% of the vote, while Utah went overwhelmingly for Ford, though they preferred **Reagan.** He joined Utah incumbent *Jake Garn* and a stellar freshman class including **S. I. Hayakawa,** Nevada's *Paul Laxalt, and Indiana's Richard Lugar.* The Republican senators were outnumbered but they set an agenda that helped The GOP take back The Senate in The 1980 landslide. His campaign was advertised by **Ronald Reagan who** said *"It is time for me to endorse a man of discipline, courage, and integrity, for the U.S. Senate from Utah. Orrin Hatch has the qualities of leadership, character, and integrity, to run this country on a clean course. Reagan* later said if everyone in U.S. Senate were like Orrin Hatch we would be debating issues like what to do about The surplus budget. In '76 Hatch's **campaign** was successful and **Reagan's** was not, but in 1980 Hatch went on to campaign for **Reagan** in thirty-two states. For thirty-six years, he has served the U.S. Senate with integrity, pride, and distinct Utah

values which have helped him become one of the Senate's true pac-
esetters.

In his long Senate career Hatch's hallmarks have included the
Hatch Amendment for religious freedom that made it harder to sue
churches and easier for religious groups to keep tax exempt status
and religious individuals to follow their consciences. He was a
champion of the Americans with Disabilities Act and has passed
legislation to make generic drugs legal and available to a wider
market so as to keep prescription drug costs down. Unapologetically pro-life he has voted with most Republicans for every pro-
life initiative in his tenure with the exception of bans on stem-cell
research. He *had authored a sixteen-page booklet called "The Value
of Life" distributed by the National Committee for a Human Life
Amendment.* He led one of the few successful fights against punishing rising enterprising and their employees through mandatory
minimum wage increases.

A longtime member of judiciary and ethics committees he has
been a pacesetter for confirming new justices and been successful
in getting **Clarence Thomas** and John *Roberts* through the process.
As an elder in The Church of Jesus Christ of Latter-day Saints he
once served as a *bishop,* a sort of lay senior pastor's role. More
than any sitting member of Senate, he has been a champion of The
First Amendment, *and touching three generations for the truth of
the First Amendment, Senator Hatch has championed the concept of
"religious freedom" particularly for those in the religious minority.
As an elder and former missionary himself, Hatch never lost his
zeal for helping spread faith, even it means a "plurality" of faiths
or at least their proclamation. As noted before he is author of the*
Hatch Amendment for religious Freedom-*like the ADA and the Civil
Rights Act of 1965-an enormous groundbreaking piece of legislation
for our rights.* Specifically in the past fifteen years, however, states
and districts have aggressively come against inclusion in that law,
and sought to limit public displays of faith and Hatch has gone to
bat for the rights of Jews, Catholics, and Muslims, and others each
time either winning the case or at least getting the community to
redress the issue from a more religion-friendly perspective. In 2008
a maniacal scheme by accrediting agencies tried to threaten the seal

on two of the most effective universities in the country-BYU and Oral Roberts University (ORU) and he easily secured participation by the legal assertion of the two schools' stated missions. Not only has he won battles for religious freedom in our own country, he has helped raise the batting average of freedom in Russia. In 1997 when the Russian parliament (DUMA) passed a law limiting the number of religions given official sanction, he championed a bill with *Gordon Smith* (R-Oregon) to withhold U.S. support from Russia if they *turned back the clock to oppressive anti-religious regimes. Hatch stood up and said "U.S. support is not an entitlement. It is a demonstration of our support for emerging democracy."* The law limited the churches with government sanction to three (eventually four-an antidemocratic measure at its core for involving the government in which churches can practice). *Yeltsin* first put forth a lukewarm opposition to the bill but it passed anyway. Hatch and Smith (as members of the Foreign Relations Committee) went to Russia in April 1998. in very courageous and politically incorrect tones, he told our (just-seven-years-rehabilitated) former enemy in the Cold War, that they were being "crummy allies" if they ever were our allies, and it would directly effect their relationship with the *world's only superpower.* Within weeks of the event, Russia officially sanctioned seven other churches including the LDS Church and three Pentecostal denominations. It is still difficult to proselytize there, and the state considers buying gifts or food for potential converts an act bordering on abuse (of whom I'd love to know?) *but the LDS Church has since made an impressive showing there, though Pentecostals, Baptists, and Roman Catholics have won more converts. In a heroic but less extraordinary measure he helped make student sanctioned Bible clubs legal and in 1986-87 he had been the* **Reagan Administration's** *floor manager for the Voluntary Prayer in School amendment to the Constitution but it failed considerably.* He was instrumental in championing prayer groups meeting before or after school as long as other non-school sanctioned activities were going on, it succeeded in part due to a Russian exchange student who testified before the Supreme Court.

Since the 1980s *when the issue became public he has been a staunch advocate for banning displays that involve desecration of the U.S. flag*. It was not the intent of the Founding Fathers to "protect that speech" it was a very serious crime in that era-like in England the original American flags were a symbol inseparable from defending the nation (in their case the crown) and British and American authorities punished anyone who mistreated it. Algerian pirates against whom we fought in 1800 made the removal of the flag part of warfare and Thomas Jefferson considered it a *crime* for American servicemen to remove the flag from American ships. We fought the ***Dey of Algiers*** a pirate ship in part based on that breech. To put it in even more personal terms this would also be akin to desecrating somebody's grave, which is obviously illegal. The extreme measures that followed were taken due to activist leanings of the Supreme Court-it was never the conservatives intention to go to extremes the Supreme Court pushed us to extremes by invalidating the laws of forty-eight states (like legalized abortion invalidating hundreds of state laws against abortion) so like protecting the unborn, the U.S. flag can only be protected by a Constitutional amendment. In various congresses Senator Hatch has been the champion of a Constitutional amendment that would make it a crime to burn or deface an otherwise *"healthy" flag* and *been* joined by *Howard Hefflin* (D-AL in 1989) and *Max Cleland* (D-GA in 1999). *While it has yet to succeed the measure cleared the House in 2006-286-130 the representatives in U.S. Congress voted to make Protection of the Flag the 28th Amendment,* but it was stopped by the Senate with three Republicans including Utah's Bob Bennett voting against it. Fortunately in 2010, Utah delegates threw Bennett out and nominated a conservative to run for his seat-while Bennett voted with the conservative members of Congress about 67% of the time, that is not very impressive, if you are good to your wife and children 67% of the days, but beat them one-third of the days, you are not a very good husband or father!

In addition to defeating other flawed amendments, Hatch has worked to reverse anti-capitalist tendencies of organized labor in creating a third force, management (as the backbone of independence) labor (as the backbone of the state) and third unions themselves which all too often seek to dominate both the individual and the state. Though at times he has been a champion of new legislation from the party that favors as little legislation as possible like **Hayakawa** he has been at times a "reluctant legislator."

He counts many among his friends *Muhammad Ali,* Facebook founder Mark Zuckerburg, and *Grover Norquist.* As a heavy sports spectator, it's a good thing Utah does not have a professional baseball team or he could no longer cheer for the Pittsburgh Pirates (I can't help but still cheer for Da Bulls) and he cannot be too much a fan of BYU football and basketball *or the U OF U fans would not vote for him.* After *the 1994 baseball st*rike he helped sponsor arbitration that led to the creation of a competitive baseball league (i. e. giving Major League Baseball- a competitor just like any other business). Hatch is a passionate Utah Jazz fan (as much as Jack Nicholson is FOR LA Lakers). He sponsors an annual celebrity golf tournament and like **Rush Limbaugh** has earned kudos as one of the country's best celebrity golfers. He has also helped raise over $10 million for Utah charities through the umbrella organization he founded to front the money, Utah Families Foundation. He has raised over $10 million for Utah charities including BACA (Bikers Against Child Abuse), Abilities Foundation, The American Western Heritage Fund, New Hope House, and Ronald McDonald House. As he pushes for more sensible health-care measures, the seventy-seven-year-old is a great example of healthful living. Continuing to golf and walk frequently or run on exercise machines, he supports healthful living at all stages and co-authored the bill tha*t created CHIP (Children's Health Insurance Program).*

Though a long-time senator and one of its top stars it was for his work on the Judiciary C0ommittee that Hatch gained notoriety during the impeachment of Bill Clinton. Along with other Republicans on the committee, he led the Senate inquiries. He was the third senator after John *Ashcroft* and *Ben Nighthorse Campbell* to officially ask Clinton to "play fair" with American people, tell the truth, and seriously consider resigning. On August 17, 1998 when instead of apologizing, Clinton did admit his sexual impropriety with Monica Lewinsky, and then proceeded to rant and rave against Prosecutor Kenneth *Starr* and the Republican controlled Congress. That did it for Hatch who had previously been loyal to his fellow party members in Senate, but also wanted to keep a degree of respect and loyalty for the Presidency, the office if not the man. Instead of seeking the American people's forgiveness Clinton did what he and many of his generation have always done, blamed others for the problems he caused. More than anything else, that convinced Hatch it was time to go on record publicly opposing the President all he could.

In 2000 Orrin threw his hat into a wide open field for President of the United States trying to defeat incumbent Vice-President Al Gore. Hatch maintained in interviews "it would take a miracle for me to win this election, but my life has been a series of miracles." *His campaign was supported by such luminaries as businessman and philanthropist Larry H. Miller,* basketball legend Carl Malone, *and* Roger Williams, *Washington entertainer who played the piano for every President since Harry* **Truman-and called Hatch the most genuinely honest politician he had known since the thirty-third President.** *As the second member of the LDS Church to seriously challenge for the Presidency, his campaign broke new ground in an age where religion was more openly discussed especially in GOP debates.* In the first debate he said it is very important to see the Clinton-Gore team gone from Washington. He later spoke of how sacred the institution of the Presidency is from *Washington, Jefferson,* to **Lincoln,** to **McKinley** who spoke of a need to Christianize our fellow human beings for whom Christ died, to **Truman** who made moral decision that impacted tens of millions of lives, to his own friend and leader **Ronald Reagan** who would never walk into the Oval Office without a suit and tie. He then proceeded to speak of how Bill Clinton had done, saying something like "I do not need to remind you people and will not even discuss what Bill Clinton did in The Oval Office, but it is time to thrown that team out." Hatch was leading the charge to put a real American in the White House and he would have been a great one. Though Hatch *rigorously* debated the other candidates in what some would call winning the debates, he only got 1% of the vote in Iowa in new Hampshire. A few weeks later he needed his campaign and he happily supported *George W. Bush* for President. It was later on Bush to come in *and give the Oval Office a good scrubbing as he had previously told* David Letterman, and the Bush team of course gave it that scrubbing literally and figuratively. *Hatch* went on to run and win his Senate seat and again in 2006, and in 2012 he was nominated to serve his state in Senate for a seventh term. I don't know if I'll ever represent Utah in anything, but at least I can say I voted for Hatch and for Bush, and if nothing else, a worthwhile thing one can say and be truly American.

In The twenty-First Century, Hatch became one of The greatest legislative assets to the Bush Administration. He helped his good friend *John Ashcroft* become attorney general. Though *the phrase is generically used for many at his level and others, Orrin Grant Hatch is a rare man who can deservedly be called* the good senator, *a man who has been true to the leanings of his conscience and an absolute value system with impeccable measures, in lean as well as robust, good as well as poor times, sacred as well as secular callings.*

In the past few years, some conservatives have said he has overstayed his time in Senate. They would say he served his country honorably, but after all his terms, it's time for him to hang it up. Indeed he helped knock down the Iron Curtain with our mutual hero **Reagan**, and his Right policies have become used up and he is now building on left-wing and centrist allies from decades as a Washington insider. While I'm not in full agreement with every word or vote he's been responsible for more in almost a five-decade public life, just as we need a new President in 2012, we must keep him in Senate so he can chair the Finance Committee and stop overtaxed wasteful spending. *The facts cannot be denied if it were not for Orrin Hatch;* **Clarence Thomas would not be sitting on the Supreme Court,** *John Ashcroft may never have become the greatest attorney general of my lifetime, and* **Hill Air Force Base** (the largest provider of jobs in Utah) *would probably have been closed.* A Utahn's *Utahn* he has struggled for tenure, not for his own sake, but so that our relatively small state, often overlooked and chided by the proverbial big boys-can have a super big boy of its own in Washington. He is also a semi-professional singer who has made CDs, though some say they would never have sold if he were not a public figure. In 2007, he supported his fellow Mormon Mitt *Romney*, the former governor of Massachusetts in his failed bid for President, but better advice and campaigning in 2012 kept the native Michigander from becoming just a winner of the Jimmy Brooks Trophy (a character on *Degrassi*-famous for finishing 2ⁿᵈ- *for* those *of* who are not big fans*)*. *Whatever else happens, Orrin Hatch is a hero of hope with a legacy for the Twentieth, Twenty-First Century,* and all future historians, an ordinary man who strove to do extraordinary things and did them because he believed in the plan of his Heavenly Father, the greatness of America, and the payoffs of honest hard work for one's values.

24

Zell Miller (1932-Present)

9 of Spades OF Hope

*B*orn in Georgia during the Depression in 1932, still a heavily Democratic but largely conservative place, Zell Miller grew up on the values of faith and country, his mother, a devout Methodist, taught him when he was young you can *have anything you want in life but first you have to pay for it. Like Curly's advice to Billy Crystal and his fellow dudes, this brief phrase stuck with him every day of his life and later was a topic of conversations with stellar members of respective fields from golfer Gary Player to Presidents Reagan and George W. Bush. If you want to be the best golfer in the world, as Player observed, you must pay for it with hours of practice and willingness to do what it takes including the bruised and calloused hands. If you want to be a writer, you must pay for it with hard work, years of possible rejection and waiting for your day to come. If you want to be a governor and senator you must pay for it by working harder and greater than all your competitors.* Early career service in the United States Marine Corps taught Miller about the value of hard work and he later wrote a book *Corps Values.*

He attended the University of Georgia and by 1961 he held two history degrees. His public service career began early and throughout the fifties sand sixties he served on the board of state corrections becoming Georgia's chairman of Corrections Parole Division while still in is twenties. He served in the Georgia senate and two years as lieutenant governor before becoming Georgia's governor in 1976, the position he held until 1992. He then taught political science at the University of Georgia.

When Jimmy Carter was running for President he was ready to run for governor of his state and succeed the penetrate farmer. Interestingly though good friends and fellow Democrats the two disagreed about a lot and the state that had previously sent Jimmy Carter to the White House let Miller be their standard-bearer and like Carter a somewhat conservative Democrat, Miller led the party to make the state respectable. The Carter recession that went national in the late seventies and eighties had struck Georgia like an old Egyptian famine and the land once burned by General Sherman's boys was burned by unemployment lines and crop shortages for several years. The great Zell reversed the trend through supply-side economics and funding the small farmers and businessmen and by the time he left Atlanta had the twelfth largest economy in the nation. No other Southern state besides Florida had ever had a competitive wage since the Civil War and country people both Black and White had left Georgia and the other great states of the Old South to find economic security in Florida, New York, California, New England, and even tiny states like Oklahoma and Arkansas. By the end of the Miller Administration tens of thousands of people were flocking to Atlanta and other cities and suburbs of the South, to find job security with some of the nation's best businesses. While great businesses like Coke-a-Cola and Fanta had long been Georgia staples, new one's like Godfather's Pizza *established by Herman Cain (*an African-American Republican). The land of the Du**kes of Hazzard was not only funny and likable (how many comedians come from the American South?)** but now a place not to be pitied but envied. Indeed the South was rising again, but not as a racist bastion of segregation **but one that would welcome anyone from anywhere to come and** own a place in The American dream. **Zell Miller had placed his state and the country on notice, Georgia was no longer a place to leave, it was a place to come.**

. With Jeffersonian rhetoric Miller spoke of great things to come for his state and our nation. He is also a lifelong member of the Georgia peace officers a civilian group that keeps order just like the Constitution intended for our citizens. The only Democratic senator to support the nomination of George W. Bush Miller tried to dissuade his state from supporting a continuation of the Clinton/ Gore policies. Though still a committed Democrat, like Hollywood figures *Dennis Miller* and Jack Nicholson who had voted for the Clinton/Gore ticket, he no longer gave Democrats a pass for unconstitutional behavior and was a voice calling his fellow Democrats to be responsible. In 2004 the Republicans found a place for him at the Republican National Convention and along with former New York mayor *Ed Koch* and Zell endorsed the Republican President George W. *Bush* while remaining a Democrat. He is one of a handful of Americans who has given speeches in various years at both major party's conventions. The party of **Lincoln** is a big tent and can find inclusion for everyone while the party of FDR has long since abandoned its principles and become just another sounding board for Socialism.

Miller left the Senate as was scheduled after the election though friends and supporters including talk-show host Sean Hannity encouraged him to run for his seat as a Republican and perhaps in 2008 he could be nominated for Vice-President or President. Instead Miller wants to devote the rest of his life to primarily state issues in Georgia again helping to revitalize his state and serve his country as a Democrat, a lone voice in the wilderness, but one who still hopes the day comes when the Democrats return to their senses so this country can again have two strong pro-America parties.

Zell Miller is pro-life pro-business and has strong views in favor of the arts braking company with many conservatives over the need to promote the arts as best as possible His *A National Party No More* told the truth about the current Democratic Party converting from the party of equal rights and helping The little guy to the party they would increase the power of special interest groups by using minorities and the poor tor trump up corporate support for their agenda. Zell Miller is the author of seven books and a lifelong Methodist. His other main interest is to see the Democratic Party, come back to one of responsibility like they were under leaders like Lyndon Baines *Johnson*, Hubert H. *Humphrey*, and *Scoop Jackson*, but I'm sure he will agree with me that the foreseeable future can see about as much chance as the elephant in the room running up to kiss a big red donkey.

25

Dave Reover

8 of Spades OF Hope

§

E nergetic, humorous, and versatile the Texas-born evangelist has preached the Gospel to more people worldwide than all the Evangelical Christians today after **Billy Graham**. Sacrificial to promote the Gospel of Jesus Christ has largely sacrificed his own reputation he rightly earned as a national figure and allowed the secular media to ignore him. David Reover was born in 1950 in Brownsville, Texas and like his father attended Assemblies of God Bible college. When the war steeped up in Vietnam and his fellow Texan Lyndon Johnson had enough sense to engage the enemy on hostile lines, Dave Reover decided to do his part for his country before going off to do his part for preaching the Gospel. Unlike other military inductees he never smoked, drank, swore, or told dirty jokes. He had already married his lifelong sweetheart Brenda and to her was faithful, never compromising with so much as a flirtatious joke toward another woman. He joined the Navy and courageously was sent to river patrol, one of the most difficult jobs in all of our military. Burning jungle brush and other survival skills may become tedious after a while but we can thank God most of us do not and never will need to become proficient in it. On one such occasion Reover was going through the process when hostile fire blew up his grenade, the jungle brush area, and the general area including his hand. Within seconds his whole face was on fire and though he eventually catapulted himself into the river his body had been seared. He immediately promised the Lord he would never abandon Him whatever this fate may be and when he got to the American hospital he had third degree burns covering 40% of his body.

He apologized to his wife Brenda for "no longer being able to look good" and she told him she never loved him for his looks. The stalwart Brenda has stuck by Dave in poverty and wealth, sickness and health for almost half a century. In the early seventies he began speaking primarily to youth, ministry in its fledgling stage, then and still only a half grown stork. To use the words of the Americans with Disabilities Act Dave Reover is an American with both perceived and real disabilities, Some tissue including part of his ear was irreplaceable and to this day he has to put on and take off parts of his body which has led to his standing joke about playing the piano by ear.He has kept his promises to the Lord and to his family, continuing to perform well as a minister which is probably the hardest job a human being can do, and this hero of hope has done it more effectively than most. By the mid-eighties Dave Reover's reputation was established as one of the greatest revivalists of the late twentieth century and he has preached to millions sometimes conducting two or three services in the same day. He has spoken in thousands of school assemblies encouraging students to stay pure, and remain loyal to family, country, and values. He also helped launch the career of Reggie Dabbs, an African-American who is an *Evangelical* giant in his own right.

Though virtually apolitical he has spoken about greatness of his country saying that while he never expected to take a bullet or have a grenade explode in his face, he would gladly do it again, or even die for his country. While some would say he has to live with facial disfigurements, they would rather die than do, ironically when you look at Dave Reover you know something happened to him, but I don[t think he looks "that bad" though I once argued with a college roommate about whether he "looks that bad." Perhaps the 6'6" Oklahoman has a higher standard of what looks bad than this homely Illinois boy. More than any other preacher of today Dave Reover has bridged the generation gap ministering to three generations and perhaps because he is an American with a disability, teenagers who struggle with parents, parents who struggle with their challenges, and senior citizens with their own dynamics of challenges can all relate to his message. While the Gospel of Jesus Christ remains relevant to all ages it is crucial for our youth because 85% of those who accept Jesus Christ as Lord and Savior, do so before reaching their eighteenth birthday. Dave Reover Ministries takes in millions of dollars every year but they pay him a salary so like most Evangelical leaders he remains well paid but by no means rich. He has served as part-time chaplain for the Dallas Cowboys. Dave Reover is still forming his legacy, as a relatively young man with much more to do and a message that must be shared by many more. This hero of hope of the Twentieth and Twenty-First centuries must have his story much repeated most importantly to point to the glory of God and what Jesus Christ can do through faithful and obedient servants.

26

Harry S. Truman (1886-1972)

8 of Clubs of Hope

§

*B*orn **May 8, 1886** in Independence, Missouri in the heart of the Ozarks, Harry S Truman was named that by his parents, un-reconstructed Southerners who still admired Jefferson Davis and thought **Abraham**, **Lincoln** was a warmonger. They named him Harry not "Harold" and "S" as his middle name after both his grand-fathers, whose names began with S. while he had no more letters or periods just a one-letter middle name. His youth was uneventful, he attended school and did chores on the farm, eventually dropping out of school so he could help support his working class family. A confirmed late bloomer Harry did not earn his high school diploma till he was twenty, took some college in his twenties, but did not enter full time. While he spent six years in The National Guard, his longer military service begin in 1917, when he was thirty-five and the U.S. entered World War I. After the war he started a hat shop in Kansas City with a friend. At the age of thirty-eight he was elected a justice of the peace, though he had not yet passed the bar exam, which he finally did when he was forty-one. Happily living on his parents farm most of his life, he married Bessie in 1916 and even-tually bought a house with her. *He also remained in the U.S. Army*

Reserves for thirty years, only resigning his non-commissioned rank when he became a contender for the national ticket. It was not however, until he became a US senator at the age of fifty when he became financially solvent. *He* and *Bessie* raised Margaret, their one child who *went on to a great career as a writer of mystery n*ovels and historical books. He loved vacationing in the Florida Keys which to this day advertises the Harry Truman Little White House where he lived along with *Hemingway* and John J. Audubon they are the hallmarks of the great vacation site. A run in with the Ku Klux Klan early in his Missouri home owning days convinced Truman of the need to shun all racial rhetoric and treat people equally regardless of their race. Notwithstanding many racists in the South of his day and considering Ozarkian Missouri as confirmed Southern territory, Truman has been tolerant and was surprised when a post-Presidential interviewer asked him about a comment he made decades earlier that while all races are equal he would shun anyone concomitants the unbroken taboo of marrying outside his race. Truman did not deny saying that but maintains that he did not remember and whole it was likely a relic from his upbringing he does not have anything against interracial marriage anymore. While it was a minor incident in his life and legacy the experience of this hero of hope serves us well to the need to be careful what we say at all times.

In addition to the values of integrity, hard work, courage, and simplicity, Harry Truman had another factor going for him throughout his life that is hard to understand but often time essential: *luck*. In 1944 people who followed politics knew of Harry Truman and he was a leading Midwestern voice for the Democrats but he was one of at least sixty-four such senators and was hardly a national figure in the pre-TV days. Needing a Midwesterner with a farming background who could also connect with Southern and Western voters to win a fourth term, FDR chose him as his running mate. Within seven months of his election the President was dead and Harry Truman was leader of the free world just as Germany was in the process of surrendering. Needing to lead the war effort against Japan he was blessed with stellar advisors on the international war front, including **George Marshall** and Henry Morgenthau the long-time secretary of the Treasury on the economic front. Making the most difficult decision a war leader ever had to make to that date, Truman ended World War II, only to send American troops to be stationed in Asia eighteen months later. It was questionable whether he would even be the Democrats nominee for President in 1948. He was shouted down at the Convention and plagued by extremists on both sides. The Democratic Communist sympathizers on the far Left rallied behind Henry Wallace, and states rights Democrats rallied behind Strom Thurmond. *With four* candidates on the ballot in all, Truman was expected to go down in defeat to Republican former New York DA and governor *Tom Dewey*. Thousands of people from New York to Ohio were lining the streets ready to welcome to the home-grown leader. They had composed a simple song all ready to be sung *Congratulations, Tom Dewey, Congratulations Tom Dewey-We'll let out a roar, for President # 34 Congratulations, Tom Dewey* and the *Chicago Tribune* prematurely called the election for him just as most Americans in the East and Midwest were going to bed *So ready were they to believe that Dewey was President-elect, the* Chicago *Tribune that prematurely called for Dewey became a collector's item and T*ruman himself was famously photographed holding one. Against all odds, voters in Illinois and other Midwestern states gave Truman the *plurality* he needed and at age sixty-one the Ozarkian was the elected leader in his own right.

As we all know Truman was able to end the war only by dropping atomic bombs on Hiroshima and Nagasaki. Here Truman became a true hero of hope avenging the only nation who had attacked American soil in 120 years and telling the world America was never to be messed with. While criticized in every generation, even some Japanese have come around to admit it was The correct decision, since they would never surrender unless The strange fire came upon them, all but a message from Heaven telling them that the land of the rising sun had seen the sunset, The flag was coming down, and only by surrendering and accepting temporary Allied occupation, would Japan ever have her day in the sun again. It was a difficult day for Truman, as it would be for any man, and though he avoided talking about it, I'm sure he shed tears and had stomach pains and had nightmares about the Japanese women and children destroyed by the A-bombs. He also knew the planned invasion of Japanese would kill hundreds of thousands of Americans. As the evil Vizzini would say in The **Princess Bride,** *never get involved in a land war in Asia.* Even the Soviet entry, could not force Japan, who believed they were in a holy war, to surrender. Fortunately, after the bombs, Japan did surrender, and regain her rightful place among the nations. Along with former enemies in West Germany, Truman built a broad coalition against Communism. Within a year of the war's closure, Russia was again flexing her military muscle in the region an internationally. Mao's China was killing unarmed Japanese soldiers as well as Westerners (including missionaries) and their own people, in a reverse of national fortune it broke Truman's heart when we could do nothing for the great Pacific tiger, our longtime ally. He could do little for the menaced nations of Eastern Europe and Asia who had capitulated to Communism.

Though only an international leader for twenty months at The time, he called on **Winston Churchill**, **George Marshall**, and other English-speaking advisors to run a broad coalition of The nations who believed in freedom and human rights. Along with delegates from The U.K, Australia, New Zealand, West Germany, France, and others, he formed a temporary coalition th would prioritize "good" countries and make it possible to resist an when necessary defeat "bad" countries. Like The bombing of Japan it was a sad, simplistic, and heartbreaking decision. Also, like dropping The atomic bombs, it was the only decision wisdom and common logic could dictate. With a speech on October 16, 1947, one of the first televised political speeches anywhere in the world, Harry S Truman told Congress that for ideological purposes The weld was now divided in half between those countries that were Communist and those that supported alternatives to Communism. Sadly that meant human rights violators and quasi-dictators including Argentina, Portugal, Spain, and South Africa became our friends. The alternative however, was to open the door to those countries befriending The Soviet Union, a fate worse (or more correctly synonymous with death for millions of their citizens). The Truman Doctrine had been expanded by Congress, and since the Republicans of that time were more likely to be military leaders, they had no one leader to either debate or endorse that highly controversial policy. Truman was probably the best political speaker of his ilk at the time in The USA, and even he took a backseat, not to The GOP's two leading stars in The States, *Bob Taft or Dewey*, no to better promote the policy, there was one man in the English-speaking world, the one who made them the winners in the hottest war ever, and was now willing to say things about the *Cold War*, few others would, **Winston Churchill.** The English speaking giant proved to be the moral example of the world who speaks her language, and having been invited by Truman, he helped enunciate the policy on May 5, 1946 with an immortal speech in Fulton, Missouri, at a college with which the President had connections. The speech better than anything else enunciated for the Western world the need to defeat Communism. Everyone in The English-spearing should memorize portions of Churchill's Fulton speech and every President and Congress has since used the **Churchill/**Truman plan to keep Communists out of power in countries and make sure their enemies are supported.

Pat Boone once shocked audiences by saying *he would rather be dead, and have his own children killed, than they be forced to live under Communism. B*ut what else could you say a the Stalinist system that murdered tens of millions of its citizens? Moderate supporters of democracy and human rights in Greece, Turkey, and Iran were the first beneficiaries of billions to keep them in the column of the good rather than Communist countries. By the end of the decade the *Cold War* was in full swing throughout the world, Russia was bad, an enemy of Russia was good, and anyone who could potentially become a friend of Russia had to be converted immediately!

With this in mind Truman and **Churchill** along with **George Marshall** led the formation of *NATO* (The North Atlantic Treaty Alliance). For the first time in 170 years of American history uniting us with Britain, France, Belgium, Luxembourg, and Lichtenstein (ten members later joined NATO-see the definitions at the end) *NOTE ALSO that by 2007, eleven other members had joined NATO* to keep Communism out of the West. **While heroically** fighting **Communism,** Truman, partly on the advice of his aide (and some would say mentor) *Clark M. Clifford,* led *Zionist* policy, becoming the first world leader to recognize the *Zionist* democracy of Israel and send them billions to fight perspective enemies both Communist and Arab. *Unlike past Presidents, promoted by a death,* Tyler, Fillmore, Andrew Johnson, Chester A. Arthur, *Coolidge, and even* **Theodore Roosevelt, the** Ozarkian farmer and hat salesman, had no choice but to act as the leader of the world, the standard for good, and the voice for world peace through the sword! THE NATO Alliance formed under Truman remains in effect to this day, and has been tremendously successful, while the support the Truman Administration pledged to Japan and other far Eastern nations (especially Taiwan and South Korea) to protect them from Communism, has been less successful as an American policy. In his time Truman got Australia, New Zealand, Thailand, Pakistan, and Indonesia to pledge support as a bulwark against Chinese Communism.

Truman's second term saw troops committed to Korea, something he maintained to be his most difficult decision, even harder than using atomic bombs, and asking Congress for large sums of money for Greece and her neighbors. Sending American men and for the first time a good many women overseas to Korea was a dangerous decision but one that integrity demanded to save South Korea from becoming the next domino in the Soviet Union's attempt to stack all the nations of the world. Like Roosevelt, *but unlike* **Reagan, he** *reluctantly played dominoes* when he could have sent **MacArthur to knock** down all the dominoes. Around this time, The Secret Service saved his life from a would-be assassination by Puerto Rican terrorists. He was also embarrassed by the revelation that one of his top aides-Alger Hiss was a secret Communist spy. Truman did not know or condone the activities of his aids, but the fact is the Missouri farmer had never met a Communist before Stalin and when U.S. congressmen including *Richard Nixon* started telling him he had Communists in his employ that sounded about as ludicrous as telling him he had large numbers of witches or Oompa-Loompas with purple polk-A-dotted skin working in his State Department. The fact is many Communists successfully infiltrated the government, because Stalin our war time ally took the struggle seriously and converted thousands in Washington D.C., New York, and even Hollywood. Truman never had an ounce of sympathy for Communism, the philosophy he most loathed but tragically as good a leader as he was he failed to do in his own state department what he was doing worldwide, purging Communist influence. He also sent military advisors to Vietnam to help the still imperialist French salvage their last vestige of empire and provide a buffer against the agitator Ho Chi Minh, who was gaining Communist converts. He was the last President Constitutionally allowed to seek a third term, but bowed out in '52 attempting to handpick his successor in Adlai Stevenson, the governor of Illinois, who was defeated in a landslide.

He died as he had lived an ardent anti-Communist and should be remembered as a hero of hope who succeeded where millions have failed, going to bat for his country and fighting to see free people continue to live free. Much like George W. Bush, the last two years of his Administration were greatly ridiculed, but history vindicated all of his *larger* decisions. He wrote quite a bit in his retirement, and is a compelling writer on mainly political issues. His funeral, the first of a President to die of natural causes since **Herbert Hoover** was mourned by millions and with *Washington*, **Lincoln**, and **Reagan,** and **Theodore Roosevelt,** he ranks with our five greatest Presidents. The standard he set for fighting Communists and supporting our Israeli allies and other freedom loving people throughout the world was carried on by all Presidents and finally his former enthusiast **Ronald Reagan,** who voted for him, succeeded in ending the Communist domino building.

27

Tony Blair

7 Of Spades of hope

I ronically a very liberal European leader who has been praised mainly by conservatives in the West, Tony Blair was born in Scotland the product of English parents and grew up in the heart of the United Kingdom. At age forty-one he became leader of the Labor Party and was the opposition leader against John Major. In 1997 Labor won their first national election in 18 years and Blair was invited by her Majesty to form a government and serve as Prime Minster. Ironically the Labor Party has been the quasi anti-monarchical party in the last century or so but Blair is the one liberal prime minister who has had good re pore with the royal family. The first liberal in eighteen years to inherit the reigns of power, he could either govern from the center, or undue a lot of very popular British reforms that had been set in place by Margaret Thatcher and John Major. Never one to accept limits, Tony Blair has combined both in a remarkable decade of British leadership. In his *The New Britain,* he explained how the British people are entering a new phase under post-Thatcher leadership that must allow all groups, not excepting churches and labor unions to take their rightful place. Unlike monar-chists, however, he maintained the New Britain cannot be dominated by a moral consensus, nor can the Socialism of the mid-Twentieth Century that came to dominate his party, really supply the answers for the Britain of today. Labor unions will get fair access to government programs but will not dominate or monopolize them. His new philosophy was what *Dick Morris* called "triangulation" taking the best of both liberal and conservative principles and forming the triangle, the third way. In so governing Blair became the first non-Socialist to lead the Labor party in a hundred years and almost comically since Britain has been half-Socialist for a century, has turned Britain back toward capitalistic principles, while America which has never had a major Socialistic party, has turned a Democratic Party that was formerly capitalist into the Socialist Party that once led Britain.

Mine is the generation, Blair said, *With more freedom than any other but less knowledge of how to use our freedom responsibly. The generation.that knocks the door of a new millennium frightened for our future and unsure of our soul.* Unlike most European leaders, Blair unapologetically speaks of "good" and "bad" even defending the good in the two million Muslim citizens of the U.K., most of whom abhor terrorism, and defines the struggle as one between the majority who have respect for the right and those who do wrong.

Blair's eloquence reward him immensely, while he had been a member of Parliament since 1983, very few people knew of his views, but understood the by his eloquence that he had a great presence as a speaker. Unlike Margaret **Thatcher** he came from a working class background and has been around blue-collar labor all his life. But unlike **Thatcher** and Major, Tony Blair uses the.best eloquent to enunciate like a born speaker, clearly delivering the quintessential British accent especially on words like *fast, past, and last.* Blair's first term saw Scotland and Wales being given their own parliaments and also granted a similar process of self-determination to Northern Ireland, but after a brief time of fighting there followed by along awaited (albeit somewhat still doubted) peace treaty in 1998, the power in Northern Ireland again emanates directly from London. When becoming a national figure Blair had always promised to take the concerns of the Welsh and Scotsmen seriously, while he claims the Conservative governments were too quick to to take the view "Well, they have no desire to separate so therefore they have to stay the same." Again, Blair saw the wisdom of a third way saying the islanders were proudly British but still entitled to autonomy within a greater Britain. The first four years Tony Blair was prime minister of Great Britain and leader of Parliament, he emerged of a great leader of Europe within the European Union, though he wisely took his cues from American economists, resisting the temptation to debase the pound and put his country on the *euro* with the rest of the European Union. He often speaks of "my covenant with you," believing his election to give him moral absolutes and mandates to choose the right, and while he may have also been friends with Bill Clinton he would never have disgraced himself and his country like Clinton did. He was leader when Princess Diana died and some say his sentimental leadership then, which included encouraging t*he Queen to go out and greet mourners, added to his* popularity. He was popular enough to get a second election, though many British Conservatives pointed out that apathy against a greater continental government that largely ignored the concerns of ordinary Britons,, caused many Conservatives to stay away from the polls.

His since published autobiography, My Journey tells how his story became intertwined with the story of Twenty-First Century America and how he started off as moderately skeptical of the idea of our greatest mutual ally. His years at the helm, his mutual trips with the leaders of Washington and London, and his friendship with President Clinton and later President *George W. Bush*, made him an ardent lover of America almost as much as **Churchill and Thatcher. Though** he both thought and governed from "The Left" his principles did not come from one philosophy and certainly not from moral relativism, as his autobiography (which came out after I published my first installment) brilliantly chronicles the steps he took to arrive at his views. They include a unique combination of Christian principles, theories of British Labor, and pragmatism, the third of which became most important when protecting a democracy of fifty million citizens and making decisions that affect and influence hundreds of millions elsewhere, what is best to protect the greatest number of people is definitely a ma*jor factor.* Most Americans knew the name of Toy Blair and were aware he was the Labor Prime minister of the U.K. but their knowledge ended there. On September 11, 2001 when terrorists bombed the World Trade

Center, Tony Blair exhorted his country to stand with America and others in the world who respected human rights and the democratic process. *He spoke of standing shoulder-to-shoulder with America, and for the remainder of his six years in office, did not once waiver from his 100% pro-America stance.* Four years later Britain was attacked on the homeland and he has continued to fight terrorism at home and abroad.

This liberal from the left wing of British politics, rose like **Churchill**, **Truman**, and **Reagan** who were the last lions of the Twentieth Century, along with his fellow Baby Boomer, *George* W. *Bush* woke up so Bush and Blair became the first two great lions of the Twenty-First century. The Anglo-American coalition came to define the *right thing,* democracies including the teenage tiger Australia, and the overachieving *double-tailed lion* the Czech Republic, also Poland and a dozen former Communist countries; plus Spain, Italy, Denmark, established democracies like the Netherlands and Japan, and fledgling ones including Guatemala, Togo, and the Marshall Islands. Sadly other *great nations, as well as barely functioning democracies,* refused to be a part of their coalition and did not give a darn if it meant terrorists got to go around killing more Americans, Britons and other free people including Muslims! Though liberal he is a stalwart freedom fighter standing in solidarity with both President Bush and New York Mayor *Rudolph Giuliani*. In visits to Washington and New York he proved himself an indispensable ally. It has even been said that he is (as was said of the other two British prime ministers in this book Churchill **and Thatcher) in the** USA as in Britain and if life were a little different each could have probably run and won as President of the United States. He was, not, however, what his enemies *painted him to be, a "Yes-man", a "wuss", or "an* indifferent political opportunist." *In fact, in all his political career, he has taken courageous stances that have* made him less popular with *his party* and at times *all* but *obliterated* his chances to lead effectively.

Though *the idea of* taking out Saddam's criminal government and the whole notion of fighting wars for "democracy and international stability" was protested by prominent Americans (including many in fields such as academia, Hollywood and media, and politicians, including former government officials) spoke out against taking the War on Terror to Iraq, many others said much worse. Most Americans were in favor of the Bush Administration's decision to take out the brutal dictator Saddam Hussein who sided with the terrorists who attacked us and refused to comply with the cease-fire agreement he had signed in 1991, the protesters were a minority as polls showed 76% of Americans were in favor of overthrowing his government and setting up a democracy.

Most of the louder protests were in Britain and the rest of Europe, and ironically Blair withstood an onslaught of criticism on the home front as did the other countries who stood by us, Australia, Spain, and Italy, had their share of protesters some anti-American others just opposing war in Iraq. To little surprise as a lifelong "global diplomat" U.N. Secretary General Kofi Anon strongly opposed regime change of the criminal government, but *Bush* and Blair stood up to the SOB who lived comfortably in America, while (by not opposing) contributing to the work of despots who belittled us and our concerns. Through the *trans-Atlantic* relationship fledgling democracies in Afghanistan and Kuwait have hatched and Iraq, once the first military pawn in the axis of evil is growing into a respectable democracy. Though many in the U.K. (including leaders in Blair's own party) did not support the Iraq War (at least without a U.N. mandate as if that body of individuals has some magical potential to decide right and wrong) he had one kindred diplomat in *Jack Straw who served as his foreign minister. One despicable criminal regime has been taken out, and Lord willing Iran and North Korea will be next (though I hope done by their own people).*

In 2004 Tony Blair won a "hat trick" third term, *a feat equaled in recent times only by* **Thatcher.** *Though hie is controversial, his people recognized his accomplishments.* His own *country faced "home-grown" Islamic terrorists on the homeland when the London subway was bombed on duly 7, 2005 killing British workers commuting on The subway.* His legacy to the United Kingdom will be an ordinary man who did extraordinary things because he fought for the good of his people and all people so that justice and democracy might prevail. In a speech before U.S. Congress July 17, 2003 he said *I know how hard it is* on America and how in *some small corner* *of this vast country out in Nevada or Idaho, or one of these places I have never been but have always wanted to go, there is a guy perfectly, quietly getting on with his life, minding his own business; saying to you, the political leaders of his country, why me? Why us? And why America? And the only answer is because destiny has put you in this place in history at this time and the job is yours to do.*

I thank God for Tony Blair and I thank Him that because of *Bush*, Blair, Powell, *John Ashcroft*, **Condolezza Rice** *Tommy Franks*, and others there is still an America and the U.S. and U.K. can still lead other democracies including Australia and Poland and help pave the way for freedom and the rule of law to become the world-wide norm. Each of these has done a special work for the world's freedom, *Bush* by building the biggest coalition since World War II and *Powell* by being the alliance builder who actually went to bat with other countries' state (or foreign ministry) departments. *John Ashcroft did the work here to insure America will not be vulnerable to terrorist attacks, and the homeland will not be struck again.* **Rice** *as leader of the branch that took to the field, and Franks as a field commander helped to provide an atmosphere of more freedom and security overseas to make terrorist attacks less popular and likely. For his personal leadership, against all odds, Blair became the most hopeful of this new wave of leaders, and thanks to them, the United States and U.K. and other democracies are still functioning. Thanks to them the world is starting to see that terrorists need to be defeated* and environments throughout the world need to be established that make democracy the rule and religious freedom through republics or representative government possible, and basically good countries among those who opposed the war in Iraq, primarily Canada and France, are electing conservative governments who will take a stand on the side of good and fight evil.

David Ben-Gurion (1886-1973)

8 of Hearts OF Hope

*T*he son of a Russian lawyer originally from Polish territory the man who would become the first worldwide leader of the Jews in modern times was born on Russian occupied territory in 1886. He began living in the land of Palestine the Biblical Promise Land in 1906 and from that point on became a dedicated Zionist. He eventually became chairman of the international Zionist Union and later the leader of the Jewish Underground with support from American businessmen and other Jewish interests. Ironically since the great land of Israel, what we call the Holy Land the places of the Bible that made the greatest contribution to religious and ethical culture of modern times, was defeated with its Temple destroyed in the year 70, it has been the most divided, disputed, and fought over land in history. It was ruled by Rome, then by Arab Muslims, then the Crusaders, followed by Ottoman Turks, then Britain, and finally in 1948 it became a nation. As chairman of the finance industry of the Jewish underground he traveled to the United States during World War I where he met a Jewish nursing student Paula Minos who became his wife.

During World War I he encourage Israeli Jews to fight in British units to defeat the Turks. Months later he began the kibbutz movement allowing all Jews who wanted to come to the Holy Land and live on communal farms. Most of the residents of Palestine did not live on *kbbituzum* then and to this day less than 3% of the Israelis do, though for a time in the forties almost 10% did. He established the movement whereby Jews in transition could live on kibbitzum or communal farms in Israel until they could get on their feet. In 1937 Ben-Gurion took a position in the British Royal Guard. A t the time he saw the British mandate in Palestine and the Jewish goals in world conflict to be one and the same since they both wanted to get rid of all vestiges of Nazi power. In December 1942 however he clandestinely helped form the Zionist armed struggle whose goal was complete freedom from the British Empire and a homeland for the Jews that answered only to Jews. On May 14, 1948 the goals of the Zionist struggle were won when the British mandate ended with the nations of the U.N. created the independent nation of Israel. To this day it is the only democracy in the Middle East and the only nation set up solely so that members of a religious or persecuted minority could have their own homeland.

Lest you be tempted to believe some of the hateful media 's hype about the nation of Israel, like America, Israel has demonstrated time and again that they are interested in peace while the other nations around especially the Palestine Authority demonstrates hatred and a desire to kill the Jews. The Israelis have dominated wars with Arab Palestinians and their allies for fifty years and have always relied on support from America and other democracies to do it.. Also contrary to popular belief America has been the nation that has most helped and befriended Israel and that is largely because of both Christians and Jews taking the lead in America and being more faithful to God than other secular governments. With **Harry Truman** like his British friend **Churchill** recognizing Israel, America can claim to be the most philo-Semitic nation outside Israel. It's a good thing, because God blesses those who bless His people, and Britain and the Netherlands have also remained friends of the Jews and continued to enjoy God's blessings.

David Ben-Gurion became the first Prime Minister and minister of defense of Israel in 1948 at age sixty-two. In 1958 during the Suez Canal Crisis when Egypt threatened to cutoff the Suez Cal's responses and the British were willing to fight them for it Ben Gurion led the defines of his people. In a way it could have been really good because if Egypt and other Arab states opposed Israel and harmed her territory it could see Britain and other democracies like France come to the Israels aid.

Ben-Gurion always maintained that no man is indispensable to the governing of the country was for that reason he decided to take what was still regarded as a premature retirement in 1953 at the age of sixty-seven and with Paula he spent two years living on a kibbutz in a desert in the Negev, resigning from the cabinet. He did, however retain his seat in the Knesset. In 1955 urged by Labor minister Golda Meir, again became minister of defense and within a year was returned to the Prime ministership by the electorate opened the door to womens' rights appointing Mrs. Meir foreign minister, arguably the third highest job. Among non-Jews the objection to the creation of a Jewish state was purely anti-Semitic, among Jews the only long-term objection was to a secular state rather than making Israel the religious mandate of Ezekiel 37-39 from which we get the song "Them Dry Bones" a reference to all of the Holy Land becoming one under the Messiah. Purely, a secular leader David Ben-Gurion would never claim to be the Messiah even on a bad satire skit, not only because of the blasphemy to the Orthodox but because like the nation he came to head, David Ben Gurion was a secular leader who went to synagogue only on the high holidays and loved to eat sausage and other pork products. He did however,along with Knesset, the Israeli Parliament, give numerous concessions to the Orthodox community and throughout the years numerous other concessions have been made particularly within Old City Jerusalem, where Armenian Christians, Palestinian Muslims, and mystic sects of both Jews and Druzes make the Jewish commonwealth a purely multi-dimensional Holy Land. The Suez Crisis could also have really bad effects if the Soviet Union came to help their Arab allies and secure canal and oil reserved or themselves it could lead to World War Three. At the time U.S. President Dwight D. Eisenhower levied both sides to be in the wrong and he was totally opposed to committing U.S. troops though he did allow American Naval ships to sail in to Suez harbor to let the Soviets know we were not idle. Fact remaining however, nothing short of a Soviet invasion of a sovereign power would get he U.S. to go to war at the time and the job was therefore that of Israel to decide along with The British and French control over the Suez. Ben Gurion's forces sailed through Sinai Peninsula taking that area and part of the Gobi Desert from Egypt and soundly defeating ground troops sent by Egypt's allies the Kingdom of Jordan and Syria. Never before head a small country won a two-front war against multiplet enemas in such a short time and the small but very well-discipline Israeli army showed itself on the scene as a major forced to be reckoned with. The British and French were on the side of the Israelis but they gave only small forces to restrain the Egyptians. Though the brief war shut down major resources from the Nile, within weeks the Egyptians de- nationalized the Suez Canal and allowed the goods to be shipped to Europe and elsewhere. As a result Egypt, Syria, and other Arab nations looked to the Soviet Union as their protector while Israel accidentally acquired about 800,000 new Egyptian and other residents. It was not however, as major as the newer acquisitions of 1967. He resigned the Prime ministership after the Suez War but remained on as Israel's President for two years a somewhat ceremonial role as enforcer of the Constitution. His Presidency included the arresting of Nazi war criminal Adolf Eichmann in Argentina. Ben Gurion laid the groundwork while an alliance between Israel and Egypt seemed about as likely as a snowstorm in the Florida Keys, the military victory led to the groundwork alliance two decades later. He also wrote letters to the Argentine president trying to avoid a diplomatic crisis between the two counterfeits since he had sent agents to violate Argentine law. Ben-Gurion gave public lectures and radio reports to teach the new generation to prepare for continued victory. Though named for the great King, he was twentieth century Israel's Moses and had to retire to make room for his Joshuas. After tendering three resignations in 1960 he retired permanently so at age 76 he left both as prime minister and secretary of defense.

In 1967 Ben-Gurion again gave advice to His country's military albeit it now in an unofficial role. At age eighty-one he was an active presence for his country when the Gaza Strip was taken in the aforementioned Six Days War. He also made several trips to America in his senior years and raised money through Israel bonds where Jewish Americans and their friends bought millions of dollars worth of Israeli investments that helped to save Gaza and the Old City which includes most of modern-day Jerusalem. In 1968 his beloved wife died. Ben Gurion died in 1973 at the age of eighty-seven. His death marked the end of Israel's *founding father.* While George Washington was first in war, first in peace, and first in the hearts of his countrymen he was first among many some w. day first among equals when compared to such standouts as Thomas Jefferson and Benjamin Franklin. Ben-Gurion has neither equal nor competitor as founding father of Israel, more than any other nation of our lifetime, Israel stands out as a place founded by the work and with the philosophy of one man,and among political leaders only David Ben-Gurion can say that he founded, built, and fought to defend a nation, and led that nation for two decades and three wars.

29

Rush Limbaugh
(1951- Present)

8 Of Diamonds of Hope

I always get quite a RUSH From hearing at liberals, Rush gush
The king of conservative Talk
Makes all in opposition baulk
Cause you can't argue with truth, only blush!
This is my own limerick I hang on the great hero of hope's beginning.

*B*orn Rush Hudson Limbaugh, III on January 3, 1951 the son of upper-middle class Midwesterners in Cape Gerardau, Missouri the man grew up just another American kid but went on to set new standards in broadcast journalism. Though he dropped out of two colleges and failed a course in public speaking by the age of twenty-one Limbaugh was working in radio and except for about twenty months in marketing for authenticity Royals he has worked in radio ever since. Fired from stations in St. Louis and Kansas City, Rush was eventually hired by a Sacramento station going there in his mid-thirties. A bachelor who had two previous failed marriages Limbaugh was spending his first extended time outside the Midwest and with no college degree and no great credentials he had to work twice as hard to prove he was half as good.

Paradoxically Rush Limbaugh could not have succeeded more. Within a short time he became the most listened to talk radio host in Sacramento. Although a staunch conservative and supporter of the Reagan Ami ministration, Limbaugh did not see himself as a political guru. He simply informed on the issues of the day in American and California politics and within a matter of months he became a popular presence at home and a sought after speaker outside California. Forming friendships with as many established media people as possible he was in Central California, not Hollywood and therefore never joined the top media establishment. His first chance to reach a wider market was a night gig as substitute host for The *Pat Sajak Show*. For the first time a national audience saw Rush Limbaugh and saw he was funny, entertaining, and likable. Within two years he was invited to New York to host a show that would be carried in over a hundred markets. By 1991 he was recognized as the modern *Will Rogers* and like fellow Missourian *Mark Twain* the standard as a commentator on what was exciting and funny about America. He appeared on "Nightline" to debate strategy in Desert Storm and his mother called the next day to tell him that his aging father saw him on TV. and could now rest knowing his oldest son had succeeded not just as an entertainer but a serious man who could be asked about policy on national television. A few weeks later his father died, though Rush graved (he was very close to both of his namesakes) he was grateful his *Nightline* appearance happened when his dad could see him. He broadcast during the **Reagan**, *Bush* 41,Clinton, and Bush-43, and Obama administrations. In spite of a brief fling with political limelight during the early Clinton years, becoming the most effective critic of the liberal President, he remained a commentator and conservative entertainer, refusing to bow to millions of requests he run for office, though he could have gotten the 1996 nomination for President if he wanted it. Another thing he has gotten famous for saying guys that he is tying half his brain behind his back something that has made it more fair to liberals and while I would never tie half my brain behind my back, God has beaten me to it *by creating me*

with a seven-year-old right side of the brain, so Rush and I have that
in common, we are both geniuses who use only half of our brains.

In 1992 he first appeared in his half-hour TV segments and published *The Way Things Ought to Be* which was the bestselling book
that year and *number one on the NEW York Times Bestseller list for*
twenty weeks. To this day it remains the third highest selling book
ever written by an American and the second bestselling book written
in the Twentieth Century. His TV. show was watched by about
twenty million a week and outshine even David Letterman while
never beating Leno or *Nightline.* Rush rooms were filled with blue
and white collar employees in all large companies in America so
that employees could listen to Rush with fellow Rush-lovers during
their lunch hours. In 1996 he had seen his TV show as running its
course though he could have stayed on he felt he was doing too
much. He has appeared at Easter Seals and other charitable events
and served on the board of several companies. His *See I Told You*
So was for a long time the fifth bestselling book of the decade and
remains a staple for conservative book lovers.

Limbaugh has created a new standard for broadcast journalism,
and his monologues and speeches have set a precedent for candid
debate not seen since the Civil War. His philosophy is relatively
simple, he is for empowering the people, getting the government
off the backs of citizens, letting them live their own lives, helping
those who fall through the cracks when necessary but primarily
helping the two hundred million Americans who are middle-class or
struggling to become so, rather than a minority who seek to live off
those who work. He lives to protect and defend The Constitution,
help people live moral and productive lives, and know their ideas,
actions, and the inevitable responsibilities that follow have serious
consequences. He is proudly pro life and has supported and won
major battles for educational freedom including the right to home-
school. He has supported the U.S. military in its endeavors to be
the greatest in the world. Though he never personally met **Ronald**
Reagan, early in the *nineties* **when** he was starting as a national
figure, the former President sent him a letter saying now that he is
retired, he is glad Limbaugh has succeeded him as the ideological
leader of conservatives. No other accolade could quite compare to

that. Still occasionally getting encouraged to run for office, it was never a choice he made, and while he remains a guru of conservatism, he rarely champions a specific cause or a candidate in a primary. In one of the few exceptions in 1993-4 when President Clinton tried to jeopardize homeschooling by passing a law requiring parents get certified like other teachers, Limbaugh with Christian radio stars led the campaign that defeated that evil legislation at the grassroots. He has maintained close friendships with both Presidents Bush and has remained loyal throughout The War on Terror where other conservatives and hosts have waffled.

In late 2003 it became reported to the media that Rush Limbaugh was fighting an addiction to prescription painkillers. About two years before he had undergone major back surgery and was living a life tormented by pain. A second surgery caused him to temporarily lose his hearing and while some attribute his remarkable weight loss to medicine he lost the overwhelming majority of The weight by 1998 before his illness. The fifty-two year-old Limbaugh twice checked himself in to rehab for prescription medication addiction and in late 2003 he was caught trying to buy the pills illegally in West Palm Beech. Given a citation and ordered to return to court, Limbaugh promised to enter rehab a third time. While his conservative allies rallied to him, he denied being a victim, while liberals cried out for his blood, the same who had long been telling us that drug addiction was a disease like pneumonia and we should never punish sick people; the same who excused Marion Barry, Paul McCartney, James Brown, Elizabeth Taylor, and others for their addictions. The Florida justice Department which had been defined under Janet Reno threw the book at the talk-show host though no one Palm Beach County had ever spent a day in jail before for "doctor shopping." Even in the case of Elizabeth Taylor harsh punishments were meted out to her doctor, not to her. Public figures in the past have urged doctors to over-prescribe pills include **Winston Churchill**, *Elvis Presley*, pioneer radio preacher *Aimee Semple McPherson*, *Kate Smith*, and Hulk Hogan. Not one of those ever spent a day in jail. The same liberals who want to tolerate many of the most heinous crimes protested for their intellectual enemy's imprisonment to get him out the way and punish him for effectively changing the nation for conservatism. Even the ACLU, his staunch enemy, after much coaxing, petitioned for leniency.

Finally all charges were dropped after Rush successfully underwent treatment. Now some will criticize my haphazard treatment of this incident, saying I'm soft on him for not coming out with blanket condemnation. To paraphrase profound pundit Ann Coulter's point, *Yes, it all boils down to a simple matter of should and shouldn't, essentially Rush Limbaugh should not have built part of his life on the need for painkillers and then broken the law to get them.* That said, what is clear to conservatives is that we have all done things we should not do and should therefore be careful saying someone should not do something, when before the grace of God, we are not much better.

Liberals seem to divide the world in half, like Whoppi Goldberg saying it does not matter how many women Bill Clinton seduces even against their will, because he has a different value system. In their world the mandate seems to be, *be ye perfect, conservatives, because your* **liberal enemies already are!** When a conservative is caught in sin, be it getting drunk, using pills, gambling addiction, sexual impropriety, or whatever else may be their sin, conservatives are able to accept that even their heroes are not perfect. They can forgive Rush Limbaugh, Bill *Bennett*, etc. because even a hypocrite, even an imperfect moralist is a better role model than someone who has no values Only to a liberal does having no positive moral values make one perfect because you can't violate a moral code where none exists. Liberals seem to think their excrement doesn't stink-conservatives know it Does. They know they have done dirty, filthy, rotten sinful acts but heroes can be people who have violated their own values. Like The liberal Methodists who paraded around Southwest Methodist University telling them not to let **President G. W. Bush put his library on the grounds, Limbaugh's enemies think their excrement does not stink, that their lack of values always trumps our high moral standards, and only they can be trusted to impose values and say who does and doesn't deserve respect. For his stalwart courage in this public debacle, Rush Limbaugh deserves more respect than all the liberals who opposed him.**

One of the most recognizable voices in America today, Rush Limbaugh has had a media presence for two decades. He has put in the English language expressions like "adult beverage" calling America the *fruited plane* calling death-*assume room temperature,* "Slick Willie" calling people *harmless little fuzz balls and bundles of mush,* calling the mainstream media "the drive-by media," "bleeding heart liberals," "illustrating *absurdity by being absurd*" and "maggot infested FM listener Woodstock crowd," and pronouncing the word *youth,* (though first done by Joe Peschi,) to sound like the Indian tribe. Impressively, he has lost about 130 pounds in his adult life, going from a harmless lovable fuzzball of 300 pounds to an average size man with a respectable frame to carry around his fairly tall body. For a time in love with his third wife Marta but after eleven years they divorced The conservative talk show host is worth over 300 million is a Midwesterner's Midwestern, like Mark Twain and other great Midwesterners he has divided his time between various states, for a time set mostly in New York and later West Palm Beach. With talent on loan from God, Rush will continue to be one of the stalwart fighters for America in the Twenty First Century as he redefined the concept of talk radio making it even more popular than much of television offerings just when it was starting to die as a genre in the 1980s.

Since I originally wrote, Rush Limbaugh fell in love and married Kathryn (Katie) Rogers in 2010. More than the other three, she seems to compliment his lifestyle, he is remarkably happier, and as his ancestors (as well as his brother, *David,* a well-regarded writer and talk-show host in his own right) produced offspring, he may well have some with Katie, maybe even a Rush Hudson Limbaugh, IV. Also very recently, Zev Chafits a Jewish conservative and former member of Israeli governments, published-*Rush Limbaugh an Army of One*-the most thorough biography of the subject to date. While for a longtime ditto-head like me, it was very little in the way of new news, it sheds much light on his life and career and is a must read for any who take the American political debate seriously. Another fact worth noting is that (though like all Democratic nominees) he campaigned hard for the defeat of Obama and spoke out critically of the new President's proposals especially on health care, he told

Mr. Chafits he would be happy to play golf with the President. The big-hearted (self-parodyingly-called) Maha Rushi would attempt some type of camaraderie or at least a mutual benefit with the seemingly impenetrable Far Left forty-fourth President, but he warned "It will never happen." When the (conservative but tolerated) mediator approached then-White House chief of-staff Rahm Emmanuel, he not only told the conservative Semite the President had no interest in playing golf (both their favorite hobby) but responded with humorless vulgarity. As usual, the conservative God-fearing man of the Right-tires to be kind and build bridges while the cold-hearted immobile self-serving champion of the Left impolitely declines. Limbaugh also hosts an annual telethon for a fight against Leukemia and other forms of blood cancer-since 1990 the efforts has raised over *fifteen million dollars to fight and bring about an end to blood cancers.*

30

William Jennings Bryan (1858-1925)

6 of Spades

*B*orn in Salem, Illinois March 16, 1860 William Jennings Bryan would go on to be known as both the great commoner and the defender of the American faith. Like many rural Midwesterners of the time His parents were both very religious but of different Protestant denominations. Bryan became a devout Presbyterian but always maintained he was simply a Protestant Christian and could worship equally well with those of all denominations. In his myriad travels around the country he also addressed Catholics, Mormons, and Jews in their respective places of worship. He graduated from the Union College of Law at Chicago eventually settling in Lincoln, Nebraska with his loyal wife Mary ne Baird.

Born for a political fight Bryan was discussing such issues from his youth. His first major political fight did not seem like a necessary moral issue it was For using silver to back federal money instead of gold. He was first nominated and won election to a seat in U.S. House from Nebraska's largest district in 1890. There the rookie congressman was chosen to serve on the pivotal Ways and Means Committee. It was then he became familiar and corresponded with many farmers and miners from the South and the West most of whom favored the backing of money with silver. In 1894 he chose not to run for his seat and instead entered the race for Senate which he lost by a close margin then began working at the *Omaha World Herald* where his oratory took a conservative turn though he remained a loyal Democrat. His oratory and rhetoric was like a true hero from plains, plainspoken and excellent and many of His local articles were read throughout the nation.

In 1896 the thirty-eight year old became and remains the youngest American to be nominated by a major political party to run fro President. In 1896 Bryan became The first candidate to travel through The nation going 18,000 miles and giving six hundred speeches though he lost to Republican William McKinley by 600,000 votes. It was an election far better attended than most today with over 90% voting in many districts because both candidates were so well-liked. He again rose to be the Democrats standard-bearer in 1900 though observers knew this election would be a slam dunk for **McKinley** and **Theodore Roosevelt**, the men who took America from rural republic to republican empire. Bryan himself had served in the Spanish-American war and came off as a supporter of some of the policies and an opponent of others, offering the voters a choice between an empire and a republic with some benignly governed territories which turned out not to make much difference in practice. Bowing in defeat after having canvassed twenty-eight states and complaining like a quintessential American cowboy, William Jennings Bryan knew there had to be more to life than losing elections. He again ran and won his seat in the House of Representatives. Once again The Democrat's standard-bearer in 1908 he ran against William Howard Taft and lost this time in a closer election this time getting a good bit of Republican support in Nebraska and The Western states. Interestingly, Bryan had much in common with two of his career rivals Theodore Roosevelt and Woodrow Wilson, both covered in this series. In the first case they were rivals and Bryan was on national tickets against both **Roosevelt** and his handpicked successor but he implemented several of Bryan's economic reforms as President. Though not always on the same page politically, **Wilson** and Bryan had much in common and as fellow Democrats were both from the Evangelical wing of The Democratic Party seeking godly principles in government which was not to become a dying breed until the end of the next decade. In 1913 Byran became secretary of state under President **Wilson.** He was the staunch crusader against involving America in World War I but The stance did not spring from a pacifist position. He believed some wars were just but at this time Americans had made a democratic decision to reject involvement in Europe and therefore sought to keep us out. After even trying to negotiate with Germany on letters that were largely rejected in Europe, Bryan resigned from the cabinet in 1915 and took to his specialty, The lecture circuit arguing against involvement in the Great War. Eventually after numerous attempts to force The Germans to honor neutrality had failed, President Wilson asked Congress For a declaration of war. Bryan, seeing his benign independence a stark contrast to The President's heroic power play just seven months into the President's second term, Bryan accepted The inevitable and became a crusader For bond drives and other attempts to raise resources for American soldiers. He even offered to don a uniform himself and fight in the war at The age of fifty-nine, and The Navy put him on a list of inactive non-commissioned combatants. In both cases he was consistent with the principles of democracy trying to stay out of war and then when war became inevitable agreeing to back it With every fiber of His being.

Though once ambivalent about Prohibition, he personally did not drink but was not sure whether it was moral to impose that standard on our nation he became the nation's top spokesman on amending the Constitution for Prohibition law. Touring the country and speaking anywhere he could William Jennings Bryan again campaigned like a cowboy for that end. He became the official spokesman for Prohibition preaching against the liquor demon in most of the states saying how alcohol needed to be buried like American always buries our enemies. He also spoke on behalf of giving women the right to vote, the first national Democrat to do so. Ironically he did not campaign for the nomination in 1920, but hoped he might get it at the last minute, but instead supported the Democratic nominee James Cox. As Bryan had been fighting the political fight of his life he won two major battles at that time when both Prohibition and female suffrage were added to the Constitution. It was a time to celebrate but for The sixty year old Bryan not a time to quit or even relax such words rarely fit into his vocabulary. His wife Mary had gotten very sick with arthritis so he moved them to Florida for the tropical climate and Bryan himself had diabetes since 1914. After a mounting drive to re-baptize the national figure in their image, Floridians nominated him to run as their senator but he again lost a close race. He remained however a prominent figure at the 1924 Democratic National Convention as he had helped to form the Party platform in seven elections and his family was rewarded with his brother Davis W. Bryan, the governor of Nebraska being nominated to run for Vice-President.

One of the most distorted and unstudied though one of the most important events in American history took place in the summer of 25. The facts that most people know is that John T. Scopes was a P.E. teacher who sometimes filled in for the Dayton, Tennessee basketball coach when he was out of town and also carried the science classes. Although neither a devout evolutionist nor particularly anti-Christian, Scopes was an agnostic and did take his lessons from the writings of Charles Darwin. A recent Tennessee law had made it illegal to promote any scientific philosophy that undermines the majority faith of Tenn. Majority, clearly an implicit outlawing of evolution. Scopes agreed to test the law by teaching evolution when he filled in for science, and was charged with a misdemeanor by Dayton prosecutors. Wanting to get publicity for their town, local prosecutors hired William Jennings Bryan to come and prosecute the case while Scopes' defenders asked New York lawyer Clarence Darrow to assist their side. When Bryan got off the train in Dayton hundreds of local Tennesseans, most devout Christians who had voted for him for President flocked to see him as though they were on some kind of a religious pilgrimage. These are the facts and these are where the facts that we know end. It was true that the Southern people treated Bryan as though he were a spiritual celebrity, but what is ignored is they also had a deferential and reverential attitude toward the secular Darrow as two national figures appeared in their town the same week. Far from trying to punish Scopes for teaching evolution, almost all of the prosecutors, police, and clergy in Dayton were Scopes' friends who talked kindly to him over lemonade at the local drugstore and wanted nothing more than a friendly competition with their town as the national forum. While Bryan prosecuted the case by saying that evolution should not be taught unless it was counter-balanced in an a way acceptable to the majority of Tennesseans, the judge agreed and at that time most Americans wholeheartedly agreed. After Bryan won the case and Scopes was fined twenty-five dollars Bryan offered to pay his fine. *Like his "conversion" about alcohol, believing it was time to have the law step in on it, he also said it was time for the law to regulate what children were being taught in school. He sternly disagreed with Darwinian evolution because it was an un-Biblical theory that said man came from natural factors, not from God, and it would inevitably lead to a social evil, where there is a hierarchy of people by various factors.*

By 1925 Bryan had happily accepted he would not be President but at the age of sixty-seven he was still looking for much to do to contribute to the nation he loved. Much of his time, however, was spent taking care of his sickly wife in a quasi-tropical climate that ironically ended up being worse for his own health problems. Sadly the oppressive 1925 heat got to Bryan and he died in a hotel room two weeks after the trial. One of the greatest Christians America ever produced, he was the forerunner to **Ronald Reagan** and had television existed not to mention radio when he was in his youth, he may have been the Rush **Limbaugh** of his era first, and like his friend and supporter *Will Rogers*, gone on to become the great photogenic hero who took the day, then ran And got elected as an older man like **Reagan.**

John Joseph O'Connor
(1926-2000)

7 of Clubs of Hope

A mild-mannered Pennsylvanian who spent most of his life quietly serving others and his Church with no experience in the
limelight in 1981 John Joseph O'Connor was the cardinal of New
York City the largest archdiocese in the American Church making
him here spiritual leader of over five million Catholics. Intestinally the cardinal of New York unlike most other Catholic spiritual leaders is expected to play a heavy political role. O'Connor had
never belonged to either political party seeing a registration with
one as a good way to alginate many Catholics in a diocese. Early in
his tenure as cardinal he got the reputation of being a radical Republican but in fact, though a mild supporter of the **Reagan** Administration, O Connor had a good man y liberal views. Hew as opposed
to capital punishment and belied that while the Democrats (and to
lesser degree Republicans) talk about jobs as a major issue both parties have failed in the far more important issue of housing and if one
candidate of either party successfully addressed the housing crisis
he would be the greatest politician to come along in years.

Of course O'Connor's most critical issue was his opposition to
abortion and for that he got protested and was the subject of hate

mail and hate articles. Some pro-abortion people have charged pro-lifers with being pro-life only to the moment of birth, and not caring what happens to anyone when death is not at stake. This indictment could never more falsely targeted a pro-life leader as John Cardinal O'Connor, a man who though never revising children provided safe and secure homes for more children than any American of his day. O'Connor believed in being pro life throughout a person's life, yes giving him the right to be born and therefore outlawing abortion, but also outlawing anything else that would harm him during life, giving parents the right to properly educate their children, helping children to be places in loving two parent families, making sure parents have the wherewithal to raise any children they bring into the world, supporting job and housing rights for these children as soon as they become adults, giving educational health options that criminalize and discourage drugs and gangs, and giving families many options and when need be money to prepare for their later years. Indeed John Cardinal O'Connor was completely pro-life as opposed to the abortion advocates who pretend to care about women but when in fact all they care about is seeing more abortions performed. O'Connor ingeniously maintained that laws are made not only to protect people and tell citizens and enforcers what to punish, but that **The law serves** *as a pedagogue, an educated teacher in its own right to point people in the right direction, and therefore even unenforced or unforceable laws are worth having if they help people know the right thing to do.* He stood up to the first woman on a national ticket, Geraldine Ferraro for saying she was Catholic and personally opposed abortion but believed it should remain legal, he confronted her hypocrisy, as she said "women should have a choice," he said *no one should* have the *choice to kill someone.* Ferraro later told the media O'Connor was right although this author always wonders why he did not simply excommunicate her!

Interestingly O'Connor struck up what may have been his closest adult friendship with the Jewish mayor of New York Edward I. *Koch.* Early in his tenure as cardinal, he opposed the mayor's policy that would give tax exempt status to groups that existed merely to promote homosexuality while requiring other charities including the diocese to take these groups as their equal. He engaged Koch at

Gracy Mansion something that many would think to be a liberal and conservative verbal shoot-out which in the end turned out to be a liberal and quasi-conservative coming together to become the best of friends. The diocese sued the city and won the issue along with allies in the *Salvation Army* and Orthodox Jewish and Quaker groups the judge ruled in favor of the religious plaintiffs, promoting the quick-witted Koch to quip "Only in New York can the cardinal sue the mayor and still be friends." *Friends is a* word not will defined in America and often used lightly but when it came to Edward I. Koch and John J. O'Connor it was a word that fit like a glove so rare among middle-aged American heterosexual men today and the two got together to write H*is Eminence and Hizzoner.*

Cardinal O'Connor saw his main objective as teaching Catholic theology and celebrating the Mass, keeping New York's St. Patrick's Cathedral strong and making sure everyone had the opportunity to receive the sacraments. On one routine Sunday a boisterous group of gay activists decided to violently protest and many were arrested. O'Connor maintains he is a firm believer in the right to protest but when it comes to the sanctity of the Church and the sacred celebration of the Mass, protesters will have to practice their rights other places. He also maintained that while we can value homosexual individuals as people the Church is *monolithic* in doctrine, homosexuality was sinful in Lot's day, in Jesus and Paul's day, and it remains sinful. He traveled to numerous countries as the spokesman for a nonprofit organization that included over fifty schools, and several hospitals and children's' homes. He opposed measures that would punish kids from Catholic schools who had to leave and get tutoring in public schools, a measure passed by the New York Court, one of the worst in recent history, in this effort he won the support of Mayor Koch. A long time battle with cancer was finally lost and John O'Connor went home to his Lord in 2000. He will be remembered as the most outstanding voice for American Catholics in the Twentieth Century and one of the greatest voices for religious education and values during one of the most exciting times in American history.

32

William Wilberforce

7 of Hearts few Hearts of Hope

O ne of the greatest compliments one can pay a speaker or historical figure in modern times is to say that this person needs
no introduction. While no one who lived in the Nineteenth Century
and very few from any time period deserved to be in need of no
introduction, sadly William Wilberforce is one who needs not only
introduction but comprehensive diagnosis and profound *exegesis* for
a generation of Americans and Britons many of whom have never
heard of him, few including me, have an adequate understanding
of his life and accomplishments. He has been compared to Jonas
Salk, Thomas *Edison*, Susan B. *Anthony* and Isaac Newton, a victim
of his own success. Unlike those people, Wilberforce never needed
such recognition in his lifetime and has only fallen out of favor with
historians after more than a century and a half of proper recognition to the crusades of anti-slavery and the need for freedom in all
countries. And while the Soviet and other nations of the Communist world and some Islamic and African nations today differ greatly
from Western morality and could benefit from his messages, to most
in the Western world Wilberforce is an anachronism, a man who carried a message that has been internalized by a world for whom his
usefulness has been outgrown.

William Wilberforce was born August 24, 1759 in Yorkshire County, England. He served for nearly half a century in the British House of Commons representing Yorkshire County, England. He served in six Parliaments, four prime ministers, and three monarchs. Ironically as a young man he twenty-one he made friends with *William Pitt*, The Younger who was also very young, twenty-four at the time when both when sought election to The House in 1780. Wilberforce won his first seat at twenty-one while Pitt lost his but went on to win another seat within a matter of months. Known for his uncommon beneficence and a testimony of the Christian life both in his anti-slavery crusade and the testimony to what grace can do in the life of a forgiven sinner, a talented politician who set out to end the African slave trade in a time when it was accepted as a necessary part of life. The slave trade was not only expected by European and other intellectuals and governments but slavery was as old as the beginning few mankind. Along with parents and children and husbands and wives going back to the days of Adam and Eve, the slave and master relationship was one taken for granted and few people (with the possible exception of the slaves themselves) ever took exception to it or though there was a possibility of eradicating the relationship any more than that of other basic relationships. Wilberforce made economic and infrastructure arguments for abolishing the trade particularly how it could benefit both European and African resources and economic, but he made it clear thought his life that his sole reason for crusading against slavery was Christian morality.

There were however, a few dynamics in The North Atlantic slave trade that set it apart from most of world slavery. The racial component was the most obvious as with the exception of Ireland and a few other parts of Europe, only an African could be taken in slavery and even then only one whose mother was born in slavery and for whom no legitimate father would vouch freedom (even an unmarried father could free a slave but only if he promised to take him into his care financially). The other dynamic (and one that also becomes a stumbling for many non-Christians reading Colossians 4:1-2 I Timothy 6:1-4 and elsewhere in The New Testament) was the little known fact that in virtually all societies of both Christian

and Islamic, slaves were largely indentured servants working ﹀
off a debt and with few exceptions were released after the period ﹀
servitude had ended or in special years. In ancient Israel the most
one could be an indentured bondsman was seven years and at various times within those seven years freedom was often purchased or
benevolently secured. The other time was the year of jubilee which
took place every forty-nine years at which time Israel was to free
all slaves, so sooner or later the clock would free slaves the masters
would not. While the North Atlantic slave trade recognized none
of these human niceties for people largely considered subhuman,
a few dynamics often go unrecognized. In 1792 when Wilberforce
was thirty-three Lord *John Grey* became the great emancipator of
Britain itself therefore freeing The slaves who lived in England and
Scotland, and with a few exceptions most of Ireland and Wales.
The bad part for the emancipated was that this dealt with relatively
few slaves actually living in Europe over 90% of the slaves in the
Empire were in African, Asian, or Western islands under the British
crown and they had to wait more than three decades for the work of
Wilberforce and the other anti-slavery leaders to come to fruition.
In 1808 Napoleon took the French out of the Western slave trade
and America officially ended the slave trade in the Nineteenth Century as did Spain and Portugal who had founded the North Atlantic
Institution. With few exceptions like Brazil and some Arab-owned
territory, no more slaves were being herded on ships to cross the
Atlantic, British, American, and other slaveholders had to rely on
internal breeding among their slaves to refurnish the "property."

At the age of twenty-eight Wilberforce the primarily leader of
the Proclamation Society the Christian arm of legislature (similar
to The Moral Majority or the Christian Coalition) in the post-Amer-
ican Revolutionary era. Wilberforce hated slavery both the idea of
man owning man and the cruel and destructive realities with which
slaves had to deal on a daily basis from their masters. As **Lincoln**
once said slavery is bad for the black man but is almost equally bad
few the White man making a monster out of otherwise descent citizens Doing hundreds of hours of interviews with other anti-slavery
observers most notably John Newton, a pastor and former slave
trader who composed the immortal hymn *Amazing Grace*, Wilber-

force saw slavery from both a theological and political perspective. He took it a step further, he sought to incorporate the greatest philosophical and moral titans of his time in the quest to free those held in bondage. When he died in London on July 29, 1833 at the age of seventy-eight having recently retired to private life, the Lord Chancellor and the Speaker of the House of Commons were among the pallbearers at his state funeral and he was committed to the arms of Jesus by a crowd of thousands of English commoners, legislators, and noblemen. His headstone notes these facts along with his reposing, *till through the merits of Jesus Christ, his Holy Redeemer, Whom in his life, and his writings he had lived to glorify, he shall rise in the resurrection of the just.*

These are the most basic facts about one of the most intriguing figures of modern times and in spite of the fact that he set out in his early twenties to accomplish a task against then insurmountable odds, and strike the decisive death blow to the slave trade itself within less than a decade, then spanning five decades of politics and prayer, dealt the death blow to slavery in the colonies as well, Wilberforce remains largely unknown and ignored, an anomaly to history. In his early years Wilberforce who differed with The church of England was an anomaly not because of his different theological beliefs nor his voicing of those beliefs but because he put off his education indefinitely because virtually all The schools in England were run by The Church and most people would just hypocritically sign on to a school they did not truly follow. He was reputed to have poor eyesight though no disability has been specified they say at times he had others read to him. He did however, become a sharp student of The Bible and literature in his early twenties. He read, heard, or meditated on the Bible at least two hours a day and The writings of French philosopher and theologian *Blaine Pascal* thirty minutes a day. He and Pitt regularly discussed established works of the day like *Butler's Analogy.*

He was only twenty-five when the wealthy slave trader, John Newton, then an atheist, began writing him and Wilberforce was the rabbi/ advisor that led Newton to Christ. Still anti-denomination though a very persuaded Christian, Wilberforce's advice to Newton mirror's Jesus' to Nicodemus, *you must be born again.* Wilberforce and Newton embraced the Methodist branch of Christianity as preaching luminaries *John Wesley*, George Whitefield, and *William Booth* (later founder of his own denomination) as well as hero of hope **Fanny J. Crosby** would do in the same century, both for that denomination's emphasis on the personal relationship with God by being born from above and the undisputed fire associated with that Church's missionary zeal. Ironically his parents were committed secularists with a special albeit understandable loathing of Methodism the way today's secularists especially loathe *Pentecostalism*. Though he loved his parents dearly, Wilberforce never let other humans influence his decisions especially when he heard and understood the will of God.

Though his good friend *William Pitt* would eventually become Prime minister and serve longer than any of the Majesty's' chief servants for over a century, Wilberforce was able to influence history against the slave trade largely because he stayed out of the inner ruling circle of Parliament. With Newton he became associated with *Amazing Grace* and he lived to see the grace being poured out both on his life and His (eventually her) Majesty's Empire. Wilberforce has been described as God's politician and along with a few from history like **Joan of Arc**, **Reagan**, and **Martin Luther King**, he can be compared historically. In another sense his exceptionalism makes him comparable to few international pioneers and world changers including *Mohandas K. Gandhi*, *Lincoln*, *and Turkey's Kemal Ataturk*, William Wilberforce rose to hear the voice of God and successfully confront a nation to heed the voice and His holy challenge. In confronting a nation, he led divine guidance to victory like only these small number of men and women (there might be others but I don't know them) you can count on your hands. In his personal life, Wilberforce married Barbara Ann on May 30, 1797 and his first book with the lengthy title *A Practical View of The Prevailing religious System of Professed Christians in The Higher and Middle Classes of This Country Contrasted with Real Christianity* sold over 7000 copies, a virtual bestseller for his day.

33

Queen Wilhelmina
(1880-1962)

6 of Diamonds of HOPE

§

*T*he most loved of all monarchs of the Netherlands and one of the most beloved monarchs of modern times was born August 31, 1880 in *the Hague outside* Amsterdam, the son of King William II. On November 23, 1890 the teen year old princess lost her father and the Netherlands was ruled by regents for eight years until she was of age. On her eighteenth birthday Wilhelmina was crowned. Unlike many other monarchs who came at the time, Wilhelmina had no desire other than to love her people, help them be their best, and be a symbol of leadership and stability for one of the most stable democracies in history. Sadly, twice in her life she would see evil people break the tough, stout-hearted spirit of the Dutch and lead her and an entire continent to the brink of oblivion. Twice she bounced back and the world will know the Dutch spirit of small real estate, immense brain and moral power, that has made a series of inland townships about the size of New York state, one of the last bastions of hope in a weary world. She ascended to the throne at a time of wealth and prosperity where her country in the middle of Northern Europe was experiencing great wealth even at a time when imperialism was dying. Spain and Portugal had lost their empires and the United States, though having inherited five colonies was using the republican method to question the purpose of colonies in the first place. Meanwhile her neighbor Belgium was becoming a power player in the world while the Northern neighbors Germany and the Hapsburg Empire were realizing the power of empire building and East Russia and Turkey were struggling to maintain their status as "big boys." Interestingly, while most people call her nation Holland she would not want to be called queen of Holland any more than the governor of New York is merely the executive of a city. The Netherlands include a series of counties and townships in and around Belgium (some were once in Belgium or ruled by France while others were former duchies or city-states) so all Holland is within the Netherlands but the Netherlands include various counties outside Holland. Dutch from Holland can be called Hollanders but remain mildly annoyed at having their country called by the name of its largest state. Queen Wilhelmina rose and in her teens and twenties continued to maintain an empire through a relatively small group of soldiers and sailors while the Netherlands was small it maintained colonies both east in Asia (the Dutch East Indies most of present Indonesia) and the Americas the Dutch West Indies, so this humble woman owned real estate on three of the world's "four corners."

On January 1, 1901 Wilhelmina married Henry and she and her prince extended voting rights to all males while adult females got the vote later in her reign. In World War I she maintained the Netherlands neutrality being related by blood or marriage to both British and German royal families while she did use Dutch troops to enforce the results of local elections in Amsterdam. She courageously took the Netherlands through the Depression and as a strong Christian she made sure her country did not suffer nearly as much as many other nations of Europe and the West. She maintained pro-British neutrality when Nazi Germany attacked Poland, but as was expected German troops attached Holland on May 10, 1940. Her people gave a brave and stubborn resistance but could not prevail and the inland townships of the Netherlands were largely surrendered with Wilhelmina being taken to spend the war years in exile in England. So loved and honored was she that the father of Corrie-ten Boom the great philo-Semitic humanitarian and Christian advocate to the Jews of Europe, was able to tell the Nazis correctly that the Word of God says *Fear the Lord honor the Queen, even in London exile, she was the reigning government and neither the Bible nor the Dutch constitution said anything about the Nazis!* While the implication that the apostle Paul would write his sacred text to Timothy with a woman in mind who lived eighteen centuries later, may sound like borderline blasphemy, to him she was the symbol of her nation and its people. Indeed Wilhelmina's autobiography *Lonely but Not Alone told of her deep spiritual faith as a Christian of largely* **Calvinistic** *leanings. She broadcast from London over Radio Orange, and the Dutch national anthem was played every Sunday on the BBC as a symbol* that the spirit of even occupied nations was not broken, *and those* nations that surrendered would *soon* be back *in full mode.* Anyone who has watched the film *The Hiding Place* remembers the booming voice of Queen Wilhelmina came on over the BBC to the struggling people of the Netherlands to continue their resistance to the Nazis. With the queen in exile her people were not silent. Though only one-sixth the size of France, and comparable proportion to the population of New York and New Jersey, *the Dutch fought on both continents to engage both a guerrilla war of sabotage on the home front as well as a very impressive air and sea war. In all the Netherlands produced approximately 200,000 troops to fight against both Germany and Japan. Since their army surrendered so early, the Dutch Royal Navy was left largely in tact and its merchant marine provided more ships than any nation of continental Europe to the Allied effort. By 1942 the* Princess Irene Brigade *was formed and while fighting mostly in the sea and air war against Japan, the Netherlands provided tens of thousands of troops to the Allied forces (namely serving the British) of Operation Overlord on D-Day. Over 10,000 Dutch civilians living in Indonesia were taken prisoner by the Japanese. While the French contribution to the overthrow of the Nazis from continental Europe was numerically greater, the Dutch was proportionally greater and, unlike the French who had 350,000 Free troops to serve under* DE Gaulle, (and eventually 1.3 million in the war) *the Dutch fought extensively against Japan.* Continuing their naval resistance they defended their holdings in Indonesia. Their success in World War II ended the last vestiges of anti-monarchical sentiment and laid the groundwork for Indonesia to become a free country. She also gave independence to several Western islands, while Aruba and the Antilles continue to be benignly governed Dutch colonies.

The recognition of the huge former colony in Indonesia, the fourth largest country in Asia, was the last achievement of her reign. After that, in declining health she ended the fifty-eight year reign, arguably the greatest in Dutch history. Her daughter Juliana and son-in-law Prince Bernhard were major figures in her reign and in 1949 she abdicated so her daughter could be crowned Queen Juliana at the age of thirty-nine. For her remaining thirteen years she stayed on as Queen Mother. In fact Wilhelmina's country has been one of the most stalwart democracies of modern times. To remain so it must continue its tradition of freedom for all of its citizens as it has long been one of the most welcoming of assimilating immigrants (e. g. Ann Frank's family) for both philo-Semitism and also be willing to assimilate Black and other ethnic minorities into the Dutch people. **The Netherlands** has been one of the most stalwart democracies of all times. To remain so, they must continue its tradition of freedom for all its citizens and assimilating immigrants (e. g. Ann Frank's family), it must remain philo-Semitic and assimilate Blacks and other ethnic minorities into the Dutch people.

34

Jerry Falwell
(1934-2007)

5 of Spades OF Hope

*B*orn in Lynchburg, Virginia Jerry Falwell *grew up knowing that his father had shot and killed his own alcoholic brother (in what was ruled an accidental homicide) and though a lukewarm Christian it was instrumental in him committing himself to faith in the Lord Jesus Christ. His father had a rough life and probably never followed the rest of his family in serving the Lord.* His mother, the irrepressible Hazel Falwell, was like no other mother of whom I have ever read or known, she was all things to Jerry, a best friend, and when he needed it his sovereign, his subject, his tutor, his student, his protector, and protected, and just a close person. *Jerry, did say in his autobiography, that his father, Carey Falwell, committed his life to the Lord shortly before his death, seventeen years after the tragic shooting.* Jerry's own brief rebellion against Christianity, mirrors fellow-hero of hope **Woodrow Wilson,** he was part of a very low-key street gang that drank a little beer, but by age eighteen he was ready for Bible college. At sixteen, on January 20, 1948, he accepted Jesus Christ as *his personal Lord and Savior.* Always a Republican, Jerry had an "Elect *Eisenhower"* bumper sticker on his car when he left Virginia for Missouri in 1952 but his main interest was serving the Lord Jesus Christ not politics.

In 1952 he entered Baptist Bible College in Springfield, Missouri was one of the hotbeds of the "Bible belt" though situated on the border within double digit miles of both Oklahoma and Arkansas. A stellar academic he soon was invited back to pastor *after a stellar academic, he was soon invited back to* Lynchburg Baptist, which was renamed Thomas Road Baptist Church under his ministry. As a twenty-one-year-old recent graduate he took the church and as a hefty seventy-year old he continued to pastor it right up to his death, rarely being absent on a Sunday except during the Moral Majority promotions and even then preaching in his church on most Sundays.

The first two decades Jerry Falwell did what every Bible-believing pastor is expected to do, preach the Gospel in season and out of season, love his flock, visit them in their homes, counsel them when they need help, and set an example of love and morality for his community. Two incidents in these years illustrate his ascendancy as a national figure. The first involves the Civil Rights demonstrations. When picketers used Thomas Road Baptist Church as a launching pad for Civil Rights demonstrations for integration Falwell got media publicity for asking them to stop. He said if they wanted to take part in their country they should come in and hear the Gospel message. This only made the protectors get louder and after asking them several times not to disrupt his services he went out with a microphone and asked the crowd to disburse from private property. He had not called the police but in a little town like Lynchburg they are bound to hear and within minutes police were the church asking Falwell what to do. He said he was not pressing any charges but he was politely asking them to leave so if they did not comply the police may do whatever they saw fit. When some got arrested that haunted Jerry Falwell for years to come that he was the preacher who let Civil Rights demonstrators be dragged away from his church in handcuffs. *In spite of this and other incidents (he later touched on as his racist past) he was never a white supremacist, and his Black friends from childhood remained his friends for life. With his loyal wife Marcel he eventually raised three children. In the second major incident* during The scandal Involving Richard *Nixon and the* Watergate, he was one of the few publically proclaiming Nixon should not be impeached. He encouraged Republican members of Congress to use their numbers to enable him to finish his term. Ironically the Republicans often called the party of opportunists did not make the exception to morality that the Democrats would. It was most conservative senator of the time, Barry *Goldwater* who would urge Nixon to do his part for America and resign. Notwithstanding Falwell's' counsel Republicans in the House and the Senate urged Nixon to face the consequence of his actions while twenty some years later it was the Democrats who used their numbers to bully the rest of the country into accepting Clinton as a full-fledged President despite his far more criminal behavior.

In the seventies Falwell began attending meetings with other conservatives though he maintained his ultimate goal was to preach the Gospel of Jesus Christ. One of The most stellar Christians of the time was Dr. Paul *Weyerich*, a Catholic layman and lawyer who had been pressing state legislatures to adopt more traditionalist values. He knew that though the majority of Americans supported his views, only a godly President could implement them because lots of career congressmen and career judges would simply overturn the will of the people in the name of "progressive liberal values." Eventually Weyerich's inner circle came to include Phylis's *Schlaffly* "the sweetheart of the Silent Majority" and *Howard Phillips,* a Jewish scholar who went on to run for President on the Constitutionalist ticket. The last member was Jerry Falwell so called the *Religious Round table because* it included a Jew, a Catholic, a Protestant, and an impartial moderator, all equal. The very wise Weyerich knew only one man could lead all conservative run-of-the mill Americans in the movement that would bring America back to God, himself too "eggheaded", the country was not ready to rally behind a Catholic woman, and in spite of progress there was still too much Antisemitism in America. Contrary to common Northeastern opinion, to lead this country one must connect with people in the South and West. That left the fiery Protestant from Virginia, and Weyercih urged him to begin a movement that could have millions of members intent on bringing people of faith and traditional morals to the top positions. Largely because of this Catholic layman, the pastor of Thomas Road

Baptist Church entered a new phase in his career, the founder of Moral Majority, the organization that would play the most direct role in electing the fortieth President of the United States.

To quote from Falwell's own S*trength for The Journey:*

I found myself sharing the platform with Catholic priests and nuns, Orthodox rabbis, Mormon elders, and pastors from Southern Baptist, Presbyterian, Nazarene, and Assembly of God (sic) *churches.* **This was not** nor was it ever intended to be an evangelistic enterprise. (ALL Emphasis added) This was ***war, and for a time we needed to set aside our differences and focus on the things that united us in common cause. To save the children,*** **Baptist preachers marched** arm in arm with courageous little Catholic nuns who had already taken their lonely stand against abortion and those who run the abortion mills. . .Orthodox rabbis in their dark suits and caps, and Orthodox priests in their ornate vestments, marched in solidarity with courageous Quakers and Mennonites who had already led the way. Episcopal laymen filled their Mercedeses (sic) **with teenagers** *from Assembly of God (sic) churches to drive into the intercity. Catholics, Mormons, Baptists, and Jews, believers and unbelievers took to the streets. . . we circled precincts, we assembled huge computer mailing lists, we sent out millions of letters and brochures. . . and in the process we helped elect a President. . . Ronald* **Reagan** *filled a vacuum on the national scene in 1980. He embodied all the views that Moral Majority held dear and his personal faith seemed genuine and relevant to his message.*

Indeed were it not for Falwell and the millions from all walks of American life and from all fifty states who lined up with him, **Ronald Reagan** may have never been President and millions in and outside of Europe may well be speaking Russian against their will today.

While his adherents were largely white, they included a good many others, for instance in Washington D.C. 85% of the over five hundred on his mailing list, and all of the local pastors with whom he shared the platform were African-American. Other conveniently overlooked facts are that the majority of Moral Majority members were women, more Catholics entered the ranks than members of any denomination, and while most   presidents were Protestants there were Jews, Mormons, and agnostics who served as   presidents in various counties. *His agenda was strongly pro-life, in fact it was largely to "push" for a Constitutional amendment that protected the right of children to be born that the Moral Majority was formed, and early on in the campaign he met with* **Reagan, who** assured him he also had that goal and would run on support for a pro life amendment. *He would, however, allow abortion to be legal in the cases of rape or the life of the mother. Like* **Orrin Hatch,** *he was not in favor of forcing people to disclose religious and other personal views and he did not want to step into the bedroom and limit personal behavior between consenting adults, he even said he would allow homosexuals to teach in public schools as long as they were not using the classroom as a pulpit to preach an agenda. A final view that was part of Moral Majority's message was unwavering support for the nation of Israel, and he staked his career and at times even his life, on Zionism and protecting The Holy Land. He was friends with every Israeli prime minister of his lifetime from* Menaham Begin on, and *Jewish journalist* Merill Simon wrote a book about his unwavering *support* for the Jewish people and the *Zionist republic.*

Throughout the eighties Falwell continue to serve his pastorate while traveling almost every week. A couple of years after the Reagan victory *they began performing the heavily conservative musical I Love America,* in churches and outdoor forums. It dealt with the Founders breaking away from Britain and their primarily religious motivation for challenging the mighty Empire to become the freest and in many ways most godly nation on earth. It contains among other patriotic songs, *I'm Just a Flag-Waving American,* which (along with Lee Greewood's *God Bless the USA*) was added to the American *lexicon* in my lifetime. Wherever the group assembled, in primarily secular forums, in addition to the keynote speaker, his "ensemble" included singers, actors, and local pastors and   representatives who defied acquaintances to appear on stage.

They were threatened on the steps of the Wisconsin state house in Madison, but courageous pastors and priests took to prayer and assertively kept the hateful bigots at bay until the police got there. He was shouted down by students at Harvard who wanted their secular rantings to outshout whatever he had to say but he addressed them directly-" I Know why you are protesting me. You have been fed so many lies-IF I believed everything you have been told about me, I would be protesting me too." This witticism connected with *the Harvard crowd* and he admitted that he had grown up with much racism and if he saw himself thirty years ago, he would conclude that man was a racist. If anything, he explained, not only was he a converted racist, but today more Black families attend Thomas Road Baptist Church and Liberty University than attend Harvard, the so-called bastion *of liberalism. Just as he was prepari*ng to speak at Yale, he was informed their president Bartlett A. Giamatti had indoctrinated incoming freshmen about the "evil nature of Jerry Falwell-perpetrating a radical assault on the nation's political values, he is rigid in absolutist slogans, absolutistic in morality. "He has licensed a new spirit of meanness in the land, a resurgent bigotry that represents itself in racist and discriminatory postures, in threats of political retaliation, in injunction to censorship, in acts of violence." Though various "translations" of what Giamatti said have been variously attributed by those present, there is no evidence he used the word "Nazi," but both members of the press and university executives and professors were comparing his deeds at that time to noted racists and anti-Semites and his attitudes to everyone from Ayatollah Khomeini, to Adolf Hitler, to Jim Jones.

While refuting all these ludicrous claims (in addition to the truth about him I have presented) could be a task for a whole other book, I will just make three points here. First, in Giamatti's delivery he used the same absolutist and I may add gimmicky slogans (as he*ro of hope **S I Hayakawa** warned against making a part of the language) he is accusing Falwell of using, and doing it without any of the facts, without stating or even implying which of Falwell's words, messages, or writings elicit such emotions, simply stating this opinion as fact and dogmatically expecting his audience to believe him. Second, though Falwell did believe in an absolute system of morality (as his critics obviously do as well, or else they would have no grounds to attack him so viciously, since obviously it is **their** absolute system of morality he has offended), each of the other accusations are a gross distortion of fact.* The values enunciated by our Founding Fathers and hence written into our Constitution, are in every sense more consistent with what Falwell and the priests, rabbis, ministers, laymen, elders, and adherents in all fifty states believe, than those Mr. Giamatti and the secular "progressives" of the left preach. He was not assaulting our political values, quite the contrary, he and his allies were working within the system to bring about the changes th*ey thought were good for America, just as the Ivy League left works similarly to champion their values. All of Falwell's "slogans" came either from the Bible or from the Constitution and its equivalent framework strengthened by two hundred years of American practice, if something is either inspired by God, or validated by the American framework, it is not a "slogan" and it is on far more valid footing than the platitudes and slogans of the Far Left.* As for a "new spirit of meanness" conservatives and their allies, are far kinder in our delivery than liberals of the past fifty years, and we are also far more likely to listen and respect the other side, and their right to speak, which makes the charge of "injunction to censorship" equally ridiculous. Never in his professional career did Falwell write or speak a word with racist or anti-Semitic implications or discriminatory postures, his America is one in which the minority is protected and every American has the right to live as they please within the law. The charge of "acts of violence" is too ludicrous to refute. Third, this diatribe was pronounced in front of an assembly of incoming college freshmen, at a mandatory gathering, almost-needless-to-say, a situation that makes indoctrination of the worst kind possible. Such indoctrination, of which Falwell was accused, all to common, is virtually an art form patented by the Left, and while Falwell and others *who* agree with him may love every opportunity to get their views out (like I'm doing with this book), a captive audience of teenage scholars would almost always be seen as an inappropriate route, and almost never would a conser*vative use such a forum to attack a single individual.*

His San Francisco meeting was interrupted by a militant transsexual named Sister Boom Boom and *though he did not address him directly, in his autobiography he said he wanted to embrace him and say, "Jesus loves you, you are just like my son, willing to live and to die for what you believe." His profound generosity and love for his fellowman helped Falwell win over a small but real portion of his critics. Many media people refused to interview him, as much like* **Dan Quayle,** *you could only hate or even dislike him before you got to know you, once people knew him they could disagree but not help but like Jerry Falwell. In a counterweight, in 2000, candidate* John McCain, *called him and Pat* **Robertson** *agents of intolerance, but Falwell later joked about the incident, wishing "a happy seventieth birthday to my fellow agent of intolerance", and encouraged the GOP, hoping McCain not be ostracized from the party, but instead be offered the job of Vice-President. He always took seriously the Biblical admonition, "When a man's ways are pleasing to the Lord, he makes even his enemies live at peace with him" (Proverbs 16:7).*

One enemy with whom Falwell has not made up is pornographer Larry Flynt whom Falwell sued for ridiculing him and his mother Hazel who died a few years before. Though he lost the case he won over many to his side and Flynt who has been credibly accused of molestation by his daughter, is hard to forgive. Though the Moral Majority disbanded in the late eighties it was only because it had served its purpose a majority of Americans were already in favor of having people of faith lead us. and twelve years of **Reagan** and *Bush* helped to prove that. He has been awarded the Friend of Israel Award by *Menahem Begin*, the highest award Israel can give a civilian. He also had a brief fling with more controversy when he took overplay Ministries in what he still maintains was an effort to restore the struggling Jim Bakker to his pulpit.

He continued to preach on TV and radio and also led a para-church movement in 2000 which may have been somewhat instrumental in electing *George W. Bush*. Falwell was ex *officio* head of the college he founded that has produced the number one debate team in America five of the last six years. In 2004 he had open-heart surgery. He died of heart failure while walking in the college on 2007. Jerry Falwell died one of the most respected Americans and one of our most distinguished clergymen ever, making *Good Housekeeping's* most admired Americans list a handful of times, including #2 on the list of most admired Americans in 1985.

35

James Dobson
(1936-Present)

of Clubs of Hope

B orn in *Shreveport, Louisiana and raised in a Mississippi town, until living in Texas for his high school years, raised in the Church of the Nazarene, James Dobson has risen to* become the defining voice of *Christianity in the 20th and early Twenty-first century.* As Billy **Graham** has become the closest thing we have ever had to a Protestant pope, Jim Dobson has become the closest thing we have a to a Protestant prophet, the lay voice of morality and hope for e American. Dobson married his beloved Shirley *August 27, 1960* and dropped out of medical school. *He* went on to get his doctorate in behavioral psychology and later taught medical students. His first book Dare to Discipline set the pace for a conservative alternate psychology and he became the more m b to Dr. Spock in one of his few "political" speeches at time saying our effort in Vietnam was justified young people growing up today need to be taught that there are issues for which to live and there are issues for which one may be called on to die. Most of his later books were written in conjunction with the colleges, so they have very little Evangelical content while being 100% **consistent** with **Biblical principles.** In the early seventies he began a monumental study of treatment of PKU a rare vitamin deficiency in the womb that results in mental challenges and the books remain the standard work in treatment of youths with PKU. Many North American libraries made some hoopla a eliminating his books in mid-seventies because he b spanking is part of effective parenting. He has always stuck behind his principles, however, that on both sacred and secular planes the best form of discipline for keeping young people in line is the occasional spanking.

A scholar and educator James Dobson taught medical and students a the University in California at Santa Barbara and other universities. In the seventies he established Focus on the Family Ministries, by going national he got millions of listeners and subscribers to his newsletter. Over twenty millions people listen to him every week and more than four million have read one or more books. The father of two, Dobson has been instrumental in teaching millions how to be good parents and practiced these methods on his own kids. Never one to seek the limelight, but only to serve The Lord to the best of his ability, Dr. Dobson has changed the world by changing the course of the American family in the last Twentieth Century. The last person to interview serial killer Ted Bundy and the last to speak to basketball legend *Pete Maravich,* Dr. Dobson had worked and played with the big boys. The basketball legend died in his arms while playing recreational basketball with The psychologist saying his last words "I feel great!"

Throughout most of his career Dobson was apolitical even refusing to sign petition for **Pat Robertson** to run for President when he was asked. While he attended the 1980 Washington for Jesus March, he saw that as church work and though leader of a para-church organization he did not see it as his duty to make political statements. Though pulling The lever for Republicans as long as he can remember, he never saw politics as his mandate. This changed in 1992, seeing the likely possibility of one of the most evil men in America, Bill Clinton becoming President he began campaigning to stop it from happening. Since, however, he was outside the political inside he did not then, have the lobbying success of a **Pat Robertson or Jerry Falwell** and he did not build personal relationships with candidates at that level like **Billy Graham. At the** time, however, he let elected officials know that he, the biggest name in radio psychology would do everything he could to see that only candidates who took Christian values and Christian concerns seriously would have the respect of his listeners.

While abortion was his primary target, as a child psychologist he did all he could to stop millions of children from being murdered, he also did what he could to stand up against Socialism, the trend toward secular Humanism in education, special rights for homosexuals, taking away gun rights from innocent citizens, and the growing tendency to get soft on crime especially crimes against children. Though still not having taken a stance to endorse a candidate, most of the Republicans both in Colorado where he settled his ministry by then and the candidates for national office courted his support. In fact he viewed all of the candidates with their negative baggage. An early meeting with Phil Gramm, a Texas senator trying to get the endorsement of Christian conservatives made him doubt he would find the type of candidate Christians can truly embrace (not just endorse) and while his political involvement accelerated, his will to endorse candidates declined. It is very ironic that the man who many consider having more direct influence on peoples' day-to-day lives than any Christian advocate of our time, did not until his senior years find worthwhile candidates to support.

His books have been both his biggest source of profound knowledge dissemination and his top source of income, since unlike radio ministry funds, he controls the overwhelming majority of his the money he takes in from book sales. In 1992 he published *When God Doesn't Make Sense, the one book in his corpus that can be termed "theological." Besides those mentioned, his two best books are the ones that answer questions from parents. It speaks out against the creeping Secularism in public schools.* While public education in America is and of right ought to be secular, groups that have a foothold in education (not primarily teachers and administrators) have gone from teaching secular studies to teaching secularism and many public schools have a decidedly Anti- Christian slant. For that reason Dobson prefers both more neutral education when it comes to public schools and government funding for religious schools and homeschooling, which was done in this country until recently and in *most other major democracies* now. Unlike Liberty University and Regents under the auspices of the Family Channel, Focus on the Family was always run by a layman, however, unlike the Christian Coalition then under the direction of *Ralph Reed,* Focus was not a purely political organization and the busybodies at the IRS could say people are giving money to a nonprofit organization not to endorse Republican candidates.

In 1996 he protested the **Dole** candidacy saying the Kansan was wanting to have it both ways on abortion and other issues and voted for the Constitutionalist Party. A previous stroke had caused the middle-aged mildly heavyset Dobson to change his eating habits. He was thinking of asking his listeners to sit out the 1998 election which, if taken seriously, would cause a Democratic landslide across the country. It would be his message to the GOP, *if Dr. Dobson ain't happy, ain't nobody happy!* In the end he relented, in the middle of the Clinton impeachment scandal. He had a second stroke around that time and like other *Evangelical* icons *is* no longer allowed to drink Coke and eat pizza and jellybeans and everything else we love to eat, he will have to settle for rice, and beans and grain cereal until Jesus comes back.

That a mild-mannered child psychologist could have such an impact on electoral politics was remarkable. He was, ironically in a position where **Jerry Falwell** had been twenty years earlier and as his supporter journalist Cal Thomas pointed out he should think about the fact t P is all about compromise, to get a bill passed Senate needs a hundred potential voters and more than four times that number in the House. While he lectured Newt Gingrich, justifiably so for not taking and r his calls, the Speaker of t H ought to be fair to a man with twenty million listeners. Encouraged to run for President himself in 2000, the sixty-four year old child psychologist did not. *Gary Bauer, a* Christian *who had served as* **Reagan's** chief domestic policy advisor *and later gone on to head the Family Research Council, a "political" division spawned from Focus on the Family,* stepped up and ran for President himself. Underrated and possibly the most intellectually qualified to lead the GOP, Bauer, a Kentucky native with more experience on national issues than any major Republican with the possible exception of **Orrin** *Hatch, though like other challengers that year for the GOP nomination including* **Keyes**

197

and Hatch, he went down to George W Bush's landslide. Dobson had no apparent problem with Bauer throwing his hat in the ring, but he later took exception to Bauer, who was a Christian leader, but he had been in politics longer, taking major leadership roles for a decade before becoming a religious broadcaster, ultimately supporting *McCain* for the nomination. The Arizonan (as noted before) had come against his allies **Robertson and Falwell**, and he and Bauer reportedly did not reconcile for almost seven years. Sympathetic *with New Hampshire Catholic Bob Smith's iconoclastic run for the White House, he later said the country* would probably be better off under George W. Bush than anyone else who had a realistic chance. In 2000 he just made those brief comments, but in 2004 he actively campaigned for the President's reelection. It was his first public endorsement for a candidate for national election. He helped the President so much it was said as Karl Rove was the architect of the campaign Dobson was construction foreman.

By the end of the previous decade he had had the worst of all possible enemies the I.R.S on his back. The same branch of government leaves left-wing bullies like Jesse Jackson and Al Sharpton alone, when you are liberal and have a few supporters, you can keep them in fear. Compromising, Dobson spawned off the PAC-which gave up tax exempt status, while Focus on the Family retains it under new board members but with him as the main radio voice. It later was broadcast under the heading *Family Talk with Dr. James Dobson* to avoid further legal entanglements, and *a shorter format "Dr. Dobson's Family Moment" is broadcast in thousands more markets. In 2008 he was inducted into the Radio Broadcasters Hall of Fame. He retired from his radio ministry to devote the rest of his life to Shirley, his two children and two grandchildren.*

For his career in family broadcasting ministry and adding his genius to about thirty books, his name says it all-like Dr. Spock and perhaps no one else in American history's name says it all, he is known as Dr. last name like very few Americans have ever been. Like others in Christian radio his audience has come to include Catholics, Mormons, and Jews while Evangelical Protestants and women with children continue to make up its majority. Sometimes mistakenly called "Reverend Dobson" **he has never been creden-**

tialed as a minster but many in the secular media think a1has strong religious values and voices them publicly must be a minister because no laymen would be that crazy. Crazy as outsiders consider the concept, the Bible particularly Ephesians 4:8-12 and James 3 puts most of the burden of publicly proclaiming the Gospel on the laymen and women.

36

Ben Kinchlow

6 of Hearts of Hope

O ne of the most remarkable but under appreciated minsters
of the Twentieth Century was born December 26, 1936 in
Uvalde, Texas. Though he was second banana to Pat **Robertson**
on the most watched Christian issues program and the third longest running talk show in television history, a leader in the Christian
Coalition, and clergyman who has interviewed some of the most
prominent Christian and secular leaders alive today, Ben Kinchlow
has seen relatively little need for publicity and has kept a low profile
while w high honors for the Christian message. He has been happily
married to Vivian since January 1959. A first career with the United
States Air Force lasted fourteen years. *His military service, could
only be possible after his conversion to Christianity, though he was
raised a Christian, he got angry at how his parents raised him, and
even at "the white man", believing Christianity and the "assimilation" largely expected of Blacks were tools to keep Black men down,
he was briefly a follower of Malcolm X and resisted fighting in the
Korean War. Like his later boss and ministry partner* **Pat Robertson,**
*he credits a friend, a white brother named John, for bringing him to
Christ, and that has helped him stay composed through four decades
of public ministry.* He is the father of Levi, Nigel,and Sean. He has

two degrees, including a post-graduate degree in business from the University of Virginia.

Jesus said like a lamp. . . Christians are to let their light shine before men that they may see their good deeds and praise our Father in Heaven (Matthew 5:16). Like virtually no other clergy or layman I know, Ben Kinchlow has done that for the past three decades. Though not usually one to take the s light literally, like few people I have seen, Ben radiates the simple light of the Gospel of Jesus Christ often without saying a word ad when a *backslidden* former Pentecostal preacher wrote a tell all book, he said there were only two living ministers he could really respect. The two were C.M. *Ward* the recently deceased longtime voice of the Assemblies of God and Ben Kinchlow.

In the early 80s Ben began his career in broadcast journalism after previously serving as a pastor. *He also became in 1979 co-founder of* His Place <u>a home for</u> *teenagers struggling with drug and alcohol addiction-making him (with* **Flanagan)** *one of two heroes of hope to start such a ministry (though if the scope were extended we could say four).He is an ordained African Methodist Episcopal minister and while that denomination is not especially a popular one for those who hold his views, they have an "open pulpit" in which once ordained, ministers are free* to preach Christianity, virtually any way they deem appropriate without being threatened for ordination, and he has chosen to keep that ordination over the years, feeling led to remain in a ministry where he can challenge others rather than the more *monolithic* alternatives. Articulate and at times funny but seeing no need to have the spotlight on himself, he became associated with **Robertson** in 1979 and in 1982 began appearing on television with him as the more frequently seen co-host and substitute host. In the mid-eighties in association with **Pat Robertson** and other CBN leaders he embarked on a secret mission to bring Bibles into Russia. He also lectured at various schools Eastern Europe and worked miraculously to see light in the darkest regions of the world. From 1979-1982 he was head of pastoral care (or counseling) to the clerical staff at CBN and for the next three years he served as the network's executive vice president. In *addition to the TV ministry he always hosted a half-hour radio show broadcast on CBN.* For nearly twenty years Kinchlow worked at one capacity or another for the Christian Broadcasting Network both ministerial and journalistic. For anyone who has seen the way he handles the mail, getting letters from viewers, reading them, and then compassionately answering their questions (particularly in **Robertson's** absence) or even more so praying for their requests, shows a man with faithful love for God and a dedicated love that wants bestowed on God's people. In a business where for every Ben Kinchlow you get at least a dozen Jimmy Swaggerts or Robert Tiltons we thank the Lord that once in a great while someone with integrity like him goes into broadcast ministry. Together with Pat **Robertson,** the 700 Club has reached tens of millions of home and sent Bibles and other Gospel materials into forty countries in dozens of languages. Even among Robertson's enemies on the far left their criticism is always directed at him and the domestic programs never at Ben. While not even a left-wing critic ever says a bad word about Ben Kinchlow, the educated observer must say *Alright, how could such a Christ-like saint have spent so many years working for and enjoying fraternal relationship with the piece of garbage you think Robertson is?*

As for defending **Robertson from** the criticism *on some alleged far-Right extreme comments the latter has made in his forty-year public career, Ben maintains that as Pentecostals or charismatics (the word is sometimes used interchangeably-but see* definitions at the end-they ARE similar but NOT synonymous)*we tend to speak the language of Zion, and others who are listening have difficulty understanding. Whether it is saying evil people deserve ongoing punishment both in this life and the next or reporting unorthodox happenings as answers to prayer, or referencing a centuries old event and relating it to the doings of God in our day, it will make perfect sense to someone familiar with the language of Zion, but may sound ridiculous to non-Christians (and even some Christians who do not recognize it) just as the* **Churchill-Chambers-Reagan-Truman-AND Boone collaboration over five decades** *to say that death by violent suffering of a whole family is preferable to living under Communism-for those outside the family of God, for whom religious and other freedoms are treated as a convenience not a necessity, makes little sense.* Often a person's spiritual language or persona overlaps with his "secular" goals and he therefore "cannot" just make the adjustment to know others are listening, so you *best speak in* "secular language." After 9-11 he wrote the foreword for a book on the Christian response to Islamic terror, and the writers made their case for a conservative message largely following the policies of the *Bush-Cheney Administration. He has since* expanded his radio career appearing more frequently and in more markets.

Though born to serve, after two decades serving the *700 Club* largely as second banana, Kinchlow decided to serve the Lord Jesus Christ at the top of his own organization, launching Ben Kinchlow Ministries in 1998. He is also the chairman of the Board of Rushmore Coffee Company. The writer *of three books he has spent his life following the Sermon on the Mount, and while noted before, his reputation* was *considered impeccable even by critics and non-Christians. Since I wrote that his ministry has changed somewhat since he is at the top of a ministry that handles a great deal of mail and broadcasting materials. I do not know whether one of the reasons for branching out into a#1 position of a ministry was so that he could follow his earthly leader (**Robertson**) in everything including as a controversialist, but in the last few years he has, in sort of a junior varsity way, done this. Though the critics of Kinchlow who would imply he has a motive beyond speaking the truth and preaching the Gospel of Jesus Christ, are (albeit almost all Black) few and far between, he has been called names, based on racist and exclusivist language, to conger **Hayakawa** again just as one can misled by the perspective of Zion, so can one with "Black talk" which it seems like his adversaries have thrown on him like biscuits and fried chicken at a Full Gospel Businessman's meeting. He cites thirty names that he has either been called or will be called for his recent ministry, all dealing with what is expected of a publicly recognized African-American. Since he had already been called some names, and knew he would be called more, he already provided his antagonists, with "descriptive phrases, for these nattering nabobs of negativity, and defenders of the arbitrarily established politically correct "'Black position'." Like **Clarence Thomas*** (though at least publicly Ben has shown a better sense of humor about it) he refuses to kowtow to such pompous prigs and professional political pragmatists who freakishly swear for a fraternal fringe of ebony edification to replace one fraternal alliteration by pigeonholing politics pertinent to another band of brothers-Pentecostals. On a more serious note, none of the racist or ethnic religion-bating-pejoratives thrown at him are fair, as the great-grandson of a slave with the same name, Ben like **His Honor Justice Thomas,** was raised by parents who never let being Black, disadvantaged, or segregated be excuses for either **racism or low achievement-**his mother earned an M.ED. He refused to have his ideas assigned to him, followed his mother's reading habits, challenged his peers and antagonists on race, and in four decades of effective ministry proved a success with which it is hard to argue.

More specifically his last few years of ministry he has (unlike in decades past) *and much like **Thomas, Alan Keyes, and other Black conservatives** like J.C. Watts and Shelby Steele refused to be a yes-man for the alleged Black orthodoxy and said African-Americans unquestioningly voting Democratic in high numbers is not healthy for their race, the party, or the country.* Like those men he has (in his words) wandered off the Democratic plantation to the Republicans who want a level playing field. He is thoroughly opposed to Blacks asking the white man to as he put in a 2011 interview with his old friend **Robertson** help "pull them up and give them bootstraps *and make us able to do like everyone else." While it m*ay not cost him what was an almost non-existent larger reputation outside the *700 Club*, it may cost him respect and even acceptance among his Black peers. While those things are good, it is better to follow the truth. When asked, however, what had become "godless" about politics, he answered both parties, as unlike the men and women of today who need to spend countless hours and dollars racking up support to make it to an office, the Founding Fathers made forming and maintaining our country a matter of hours of prayer. While both parties are reluctant to do this today, the Republicans (with some exceptions) are simply not partaking in such proclaimed prayer campaigns during the election and legislative seasons, while Democrats, are actively opposing it and (again with a few exceptions) making public displays of godlessness a virtual litmus test for good Democrats. He further explained that his fellow African-Americans are like him far more likely to attend church, pray at home, oppose abortion, discourage homosexuality, and desire to keep marriage between a man and a woman-than elected Democrats in all fifty states. While he considers voting for Democrats, particularly those of the Obama agenda a combination of being immoral and/or stupid, he knows the overwhelming majority of his fellow Blacks are neither. He asserts they are misinformed which he asserts is the most dangerous thing one can be as a Christian, a voter, or a citizen. He concludes that like other obstacles African-Americans have faced this lack (or intentional distortion by some leaders) of information can be overcome. He along with the conservatives I named and others I may profile in future books hold the key to ending that distortion and bringing this great people who overcame centuries of slavery, abuse, racism, and deliberately enforced lack of advantages; to overcome the less punitive but equally ominous peril of political and social distortion. Also in his desire to advance the truth and set an example for others of his religion and race, he has emphasized support for Israel giving money and joini*ng his business dealings to the mutual benefit of the Zionist republic.*

For these facts I have stated in the two "incarnations" OF Heroes OF Hope-*I submit to you that Ben Kinchlow has become a Twentieth and Twenty-First Century example of the Sermon on the Mount more than ninety-nine percent of Christians and pastors. He has stored up treasure in Heaven that no one can steal, and while his heart is there, he is continuing to remain vital and active more so in his seventies than at other stages, like our mutual hero* **Pat Robertson** *he has taken good care of his health so to continue a ministry into advanced years, I hope and pray works wonders in this century better than the last (maybe I can even be invited to his eighty-fifth birthday party or something). Both the storing of his treasure and the number of healthy years he can accumulate on earth, mean when the Lord takes him to that place, he will go where his treasure in being sown into a crown for many years. While you know by now* that I have a certain diarrhea of ideas without necessarily being high on the blood pressure scale of profundity, if my calculations are anywhere near correct, one man who will have a crown of life full of enough jewels to make Zsa-Zsa Gabor scream, that Christian is Ben Kinchlow.

37

George Marshall
(1880-1959)

7 of Diamonds OF Hope

*I*n 1880 George Catlett Marshall was born to a financially secure family in Pennsylvania. The easy-going Pennsylvanian would go on to be one of the most distinguished figures in American history. Interestingly enough, he never sought the limelight but had it thrust upon him. American will always remember G M for being on e of our inmost disturbed generals and later doing on to make lasting peace in Europe. He would go on to serve on the front lines of World War One with the legendary General Black Jack Pershing becoming one of the first Brigadier generals in American history and later winning five stars becoming only the fifth ranking general to do so, military intelligence officer he got his fifth star in the 1930s and in 1939 became chief of Naval Staff for all forces in the Pacific. It fell to Marshall to prepare our forces in Asia and with other forces there he made the mistake of deceiving the Philippines could be attacked and thus preparing them fully, but not Hawaii who was unprepared for Pearl Harbor. In spite of the infamous attack however, American forces fought back and Pearl did not became the great victory for Japan it could have been against a weaker enemy. Marshall had previously supported the Lend Lease Act to Britain and measures that would create a stronger alliance with Britain and many believed it would provoke Germany and The Axis Powers to war against us. He was one of the first to say Germany (the European axis countries) were to be the more formidable foes in the war. Strategy and history prove him right, although *it should also be noted that we should have worked harder on overall strategy to Asia (not just defeating Japan) but carving out a military strategy and legacy that would prevent future Asian wars. He was with Roosevelt* during the initial planning stage and throughout the war, more than any other American was responsible for planning the strategy and execution of World War II. He was also with FDR and other Western allies in Quebec and with all the Allied leaders in *Tehran and Yalta. Interestingly, that was one of the most strategic meetings of which a leader could ever be apart, as* while we were trying to work with our Soviet allies to defeat Germany, we were, in the case of our ally Stalin, trying to beat the Soviets to Berlin and therefore had to work with **Churchill** and Stalin to defeat our enemies while at the same time working within our own country to outplay and defeat our ally as well. Shortly after the war began, he convinced filmmaker Frank Capra to make war films to help increase the morale at home.

Though a great commanding officer for most of his life in 1942 Marshall accepted that most of the remainder of the war years would be spent at a Washington D.C. office though he did frequently travel to Europe inspect troops and advise the other national leaders. He disagreed with his successor in the Philippines Admiral King, saying more money and resources were needed to take Germany out of the war first and his advice was heeded but the Present. In 1943 he helped devise the strategy that led directly to the liberation of France. He coined the phrase "War in a democracy is no bed of roses." When President Roosevelt died, he accompanied President **Truman** to Potsdam at his first inter-Allied meeting and was also present as an American delegate at the first United Nations meeting in San Francisco.

George Marshall is a hero of hope primarily because he resisted the all too human temptations to sign or push for any post-war treaty that would further punish Germany for behavior that would merit it. Marshall, **Truman** *Eisenhower*, British Gen. Bernard Montgomery, and other Allied leaders made the brilliant derision, some would say with divine guidance, that Germany had suffered enough after all the bombing. They wisely decided to round up the greatest German war criminals especially Martin Boorman, Erik Reader, Herman Goring, Albert Speer, and others, and a handful of doctors and lawyer and other political people to be tried in Nuremberg. Hitler, Himmler, and Goebbels had already committed suicide and though Martin Boorman Hitler's former right hand, was immediately arrested, he escaped from a British prison only to fall dead weeks later trying to get out of Berlin. In all, twenty defendants were tried by the military tribunal at Nuremberg and twelve were sentenced to death, three got life sentences, and two got prison sentences, while three were acquitted. The doctors and lawyers were sentenced to prison by a separate American tribunal but like most of the other Nazis, they were eventually released, and forgiven, some went on to lucrative professions even after being convicted war criminals. In the movie *Nuremberg* produced by HBO, the American prosecutor Francis Biddle said we have enough evidence to hang half the country. That may have been a *only slightly hyperbole* about the German people who had clung to Hitler like a father figure and carried out terrible policies. Instead of hanging half the country, Marshall led the American occupation forces to come down on The side of forgiveness, and rebuild Germany as **MacArthur** was doing in Japan. Marshall was also instrumental in deciding that Italy, though a longtime Axis member, had also suffered enough and not punishing them further. The last of the Italian prisoners of war were released around the time Marshall took over in Berlin, though a few of the worst offenders like American-born poet Ezra Pound would face some justice.

At the end of 1946 he went home to what he thought would be quiet retirement. At age sixty-five he went back to his Virginia manor. Instead he was called back in 1947 to be secretary of state, and though he held the post less than eighteen months, he laid the groundwork for The Marshall Plan. In it Marshall led the occupation forces in Germany along with our British, French, and Dutch allies, to advance millions of dollars to revitalize the German infrastructure and help the economy of West Germany while at the same time giving generously to other countries in Europe who had been our allies and victims of Germany. The funds helped to feed and house tens of millions of people who were barely surviving. Another controversial decision was supporting The **Truman** D*octrine whereby t*he nations of Europe who were anticommunist got first preference and were automatically our allies and entitled to American assistance because they were joining us in opposing our new enemy, The Soviet Union. With **Truman** he endorsed the West German policies of *Konrad Adenauer* to counter the Soviet blockade which led to further division between Eastern and Western Europe not repaired for forty years. Though West Germany was happy to allow dissidents and other troubled souls from the East to find refuge in their country, the Soviets later built the Berlin Wall which kept them out. But Germany and the rest of Western Europe was able to rise from the ashes in what is known as the economic miracle that *Paul Johnson* ingeniously declared the European *Lazarus in Modern Times,* largely due to the Marshall Plan. Following surgery on his right kidney, Marshall retired to quieter life. He did, however allow himself to become President of The Red Cross. Following a cabinet shuffle in 1950, he was secretary of defense for three years, a role in which he clashed with fellow hero of hope, **Douglas Macarthur. Both** saw the need to defeat Communism and perhaps even reinstate China into The Allied camp, but unlike **Macarthur,** he was not willing to risk World War III. He held the American forces south of the Korean Thirty-Eighth Parallel which almost insured half of Korea would remain in the Chinese and Russian camp.

In 1953 Marshall was awarded the Nobel Peace Prize for being The one most responsible for The European miracle, he was the fourth American to win the award (four out of the first five are entries in this book, only Cordell Hull is not). When *Eisenhower* became President, he retired permanently, a man who had served his country as well as any general. Eisenhower did give him one assignment. In 1955, he was sent to be the U.S. official representative at the coronation of Queen Elizabeth. It was a source of anger to some Britons who felt the President should attend himself.

Several accolades can be hung on the end of this great man's career. **Harry Truman** said "many Americans gave their country exemplary service during the war, George Marshall graver her victory." Marshall entered Buckingham Palace in one of the few times when England did not have a reigning monarch, *George VI* had died and his daughter was going to be crowned that day. The room became electrified to welcome this American who helped save London. Marshall was escorted on by British security and Londoners gave him a standing ovation, with pomp usually reserved for the monarch or at least a member of her family. For a few minutes he was the most beloved person in London and he did not believe the cheers were for him, he felt the Queen (who became the Queen Mother, the most beloved royal family member in history) must be in the room, but she was not all the Londoners and others were cheering for George Marshall, the American who brought peace to Europe and renewed prosperity and democracy. This was perhaps the Pennsylvania's most enduring memory. George Marshall enjoyed horseback riding and had two and a half years of marital bliss with his second wife Lilly, a native of Georgia. His *first wife Katherine Tucker, a native of Texas had two sons whom he primarily raised after she died in 1927. He loved them very much and was primary parent to three, including his stepson Alan who died in World War II during the Battle for Rome. Like his stepson he was buried at Arlington National Cemetery, near their last home in Leesburg, Virginia.*

38

Edward Flanagan (1886-1955)

5 of Hearts OF Hope

E dward Joseph Flanagan was born July 13, 1886 in Laebeny County Roscommons, Ireland. His brother who had been ordained a Catholic priest went to serve in America in 1904 and Edward followed that year living with His sister Nelle. He attended Mount St. Mary's College in Maryland and in 1908 began attending New York Seminary with the goal of becoming a priest. It was there he did his first parish ministry visiting T dying in hospital wards. W that had anything to do with the young man's own health problems is u but during His stay in New York he developed a major lung ailment and had to leave seminary. Returning to Europe, he tried several seminaries until finally being advised by doctors he could attend one in Austria because alpine air would not inflame his strained lungs. Ordained a priest in 1911 he was wanting an appointment in America and after his health records checked out he was assigned associate pastor of St. Patrick's Church in Omaha, Nebraska. Boys-Town MC1

In three short years of ministry he developed a great burden for youth and at the age of twenty-eight he founded the Pioneer Workmen's' Hotel to rehabilitate delinquent and needy youth. He worked with the juvenile court in Omaha who were more than happy to send less chronic cases to the care of this loving clergyman willing to take them in. In 1919 the home was renamed as Boys Town, Douglas County. Developing it like a city, all its own, in 1936 it was officially incorporated as its own city holding elections among the residents for mayor and other "municipal" positions..

Father Flanagan emphasized the point that when it comes to educating boys it is all about the environment thinking, and the training. Drawing freely from psychologist Erich Fromm, he took this triangular model starting with improving a boys' environment. He maintained that if a bad environment can contribute to making a kid bad, a very good loving, welcoming environment certainly could contribute to making a good kid. The second part was nurture, and that is where proper training comes in. Unlike other ecclesiastical behaviorists and and judicial role models of the day, he did not see discipline as the most important factor. He wanted an environment based on making each child know he is loved by both God and man. When kids know that it is easier for them to learn good habits since most of the delinquents and underprivileged youth he knew had grown under the absence of love. He also emphasized punishments and rewards. Finally the third part of the triangle is thinking. It has been said that a neurotic is a person who, in youth, learned purpose defeating and destructive behavior and took it *with* him into *adulthood*. A large part of the battle, perhaps, even half the battle is getting the child, whatever his nature and whatever his nurture, to think with the skills that are valuable in the adult world.

Such positive values and ideals will help kids grow to young men who rise in faith and in life not only for themselves but to better serve their families, being friends, and better helping society at large. Though a small-time and locally based operation, by 1938 his program was being discussed all over the United States. Edward Flanagan was a pioneer and like David *Wilkerson* who founded Teen Challenge, he built a Christ-centered program, based on building youth up, and started locally, but eventually contributed to the redemption of hundreds and by extension touching millions of lives. He also publicized his organization by getting speakers like *Babe Ruth and Jack Dempsey* who gladly came and endorsed the program. Ruth himself was an orphan redeemed by Catholic outreach and his love for baseball first came from a cleric named Brother Matthias. Father Flanagan became a U.S. citizen. He served on the Omaha Welfare Board and National Board of Catholic Charities. Hollywood made two movies about Boys' Town which starred Spencer Tracy as Flanagan.

Eventually Attorney General Tom Clark asked him to serve on National Panel of Juvenile Delinquency. He traveled and discussed his program and its success in Europe, Japan, and Korea. In 1955 he was on his second major international tour of children's' homes in Europe and on a particularly strenuous series of visits he died in Austria, at a home he was visiting (though tragic it was fitting he would die in one) at the age of sixty-two. One of our great heroes of hope, Edward Flanagan saw hope where many deny it, in faces and hearts of young boys who were poor and often times criminal and transforming them into useful productive members of society, something that many of era believed could not be done. Today partly due to his example, virtually every state and many foreign countries sanction rehabilitation programs for children and teach penitent rather than punitive ways for dealing with most wayward children and teenagers.

39

Lech Walesa
(1943-Present)

4 of Spades of Hope

*L*ech Walesa was born in 1943, the son of working class Poles. A war baby he was born in the center of one of the greatest series of events in history in, the watershed of Central Europe. He was born in a country that had a great historic tradition of over two thousand years, like Israel and parts of Mexico, one of the most disputed pieces of real estate in the world. Ironically, the Communism that seized his country shortly after World War II was never accepted by The majority of Poles who continued practicing mainstream Catholicism so much that by 1979, there was a Polish Pope. He *married* Danuta *in 1969 and they have eight children*. In that atmosphere, Lech Walesa rose to be a man, loved and feared by Church and state, who would have more impact on that region than any Pole in half a century. Not only did he effect his native Poland but transcontinental matters as well. In 1982 he was elected leader of Solidarity, then a labor union, for blue collar workers, it became second most popular political movement in Poland. He was briefly jailed with other members of Solidarity. Facing on and off oppression for a decade, by 1989 most Poles were behind his political stances and it was clear Poland would dissolve its Communist government and elect him or someone who shared his republican ideals.

By the mid-eighties he was also recognized in the West especially America as a spokesman for democracy in a land that badly needed it. In 1983 Walesa was awarded the Nobel Peace Prize for his stance on a free Poland. Throughout the 1980s Walesa, along with Czech *Vaclav Havel,* was the greatest symbol of Eastern European *freedom in resistance to Communism on both sides of the Atlantic. Other awards he won around that time included* Time's *man of the Year the Financial Times Liberty Medal, and in 1989 the Presidential Medal of Freedom* from President George Herbert Walker Bush. Interestingly before my lifetime only two non-Americans (Lafayette and **Churchill**) had been honored at that level-in the past thirty years at least eight have. Perhaps this shows The more global shift in American thinking and who is directly involved in American affairs (or with whom we get directly involved). As a Labor leader, he led the movement of auto assembly workers, though he spent most of his life as an electrician. The publicity was new and never expected, but he traveled the world giving speeches about it and the Russian and Polish Communists could not "conveniently banish" him as they did many of their enemies. Especially in America, he was honored and gained a cult like following with millions of Americans, including millions of Polish and other Eastern European descent, who had personal as well as political reasons for wanting their ancestral homes freed from Communist domination.

*Just as Americans and others justly feared the domino affect of Communism in the '20s And '50s and '60s, by the late 80s Communists in Europe had good reason to fear the reverse domino affect, people would knock down all the Communist domin*oes. By the late eighties it became clear Communism could not retain a stranglehold on countries where it was not wanted, and if a religious country like Poland could change because The people, even an oppressed people spoke, things would change in other places, both more secular Eastern European nations as well as Muslim ones as soon as The people have spoken. In 1989 Lech Walesa became Europe's first domino knocker downer--Poland became the first country to declare reverse domination from Soviet Union, and for the first time in forty-four years a non Communist government won a majority in Poland's legislature. Poland was freed by the good fight of the good people led by hero of hope Lech Walesa. In 1990 Walesa was elected President of Poland making him the first European to win a democratic election in Eastern Europe since before World War II. He saw Poland go through a historic change and while remaining Socialistic it brought a number of reforms leading to evolving capitalism. *Like many* Socialists he tried the precarious measures of balancing state management and individual liberty to impressive results, but did not gain the lifelong dream conservative free enterprise systems have won in middle-size powers including Canada, Chile, and South Korea, nor the mega-economic miracles of post-war societies in Germany and Japan. While his five year presidency was less impressive than his fourteen year fight with Communism, it was the most exciting of any previously oppressed president in modern times. In his justified defense it is hard to turn a country from Communism to capitalism, and he laid the groundwork for Poland to become capitalist and eventually join the European Union (which they did in 1998). He is a serious Catholic and so devoutly pro life he said he would resign as president if the courts make him enforce any larger European abortion laws. Poland has (during and after his term) one of the strictest abortion laws in the Western world-it is legal only in a few hard cases. Nonetheless he championed Poland becoming a member of NATO (which they did three years later). While his critics say he did not set a good enough economic turn for gradual transition, most likely the reverse is true, his government used the free enterprise system, but was not capitalistic enough to end punitive measures on big business or encourage enough small businesses *to succeed as a modern state of comparable size like Australia or a small but heroic one like Israel and Singapore. All of the countries I named are former colonies which rose from Socialism to dominate (at least economically) a region. No doubt he took a new free country, and turned it into a very impressive one and no other Communist country has made such a swift transition to freedom.* In 1995 he was narrowly defeated for President by Aleksandr Kwansniowski..

Both during and after Walesa's service as head of state, Poland primarily championed two outlets for capitalism, trade with Western *and Central* Europe, and most heroically computers, which, taking the day in the early Twenty-First Century, made Poland an economic powerhouse, that set the pace for it to be the Canada or South Korea of its day, achieving more within this generation than any country with the possible exception of East Germany. It served as a moral example to its neighbors, particularly the Czech Republic and Hungary, and likely a moral example to similar size powers battling totalitarianism, including Cuba, Argentina, Vietnam, and possibly even the two much bigger examples Russia and China. This may sound grandiose and I do not mean he is single-handedly responsible for all this. I do believe he had more to do with improvements in neighboring countries formerly occupied by Russia than any single individual and since the former non-Soviet but Soviet dominated new republics are all smaller it would make sense they would look to a Pole as their example. He is no longer a force in Polish politics but he still gives speeches as a hero there and elsewhere in the world, specifically to celebrate the freedom of his country and the end of Communist domination in Europe.

Because of Poland's history even after two major wars, and her reluctance to take in immigrants rumors have surfaced that Poland today and even Walesa himself have antisemitic tendencies. This is not true, in 1991 democratic Poland renewed its commitment to religious freedom and inclusion *of all its people and while very few Jews still call Poland home, there was no discrimination against them.* He built bridges with Jan Karski, the late Polish patriot who resisted the Nazis and fought to smuggle Jews, getting hundreds out of Poland and later *winning the Nobel Peace Prize. He also created a Warsaw ghetto museum to honor the brave but doomed Jews of Warsaw who stubbornly resisted unto death. Walesa sensibly said despite the plague of Polish antisemitism, Jews and Poles were kindreds in suffering at the hands of the Nazis. He has also had meaningful dialog with Holocaust survivor and fellow Nobel Prize laureate Eli Wiesel. And in the late nineties and early 2000s Poland itself became a popular haven for European immigrants of various religions, a situation unthinkable just a few years ago.*

There *did,* however surface *bad blood between Poland and the Obama Administration* when *the* forty-fourth President was in Warsaw, Walesa as an ongoing symbol of his people's freedom refused to meet with the man who reversed the Bush policy to keep American weapons in the heart of Europe to guarantee the safety of Poland and her neighbors. Leaving the meeting, he asked the Polish embassy in Washington to complain about the change in U.S.-Polish relations. *When he took the **justly labeled Wrong stance,** Obama refused to see him in Warsaw when* the President visited there, saying his statements were too inflammatory. Obama should have learned a few things about watching his mouth, in a May 2012 speech awarding Polish hero John Karski a posthumous medal, he made reference to *"from a Polish concentration camp" he later corrected it to say he meant a German concentration camp in Poland,* but it already justly inflamed a lot of people that such a gaffe could even be possible from someone at his level. Indeed, this should seal the last nail on the coffin, Polish Americans should not vote for his reelection. Obama "got back at the Polish hero" for his principled stance by not inviting him to a White House gathering in 2012 when the widow of Karski was honored in Wash*ington.* Obama snubbed his fellow Nobel laureate, though Walesa won the award as a true hero, and I'll be polite here and say Obama won the Nobel Prize for being a silly goose. Poland was the USA's friend when we badly needed her, during the War on Terror and in Operation Iraqi Freedom where much older democracies floundered, and we were helped because of the involvement of Kwansniowski, the more conservative president (politically though not personally) than Walesa. Poland has been our friend since freedom, and we should be there friend every step of the way. We can only expect the next Administration to be better to our precious Eastern European ally instead of the current Silly goose-in-chief.

In 2002 Walesa was one of five men to carry to represent a continent, carrying The Olympic Torch of Europe in the Salt Lake City Winter Games. Lech Walesa remains one of the greatest symbols of freedom and democracy alive today. Due to his stalwart leadership among other factors, in sixteen years Poland has gone from being one of the most oppressive countries in the world to one of the freest. More power has been transferred to the people and particularly The business community than anywhere in history, with the possible exception of Germany. When he won his Nobel Prize his career to that point had been summed up in what was then his legacy, as he had just reached his late forties and was starting to enter the years when grown men really accomplish something. The key at the time was his organization was so successful, the Communist Prime minister Jarazelski had to negotiate with Solidarity. The Nobel citation said *this is homage to the principles of victory, with a belief in peace and a vision of the honest courage to follow his call.* That is the legacy of Walesa, who in the term (nine-fourteen years later) put his country in the camp of the U.S., U.K., and Israel having power in the hands of the people. Though he is no longer a force in Polish politics, he gives speeches throughout both Western and Eastern Europe as one of the greatest leaders of our time.

40

Richard Simmons
(1949-Present)

5 of Clubs OF HOPE

❦

*B*orn in New Orleans shortly after World War Two to conservative parents who had previously moved from California and
New York, he was raised in Catholic school but not baptized Catholic
until he was 16. His mother's parents were Jewish immigrants from
Russia. His birth name was Milton Richard Simmons and it was
not until he was eight that he had the privilege to travel to Sarasota,
Florida and meet his name sake "Uncle Dick." The two remained
close throughout life and young Milton decided then that like his
uncle he would go by "Dick" or "Richard." He never minded being
called "Dick" or "Dicky" but wonders even today why some people
call him "Mr Simmons." From an early age he had a phenomenon
vocabulary as many of Catholic schools and went on to write eloquently. Early in life he had the opportunity to study abroad and went
to Italy where he primarily studied his favorite topic in life food!
Interestingly enough places like Italy and Greece provide one of
the greatest opportunities to study food while most Mediterraneans
may have an addiction to it, they also have an addiction to walking
making obesity the exception. Fittingly his first word was "kitchen."
Richard Simmons became very obese during his time in Europe and

returned to the States close to 400 pounds. Though he struggled with weight problems from early childhood, food was his favorite part of life, after all, at this point, having recently lost Uncle Dick, he came to realize a human being can die from overeating. Wanting to excel in all he does it was not enough for the twenty-something Simmons to take weight off himself, he started an entire business and exercise network based on being the best you can be through health, nutrition, and exercise. Often seen leading exercises in a red leotard, the then impressively thin Simmons led an audience of about a hundred. He also started his Simmons exercise studio which at the time also included a salad bar so dieters could come in exercise, eat, and meet with like minded health enthusiasts all in one. His television audience ranged from three hundred pounders and others almost literally "dying" to lose weight, to thin builds committed to staying in shape. He went around preaching The good news about weight loss and exercise in malls and wrote a series of books on the subject including *Never Say Diet*. He may have been the first great American to discourage the use of the word preferring "meal plan" or "eating program" to emphasize that it was a healthy lifestyle not the gimmick or temporary relief dieting has become. His Slimmons-TM food includes tasty pretzels and while not as poplar as it once was still brings in revenue. By the late eighties his television career was less than it had been before but he continued to remain one of television's most recognizable faces playing a recurring role on "General Hospital." His first book took a stretch on #1 New York Times and sweat up and down the list for fifty-six weeks. In 1979 he won his first Emmy dedicated to his father who died recently but thankfully lived to see his son become a success. On a later trip to Rome he met Pope *John Paul*, II. He also gave good performances on game shows becoming the first person I remember to get 200 points by himself in the *Family Feud* bonus round, something obviously done by intelligent people. He also invented Deal-a-Meal a plan to count calories every day and eat enough to get the foods you like and the calories you need without overeating. While obviously airing some of his issues in public Simmons hates when others mock them as he briefly had a feud with late-night talk show host David Letterman. He also has a "thing" for not being taken lightly and in a similarity with people with disabilities, he has often reminded people that there is nothing "cute" or gimmicky about what Richard Simmons does, if they had thought of building his career they would be very rich today. He also wrote a book about exercise for the Disabled.

Remaining a champion of health and fitness in four decades, Richard Simmons will long be remembered as the man who taught America exercise is not just for jocks and military people it is needed for all of us. *In recent years he testified before Congress encouraging the physical education requirement* to be continued in public schools, though currently only the state of Illinois requires it to be taught in all four years of high school. A lifelong bachelor he summarizes his life *By* devoting my life to my work I live an extremely structured, cloistered life. I know what I'm doing every minute *of ever day because it is so scheduled. It's hard to have a normal life when you have work as I do. That's the life I've created, that's the life I've chosen. It's like the priest who chooses to be celibate, it's a calling. I've chosen a public life rather than a private one. I don't have a traditional family. My family is thousands and thousands of people. Those are the people I love.*

Surprised I included Richard Simmons with **Lincoln** and **Teddy Roosevelt** on this list? If you are over fifty or under twenty you may be. But for those of you who grew up in the seventies and eighties who did you see every day on tv? If some of your heroes included Ronald **Reagan**, James **Dobson**, Rush **Limbaugh**, Judy *Blume*, and Bill *Cosby*, as mine do, notice Richard Simmons has been in our lives longer than any of them! Unlike other entertainers who have their brief time in the limelight, Richard Simmons has remained a force in America throughput the nineties and the Twenty-First Century. His autobiography *Still Hungry* is one few the most impressive tales of ups downs and ultimately *back up for good* ever articulated by an American. Often believed to be gay few what some would call his gender non-specific demeanor in 2003 he denied the allegation. Millions wonder why he did not deny it sooner when he was building his career, others asked why he did not simply come out sooner, in both cases Simmons was being fair to all groups involved if he had denied homosexuality in his twenties it would look like he was putting homosexuals down, by waiting until his fifties to tell the truth he could be an established figure who may or may not be gay; and remains private about his sex life. After all he does not act gay he simply *acts like Richard Simmons that says it all!*

Also in his early fifties the pop icon slapped a man who was heckling him in an airport after both men were walking off the plane. Though I have whitewashed some of the heroes of hope's peccadilloes I want to deal with this incident because I see it as significant. Honestly I can see both sides of the issue. Here a fifty-year-old man who was a multi-millionaire is being mocked by an average Joe while both are getting off the plane. From our hero's perspective, having long been called a wimp and considered by his fans, one who is in great shape, but for limited greater purposes, wanted to prove he was not a wimp and could hold his own and take his chances in a fight. Furthermore, often being ridiculed by those who are not his fans, paradoxically for being fatter than he should be, or for making a lot of money off other peoples' problems, Simmons, in a momentary fit, showed he was a red-blooded American male, after a taxing flight, and probably a long day, wanted to prove he could hold his own with the big boys. From the other man's point of view, he was just getting off an airplane, and seeing a celebrity, something we do not get to do every day, he probably wanted to get a cheap laugh and perhaps score points with his girlfriend or whomever he was with. While he found Simmons an easy target (in fact the fitness guru said "It's not nice to make fun of people who have issues") as whatever America knows Richard Simmons for, being a tough guy tends not to be one of them. In Simmons' defense, however, the man, like many who insult people with disabilities, was having selective fun with a celebrity. If Hulk Hogan or Mike Tyson had gotten off the plane he probably would not have made fun of their issues. On the other man's side, being a rich celebrity should mean Simmons is expected to have more restraint and be able to take a mild joke, especially in an open place like an airport. In this way I consider both men as having valid points, but in the end, when officers got there to learn that one man in the situation was a three-hundred pound biker with a habitual criminal history, no charges were filed against the hero of hope.

Simmons has impacted millions of Americans for good health in two centuries. He considers himself Roman Catholic, but his religious views are unclear beyond basic theism. Apolitical in message, he was willing (albeit unable) to fight for his country against Communism, something a lot of bigger but by no means better men would never do.

41

William McKinley (1841-1901)

5 of Diamonds of HOPE

B orn in Ohio during the first economic boom to give America a place among the nations, William McKinley lived in a relatively comfortable family. Early on he joined the Union troops and was a hero of the Civil War earning the rank of major. After that he worked in a bank eventually working his way up to be the president of several Ohio banks and one of the most eligible bachelors in Ohio, a prize landed a beautiful epileptic named Ida who loved him for life. An impressive governor of a very impressive state, McKinley earned a national reputation and was asked t head the Republican Party ticket in 1896.

According to this series 1896 and 1900 was the only time in American history when two heroes of hope topped ballots as McKinley ran against William Jennings Bryan. His opponent traveled all over the country which was not don eat time McKinley thought it more prudent to campaign mostly int eh states that were near Ohioan nearer Washington, D.C. While the incumbent Predestine Grover Cleveland may have had ambitions to seek a third term, neither he nor Bryan could withstand the very strong competition by William McKinley who ran on the gold standard. Maintaining that gold has been the standard for wealth dating back to Biblical times, he believed only a system strengthened by gold backed by the ancient precious medal could continue to keep the American economy growing. In this he successfully convinced his listener over the more intelligent and articulate Great Commoner to win the election by a respectable margin though he did not win a single state in the South.

In becoming the twenty-fifth President and the third from Ohio the state that may well be defined as providing a microcosm of the nation, William McKinley had a popular mandate to govern. He is easily our most underrated President as more territory was added to America during his terms than all but Jefferson and Polk. Utah had p joined the Union as the forty-fifth state and it was up to McKinley and his supporters to prepare Oklahoma, Arizona, New Mexico, and Alaska for statehood. Interestingly Hawaii though situated three thousand miles Southeast of California in what some people call Oceania, being geographically equally close to Australia, which was then still a British colony. Ironically, however, Hawaii was practically two countries one a kingdom ruled by Queen Liliuokalani, the other half including the island of Hawaii proper, made up primarily of American businessmen who recognized *American* Sanford P. Dole as their leader. Like past American leaders, McKinley wanted to get the beautiful islands into the American sphere, but wanted to inherit the so-called kingdom in such a way that did not alienate the island's Polynesian residents.

The greatest crisis of his Administration, however took place with our neighbor to the South, as she, the good island of Cuba, was being menaced by evil occupiers from Spain. When the Spaniards continued to steep up their oppression on Cuba McKinley found two champions for intervention. One was the American stalwart newspaper owner William Randolph Hearst, a man ridiculously characterized in a movie some misguided critics consider the greatest ever made. The other champion of freedom through intervention was Cuba's own *Jose Marti* and though he was murdered weeks before McKinley came to power his followers cried out in the spirit of remembering Marti, and McKinley finally responded. Hiring the forty-year-old **Teddy Roosevelt** to lead trans-Pacific ships the

United States embarked on what was the greatest Naval mission ever done to that time. While most of Europe laughed at the audacity of these strange colonists three thousand miles across the coast of England trying to overthrow an empire, we got one stalwart ally in England herself. It was the first time the trans-Atlantic relationship would be born, and ironically enough it was the father of Trans-Atlantic relationship, **Winston Churchill** himself, only a teenager at the time, who wrote home to his family friend the Prince of Wales urging support for his cousin in America. Because of **Churchill** and other great Britons America had support to begin the most monumental Naval undertaking since the Spanish armada.

Paradoxical as it seems, most observers thought Spain would win the war. America at the time was still seen as a lucky confederation of states, and at this time also a confederation of three races, thigh united by the English language, divided in many other ways. Like Britain, France, Austria, and even the Netherlands and Turkey, Spain was seen as a great and mighty empire with history going back over five centuries. America was definitely the *awkward Eeyore of the imperial game, one with barely a relationship to the parents from which he sprang, and no expectation for offspring to spring from his loins.* Instead the Ohioan proved them all wrong and like our future encounters in Grenada and Desert Storm, the Spanish-American War was hardly a war at all but more of a vacation for great warriors to fight, win, and come home.

The Cuban resistance was vindicated within a week and Spain released its hold on our neighboring island. Forces under **Teddy Roosevelt** fought on Puerto Rico in both land and sea while the father of the Rough Riders, a practical teenager oath the time (forty was a man then,as was nineteen neither tend to be today), led the first great amphibious military outfit up San Juan Hill to conquer that good island for the good Americans. Teddy had also been studying the ramifications of Spanish rule in an island few had heard of before the Philippines but with Cuba and Puerto Rico being won in two weeks, **TR** and his forces decided to take a real challenge sailing to the Asian waters and crushing the last holdout of Spanish resistance. Spain then surrendered on our terms and Guam was added to the American Empire while Hawaii was also annexed. A little over a century later, Hawaii is a proud state of the Union, home to some of our prettiest contenders for Miss America and home to a disproportionate number of military officers and successful people of business. William McKinley paved the way for our fiftieth state to become America and Hawaiians and those who love them thank him.

In defending our taking of an overseas, island William McKinley became the first and still the only President to explicitly claim a divine resource saying, "*I am not ashamed to tell you people that I got down on my knees and prayed and the Lord told me. . . hate them, and civilize them, Christianize The Filipinos and do our Best for them as fellow human beings for whom Christ died*. Some would say by claiming a divine source, McKinley was simply putting an American spin on a European concept that was used for centuries to take other peoples' land. But when we inherited the Philippines it was a backward colony of various island peoples with Moorish Muslims, Roman Catholic Christians, and practicers of ancient tribal faiths. Only forty-three years later the Philippines had gone through a historic transition like no other colony in history, still a land of religious pluralisms and tolerance, when Japan attacked them forty-three years later thinking they would be welcomed as fellow Asian liberators, they become the only colony to fight for their so-called oppressors in a guerrilla war that took out tens of thousands of Japanese and helped the Americans in shortening the war by perhaps a full year.

Ironically, McKinley set out to win a war for liberation and instead became the first President to inherit an American Empire. He and his successors were left to decide what to do and like true believers in democracy they affected it ingeniously, Cuba was immediately given its freedom and remains an independent covering today; the Philippines were looked after as wayward children promised freedom as soon as they were ready and the majority of Americans and Filipinos bonded together to make World War II their time to arrive as a nation in their own right which they have been for fifty-two years; Puerto Rico chose to stay a part of America without yet having become a state in 2007, similar status is owned by Guam; while Hawaii remained a territory benignly governed by joint American and Hawaiian authorities until 1959 when by democratic choice it became the fiftieth state. No other President had such a global impact in transforming the United States from rural republic to republican empire. Re-elected in 1900 by the greatest landslide then recorded,as one of eight great wartime President McKinley made his other lasting legacy choosing the rising star **Teddy Roosevelt** as Vice President. Like I said before Teddy was at an age barely above kiddom by our standards, but in his generation like John Kennedy's, a man grew up at eighteen or nineteen, unlike today. Sadly the great McKinley was gunned down on a trip to Buffalo, New York, by a Polish-born anarchist named Leon Chozog and he died in a hospital after intense treatment. McKinley left a wonderful Christian impact as a hero of hope on his two daughters Ida and Kathrine while his stalwart wife buried him. She became a constant memorial to him in the eight years the Lord let her continue living. Like **Lewis** every day for Ida was a memorial and time of mourning from the supremely loved spouse to the fallen hero who died much too young while bringing hope to millions.

42

Christian X
(1870-1948)

4 of Hearts of Hope

§

*T*he man who would reign over Denmark longer than any other in recent times was born in Copenhagen and named Christian in 1870, the son of King Frederick VIII. Like very few heroes of hope but including **Truman**, **Chambers**, and **Nightingale**, more than anyone else in this series he would grow up to live up to his name. He was the first monarch of his illustrious family to have a distinguished career as a scholar and he later made the conscious choice to join his nation's Army. Although since the Middle Ages Scandinavian military have been so in name only he knew the odds of an attack on Denmark were slight, yet anything is possible and he made the courageous decision to join his own military and take the chance of dying for his country. At age twenty-eight with his coronation, and subsequent marriage to Marie, Denmark remained a small fairly close knit group of counties slightly larger than New Jersey with about the population of Illinois, several small city states from medieval Scandinavian times, still made claims to own small parts of the Kingdom. In 1920 during the Easter Rising the rebellion of a small duchy (in other words a city-state about the size of a county run by a duke)

Slussivigibod rebelled, Christian made the political decision, the last of a monarch to do so in Danish history, to bring the final rebellious towns under Christian X's Kingdom with a bloodless coup. Unlike many Twentieth century monarchs particularly of the European stripe Danish kings continue to play a major role int eh governing of their nation. Christian appointed cabinet minister with the help of Parliament and also sat and made decisions with Parliament sometimes five days a week. He appointed all of his own Prime Minsters though political popularity in and elections of Mps played the pivotal role.

More than anyone else Christian lived up to his name when World War II began. At first the great Dane, committed the Kingdom of Denmark to neutrality though he personally had a preference for Britain and The other Allies. Unfortunately as a small nation with more than half living in and around Copenhagen, there was little he could do short of soliciting help prom foreign nations. With his neighbor and friends Norway immediately declaring hostilities, Christian was torn between wanting to help the British, French, Norwegians,and their allies defeat the Nazis and wanting to avoid sending his people to war at all costs. In the end the latter was his choice he chose to forgo hostility that Denmark may avoid becoming a war zone. Months later in April of 1940 Norway gave the Nazis their first test as an army but in the end the Germans overwhelmed the smaller nation. Although he sent a number of troops to the Norwegian border to keep the Germans from entering there were few troops and some of them were even the local police force. Within days after that, Germans took over Norway, they forced Christian to come to the Norwegian border and sign a neutrality pact. From this point on Denmark was committed to a potion of subordination to the Nazis, and while most of the Danish people supported Britain and The other Allies, it was in a state of non-belligerency while accepting Nazi officers in their police departments and other ranks. Christian believed that by allowing the Nazis to have some influence over his country he could continue to let his officials from elected membership of Parliament on down to police and disaster relief workers, school teachers, and the state church (Evangelical Lutheran) continue to do their jobs with as little foreign harassment as possible.

As you know from the rest of these articles I'm no pacifist, and for the most part I favor military action against evil people when it can serve a constructive purpose In this case, however, Christian did the only practical thing imaginable for a small country against a large and self-possessed invader. After being invaded he made the wise decision to let the Danish protectorates in Greenland and the Camorros Island be administered by the United States to prevent a Nazi attack on those islands.

Christian X is included on this list because he and the other heroic Danes did one of the most heroic things in World War II. When the Nazis were rounding up all Jews and other "enemies of the German Reich" in their conquered nations. virtually all countries sat by and did nothing if not actively assist Nazi Germany. France, which was divided between the pro-Nazi Vichy government and the Paris government which was Nazi occupied, cooperated in handing over the Jews, while Italy which had been Hitler's ally fought to smuggle some Jews across the Greek border without taking an active interest in their fate at large. Jews of Eastern Europe fared even worse while Poland, Lithuania, Latvia, Ukraine, Slovakia, Slovenia. Croatia and other countries saw handing over innocents as a small price to pay for not suffering more in the war. While a remnant of brave and moral souls from the Netherlands, Switzerland, Sweden, Greece, Italy, Germany, Austria, Bulgaria, Hungary, and even Axis Japan put their lives on the line to save Jews, they were just that a remnant, and the overwhelming majority of Europeans sat by while Jews were murdered. Denmark was the exception to this! Within weeks of taking over Copenhagen, Hitler demanded that all enemies of the Reich be arrested and handed over to Nazi authorities. This was almost exclusively for Jews because Denmark had almost no Gypsies and while the Nazis captured or killed hundreds of Danes with disabilities, they were no longer perusing all mentally disabled whit some exceptions like inmates in various hospitals and group homes. For Denmark's case the enemies of the Third Reich largely referred to a little less than ten thousand Jews who would be required to wear yellow stars of David. Christian X, *who of course was no more Jewish than Mickey Mouse,* said he would be the first one to don the yellow star. In making this offer he sent the obvious message, if you mess with one Dane, you mess with us all, from the King on down. We know he daily rode horses through Copenhagen in breathtaking fashion, and some Danish and foreign sources say at this point he sometimes did it with a yellow star of David on his lapel. While history disputes whether it was ever actually done, he and his fellow Gentile Danes, were ready and willing to wear the yellow stars to confuse and frustrate the Nazis. Either way, he acted in accordance with the spirit of that promise, mutually so for the nation he led, and as he rode through Copenhagen, and was greeted by loyal subjects, the Jewish population knew he was a hero, risking his life to stand up for them.

The Nazis never gave up easily and they gave commands to the local police that they would arrest all the people in Copenhagen with Jewish names with or without local police cooperation. The heroic Danish police under the influence of the great Christian, went out that afternoon to warn all the Jews they could that the Nazis were coming. The local Red Cross and churches throughout Denmark put up all the money they could to smuggle approximately seven thousand Jews to neutral Sweden. The only Jews who were home when the Nazis came were those who had missed or ignored the Danish polices' messages. Though the Nazi troops arrested about 1100 Danish Jews and took them to the camps Christian and others within the government continued to visit the concentration camps, deliver food and other amenities to imprisoned Jews, and make phone calls to the Nazis inquiring about the safety of their fellow Danes. While their neighbors were in prison, thousands of Danes in and around Copenhagen fed their animals, tended their gardens, took their mail, watched over their belongings and made sure in less than five years when the Danish Jews got out of the camps, they returned to virtually the same surroundings as they left. the heroic Danes led by the great Christian set an example for the world to follow.

Tragic lessons, however, are implied when we compare what Denmark did to what the rest of Europe did and how what worked there could well have worked with more moral people in protecting over five million other Jews and a least a million other victims. Christian continued riding his horse through The streets almost every day. Shortly after a birthday card from Hitler was answered with a form letter on November 9, 1942, the Nazis decided to clamp down on the Danish "protectorate." Danish police and civil servants were under more stringent control and Nazi officers could burst into teachers' classrooms at any time and monitor the lessons.

King Christian himself was no longer allowed to ride his horse though he had survived a previous injury which resulted in surgery on part of his right arm. The King was kept under house arrest for most of the next two years while his officers brought messages to Norway and when possible to England that they were now in th oar against Hitler and would resist Nazi occupation whenever and however possible. Though no Danes were able to join the war effort from that time (a handful were fighting in the Norwegian Army) and a few thousand had joined via-the Norwegian king's London government in exile. Denmark was thus recognized as one of forty-four Allied countries and therefore became a founding member of the U.N, on October 23, 1945. Christian returned to the streets with a hero's welcome after the Germans surrendered. He died of quasi-natural causes in 1948 at the age of 78, though he was at an age even above average for life in his day, it did follow complications after a horse riding accident in Amalienboy, Denmark. He will always be remembered as the Great Dane who outshone all of Northern and Eastern Europe, the **Churchill** of the small countries, defying the most powerful continental army of his time knowing it could result in his death, but choosing to put himself on the line that Denmark, Europe, and thousands of innocents might live.

43

Fanny J. Crosby
(1826-1915)
L1tAS 8th including NUMBER

4 of Clubs of Hope

Blessed Assurance
Jesus is mine, O What a foretaste of glory Divine, heir of salvation
purchase of God, born of His Spirit, washed in His blood
THIS Is my Story-This is my song, praising MY Savior-All the day
long, this is my story This is my song, praising my Savior all The
day long.
Perfect submission, perfect delight visions of Rapture, now burst on
my sight
Angels descending bring from above, echoes of mercy, whispers of
love!

*W*ith these and many other simple yet profound words, Fanny J. Crosby became The queen of American hymn writers. Born Frances Jane Crosby on March 2, 1826 in Putnam County, New York she was blinded as an infant. Well-versed in Scripture by her teenage years she quote hundreds of texts and had already written numerous poems and songs. She wrote for The *New York Times and* addressed Congress at the age of eighteen on The need to make writing and other materials available to The blind. She met with President Polk and had also been an acquaintance of Grover Cleveland who as a young man took dictation for her. She taught English rhetoric and music at the New York Academy for The Blind. She married Alexander von Alstrum, a blind teacher from whom she was later estranged. She had one child who died in infancy. She is the writer of over a thousand songs including "Safe in The Arms of Jesus" which was played at *U.S. Grant's* funeral. She i famous for "Pass Me Not, O Gentle Savior," "I AM Thine, O Lord," and *Blessed Assurance from which the epigraph was taken* and it has been sung by almost everyone who has had even a transient relationship with a church. Ira Sankey and *D. L. Moody played her* hymns at revivals and into The late Nineteenth Century she played them as staples for *altar calls* at meetings of various denominations. She was herself involved in thousands of revival meetings though as a singer and piano player. Along with John and Charles Wesley and *Wilberforce* she was one of the five most famous Methodists of her time, and though she was not a contemporary with The Wesleys she was recognized as their most noteworthy heir, continuing the on fire missionary zeal of that Church into The Twentieth Century. They were "the Pentecostals of their time" something that surprises many of today's Methodists who see Christianity more as a way to encourage people in this life rather than effect the next. She was one of The to lead the revivals of the YMCA, which is another once devoutly Christian and missionary society which has also become a lukewarm service station. Like other heroes of hope she brought the light of the Gospel to millions during and after her l and her songs will be sung for as many centuries as our Lord delays his coming and most likely for eternity in Heaven. She lived to the age of eighty-nine poignantly stepping on to a carriage around that age singing "Blessed Assurance" which the carriage driver knew was written by Fanny J. Crosby, and then spent the rest of the ride convincing the driver that she really was Fanny J. Crosby. On February 12, 1915 she was taken home to be with the Lord. She is buried at Bridgeport, Connecticut where she lived with her sister.

I will end the entry on this brilliant hero of hope with her own hopeful words from "Draw Me Nearer

"O the pure d of a single hour that before Thy throne I spend When I kneel in prayer, and with Thee, my God, I Commune as friend to Friend

Draw me nearer, nearer Blessed Lord, to the Cross where Thou hast died. Draw me nearer,. nearer blessed Lord, to Thy Precious Bleeding Side!

There are depths of love that I may not know till I cross the narrow sea.

There are heights of joy tat I will not reach till I rest in peace with Thee!

44

Douglas MacArthur
(1880- 1964)

4 of Diamonds OF Hope

*B*orn in Little Rock, Arkansas in 1880 Douglas MacArthur was always in a military family as his father Art had also been an imposing general. He was a lukewarm student until the age of 19 when he entered West Point Military Academy and excelled at military maneuvers and other subjects. He rose through the ranks, becoming an officer early in his career and by age forty-two he made brigadier general. Sent to command troops in World War I, MacArthur earned an early reputation as a war hero. The inter-war period was very difficult on lifelong soldiers. Through The first war, he was experienced and believed himself to be an ex-military officer, thinking it would be his last taste of combat. His next assignment was teaching at West Point. Thinking the time for war had ended, he was not crazy about teaching new soldiers skills to prepare them for war, preparation for they would probably never need. He was then assigned to five years in the Philippines. He went with his new wife Louise,a Pennsylvanian., to command soldiers on the Pacific island.

Like many who lived in this era particularly those with military background, MacArthur saw two major problems creeping into America apathy about our future and excuses for Communism.

While the worldwide Depression made it hard for average Americans to be apathetic with poverty all around them, that only made Communism seem less a to some in the political left or center. He hit hard against Communism, the philosophy that could well destroy America and the world, even when she was on top, and with its gaining footholds in Eastern Europe and Asia, it may have been part of the reason we considered the Philippines unprepared for autonomy until the forties. He warned about Communism back in the States prophetically so, it was a fledgling party, but by 1932 Josef Stalin had the American party like all of worldwide Communism under one military umbrella. Though one of over six hundred U.S. Army generals he was named to the second highest post. Reassigned to the Philippines in 1940, he was prophetically warning about Japan's desire to advance militarily even as Japan and America continued to exchange ambassadors. It seems ironic why we did not send the Japanese delegation back while until 1941 the overwhelming majority of Americans saw no need to provoke Japan or Germany and every reason to avoid war at all costs. Shortly before he had married Jean Faircloth and The two remained very much in love and raised his one child, Douglas MacArthur, Junior.

Ironically MacArthur and others in the Pacific front were expecting Japanese attacks on the Philippines and possible Dutch or British holdings in The East, not Hawaii. When Pearl Harbor hit, he like most of his fellow Americans were shocked, finding out about it just hours after the bombs first fell in Hawaii. He had his own ideas for strategy, but as a patriot, stuck to taking orders. He wanted to fight to the last man with American and Filipino troops around Manila, but was early on asked to retreat his forces to the island of Bataan. The determined and some would have then said divinely inspired militant Japanese attacked even the far flung island of Bataan and soundly defeated American and Filipino troops. As usual MacArthur wanted to fight to the death, he was ordered by the War Department to vacate becoming set on Australia as a military base. In a famous message to the territory and its American forces there MacArthur spoke the famous words *People of the Philippines I shall return.* What followed was the infamous Bataan Death March in which over 12,000 Americans and Filipinos were marched through the island to prison camps where more than a thousand died and the others were used for slave labor in the Japanese war machine. For the next two years MacArthur lived in a large house in Australia paid for by the American military. He told reporters Bataan is leek ea child in the family who dies, she lives in our hearts every day.

Little was written about his war years until after his death, as it was the planning of very special and secret strategy. His love for his country would have compelled him to fight for his soldiers while that same love for his country was the one thing that made him obey her orders and remain in his quarters. Instead he spent the time studying the enemy and reporting on Allied strategy in the Pacific to American and Australian military personnel. In 1944 the soldier was let out of hiatus with an impressive array of American, Australian, New Zealand, Chinese, and Filipino troops which came crashing first into New Guinea where they scored an impressive victory. In October 1944 the forces returned to the Philippines this time turning the tables on the Japanese for the decisive battle for the Pacific. Getting his chance to broadcast on radio he again salespeople *of the Philippines I have returned*. The islanders made visits to h base welcome him and his troops as liberators and carrying out the war when possible to kill as many Japanese soldiers as possible. Interestingly imperialism is one of most negative subjects of history today. Thankfully, that is history and Asian, African, and Latin American, and other former colonial peoples are free to determine their own future. That said much of the value of imperialism depends on the virtue or vices of the imperial power, as Eastern Europeans occupied by the Soviet Union and later long-time holdings of Portugal were willing to fight of the "enemy" because they hated the imperial power, while throughout Asia, even as Japan claimed to give Asia back to the Asians, only Thailand saw the Japanese as benevolent. Colonies and former colonies happily joined their alleged oppressors to fight Japan otherwise the war could not have been conducted as it was. Indians and others of the subcontinent happily volunteered for the British Army (while their own neighbor in Ireland refused) even South Africa happily fought for Britain while tens of thousands of Indonesians fought for their Dutch colonial possessors. No other colony fought as valiantly as the Philippines. In fact there was a brotherhood between American and Filipino troops, largely due to Macarthur's leadership and it was easy to forget who was who it was simply joint American-Filipino effort that helped save the war for the Allied cause and help shorten it, some would say by a year or more. He led troops that took the Allies through three decisive battles against Japan, and if the atomic weapons were not used to end the war, he would have been the leader of the final battle to invade and conquer Japan itself. For a year MacArthur remained on the Philippines, practicing daily commands from the American office until the Japanese surrendered unconditionally. On September 1, 1945 MacArthur was allowed to sail to Tokyo Bay and officially receive Japan's surrender.

It should be noted that Japan started one of the most brutal and non-sensible wars in human history. As Churchill said "However sincerely we try to put ourselves in another position we cannot understand another man's perspective where reason offers no key." Both Germany and Japan waged brutal, aggressive, immoral, and illegal wars for no reason other than military advancement. Like the Germans, their Japanese allies had in mind domination of a continent, and brutal mass murder of many innocents. They killed those they thought to be inferior, particularly The Manchurian Chinese, but also but also large numbers of Tibetans, Koreans, and Filipinos, and used racial torture and slave labor on American, British, Dutch, and Australian prisoners. Today it is popular to whitewash the crimes of Japan because they made such a radical change and is today one of the West's best friends. It should be said without qualification that both Imperial Japan and Nazi Germany were criminal regimes who killed millions of innocent people and force fed their youth a diet of hyper nationalism, an irrational worldview. Now that the war was over, MacArthur and the overwhelming majority of Japanese believed it was time to introduce a new worldview. Some were surprised at Macarthur's benign rule but in fact it was the only way to logically lead a proud and now totally defeated enemy.

MacArthur's **first major act as head of Allied Occupation Forces on Tokyo was to communicate what became the accepted Western position that Emperor Hirohito was simply a ceremonial leader and had no culpability for his peoples' crimes and**

was not be considered a war criminal. *Although never especially close, MacArthur and Hirohito developed an enigmatic friendship, and MacArthur,* a devout Episcopal who saw his work in Asia as part of a divine challenge to bring Christianity to The Far East, where it was not the major religion, influenced the Emperor who might have opened up to Christianity though sources dispute the result. Nonetheless, the two led Japan into a period that saw democracy, equality for women, labor organizations both economic and union, educational reform, and religious freedom. Along with other members of the occupation forces from America, China, Australia, etc. he wrote the modern Japanese Constitution which though modified a little in the 1990s and twenty- first Century largely still in use. What was confirmed is that Hirohito offered to make Christianity the official religion of postwar Japan but MacArthur advised against it, agreeing with **C S. Lewis'** quip *When Christianity does not make a man much better it makes him much worse.* This is constituent with the belief of Christianity and most religions that it cannot be forced, it must be accepted in a man's will, and is especially true of Christianity which requires an assent to both intellectual facts as well as an embrace of a relationship with God, to serve the Master.

For five years MacArthur was the powerful person in Japan ruling the country benignly along with Hirohito and Parliament. In 1953 Japan was given the right to elect a prime minister still ruled by a combination of parliament and occupation forces for three years and in 1965 Okinawa, the last American governed island was handed back to Japan officially ending the American occupation.

In 1950 MacArthur then age seventy was called to command troops in Korea. In duly he appealed to U.N. forces to send more and officially became Supreme Allied Pacific Commander over troops including Canadians, British, Australians New Zealanders, Taiwanese, Thai, Dutch, French and Belgians. Chinese armies withstood benevolent requests by the United Nations to negotiate with the Armed services committee though China was not yet a member of the U.N. because its seat was held by the nationalist Republic of China (modern Taiwan).

Instead Chinese armies occupied North Korea to help the follow Communists fight their neighbor in Seoul and gave the North Koreans weapons used to bomb targets in South Korea and also American military instillations and French targets on Indochina. MacArthur wanted to bring in more troops and along with our South Korean allies go in and invade Pyongyang, the capital of North Korea, since we could easily end whatever military success North Korea was having in a matter of days. **President Truman** was against it, fearing Russia would enter the war, and ordered MacArthur to retreat to the thirty-eighth parallel and lead Allied and South Korean troops to withstand the conventional air and land war. MacArthur retreated but continued to make inflammatory statements in speeches before troops at South Korean colleges so Truman relieved him of duty.

Within a year **Truman** was retiring and many Republicans wanted to get MacArthur as their candidate for President. Instead the 72 year old Macarthur endorsed his good friend and fellow general Dwight *Eisenhower* who became the thirty-fourth President When Ike asked his friend about the best way to end the war Macarthur advised the President to drop atomic bomb North Korea cl them as one Korea under Seoul, and also bomb China then go in an occupy with our Taiwanese allies. Eisenhower disliked the idea and ended more peaceably but perhaps current realities have vindicated MacArthur's ideas. Perhaps a more hawkish stance, the only thing that gets Eastern, Communist, or terrorist enemies' attention, would have brought these countries in line sooner. **Fifty-five years later North Korea is still our sworn enemy** and they have nuclear bombs. *If Eisenhower had listened to MacArthur and put him in charge of strategy in '53, North Korean and Chinese cities would be turned into something worse than Hiroshima and Nagasaki and we would not have to worry about their nuclear bombs. Instead, like Japan they would be debating about nicer things, like where to hold the chili bake off or what singers to invite to cut the ribbon at the new car lot.*

MacArthur left the military and went on to give speeches throughout America. Almost half a million people heard his San Francisco speech, the first speech he gave in American in twelve years. A similar number lined The streets to welcome him back to Washington D.C. As our greatest war hero ever, and he addressed a joint session of Congress. At that time he was also presented with a special display of medals he won throughout his career starting with World War I, for heroism on the battlefield. He became chairman of the Remington Rand Cooperation. In a sense he was enlightened and well beyond he lie of political correctness that the educated Americans and military leaders are still in. In 1942 MacArthur advised the War Department that Japan was the tougher enemy and we had to put the total war effort into their defeat. Another hero of hope, George **Marshall**, got them listening when he said Germany was the greater threat. After the war MacArthur advised **Truman** who was wisely putting all effort behind defeating the Soviet Union without war, saying yes that was important, but Communists in China and other smaller Asian and African nations could pose a greater threat to the American military.

His views were largely ignored and today Communism is dead in Europe but not Asia or the third world. Today so-called Third world nations posing a threat to each other and by extension to us could be a greater threat than Nazi Germany and Soviet Russia ever were. His voice should have been heeded and perhaps today The world would be made safe for democracy. Instead American presidents and military leaders have kowtowed to The United Nations and The politically correct. Now we have nations as diverse as Iran, North Korea, China, Cuba, Vietnam, and possibly *even Venezuela* and Syria who could all be threats to the great American eagle. In Mac's day it was only two non-Western countries and his simple advice was bomb then now that they have already struck and they will never be a problem again. Instead the politically correct say do not bomb them, talk nicely to them, try to live in peace, and instead we sit and watch as they line up at least seven d that can stack and all attack us together.

As an extension of his military awards and in recognition of his courage in war and strategy MacArthur was given the Congressional Gold Star, his nineteenth medal for his military excellence. Recognizing his greatness just a few months before his death *President Johnson* gave him The Presidential Medal of Freedom, his first and only award as a civilian which was *inscribed, to the Liberator of the Philippines, Protector of Australia, Conquerer of Japan, and*

*Defender of Korea. His last famous speech was fittingly to a gradu-
ating class of West Point from which I excerpt the following:*

*Duty, honor and country, words that teach you. . .to stand up in
storm but to have compassion for those who fall, to seek to master
yourself before seeking to master others, to have a heart that is clean,
a goal that is high. . .to reach into The future but never forget to first,
to remember to laugh but never forget to weep, to be serious but
never take yourself too seriously. . .that you may know the simplicity
of true greatness, the open mind of true wisdom and the, meekness
of t. strength.*

Douglas MacArthur died in 1964, age eighty-four, at his home
in Arkansas.

45

Herbert Hoover
(1874-1964)

3 of Diamonds OF Hope

A wise man named Archibald Bunker once got off his patented turlet long enough to sing with his wife *Mr. we could use a man like Herbert Hoover again.* Though a standing American joke, Archie and Edith were dead on about that. Born August 10,1874 Herbert Clark Hoover in Iowa the thirty-first President studied engineering at Columbia later becoming a civil engineer and the first President to become a self-made millionaire before his election. He helped engineer thousands of roads and waterways in Europe and Asia briefly living in China and learning to speak fluent Mandarin. For three years during the war he headed up the civil Engineering Division in Europe saving France and Belgium from starvation and later headed the U.S. Food and Drug Administration Under President Harding he was appointed Secretary of commerce a role he held for eight years making him to date the only President to rise from a cabinet position to chief exec. In 1928 he ran for President choosing Charles W. Curtis a native American from Kansas to run as Vice-President. Easily defeating Democrat Al Smith, the mayor of New York, Hoover became our thirty-first President. Hoover was the first and only President to refuse a salary having already been a millionaire as a scientist. A likable leader with personable skills, he presided over the Stock Market Crash in 1929 while not being his fault he took the blame for what often became called the Hoover Depression.

Ironically as a citizen Hoover could have done far more but as President he was shackled by the laws already in place and had to allow the Depression to ruin its coupe and business to eventually make a comeback. Contrary to popular belief, he did not see fit to change the laws, while his successor FDR revitalized the economy with a myriad of illegal unconstitutional measures that made America the greatest debtor nation in history and almost bankrupted us by 1968. In another irony when the Depression and the war hit Herbert Hoover was a more intelligent and more experienced man than FDR just like *Neville Chamberlain* in Britain was more intelligent than **Winston Churchill.** In this case however, intelligence took a backseat because both FDR and **Churchill** were better at connecting to people and both led their countries through the war. Hoover passed a variety of legal measures to contribute to the livelihood of poor people who had seen better days, particularly farmers who learned to sing the famous song, *Brother, Could You Spare a Dime?* Like no time in American history thousands lined the streets some were wearing suits and fancy clothes from their better days, many were unshaved and unshowered, some were illegally entering trains. He could not have have changed the current economic situation or built up business better than it already was without amending the Constitution to favor Socialism. In 1932 this reached a climax when agitators who had served in World War One decided to organize what they called a "Bonus Army" a group of soldiers petitioning Congress for early pensions. Though it passed the House and failed in Senate and Hoover, again upholding the law asked the protectors to accept the wait a few years for their pensions to kick in. About 10,000 protectors took to the streets and rode the rails from several states to Washington, Maryland, and Virginia, walking to the capital to demand their pensions. For some, what Hoover did was unforgivable, but again he was only following the Constitution. After several days of protests he announced that the voices of the protectors had been heard, yes, they had demonstrated under their

First Amendment rights and now it was time for them to go home and let the law take affect. When thousands refused he called in his own Army against these dough boys, the former members of the Army and hundreds were arrested. Ironically, the two leaders of the Army who quelled the insurrection in Washington were **Douglas Macarthur** and Dwight D. Eisenhower, both of whom have gotten over the stigma to become American icons in their own right. Some people can never forgive Hoover for using our own troops to quiet our former troops but it was the only stance the Constitution could have allowed. Like the Whiskey Rebellion and the XYZ Affair at the turn of the Nineteenth Century, this one saw us in danger from capitalists in one of our own states, the other saw us in danger of following orders from France, a group of Americans were undermining the government and the military is the only wing of our government with the power to bring insurrections under control. Hoover felt bad for the veterans who were struggling to feed their families and pay bills during this most difficult time in our economic history, but their voices had been heard and it was time to use our Army to come and quiet them. Most of the World War I veterans were not protesting and most of those who had, had already left. Those who refused were arrested by troops under **MacArthur** and Eisenhower and the insurrection quieted down. In 1932 he was defeated in his bid for reelection, losing in a landslide to *Franklin* D. Roosevelt.

Many Americans especially **of my age and younger believe all Presidents and politicians are philanderers** and have many mistresses. Nothing could be further from the truth. If you were to write a book about Presidents' mistresses it would be a very short book, only a few have had multiple sex partners, The overwhelming majority have had only one, a wife. **Hoover like** *George Washington*, the two Adams, *Madison*, Monroe, **Abraham Lincoln**, *U.S. Grant,* **Theodore Roosevelt, Wilson,** Calvin *Coolidge, and Truman, LBJ, Nixon, Ford, Carter,* **Reagan,** *and the Bushes, as well as prime ministers* **Churchill, Thatcher,** *and* **Blair, and President Walesa, all experienced the bliss of having sex early in life, often, and always with a spouse. In other matters of personal morality including economics Herbert Hoover was a man of impeccable character. He also supported Prohibition believing we were at a time in** history when teaching people to drink responsibly had failed to be the American way of life and while otherwise disciplined and hardworking, Americans tended not to be trustworthy at walking away from booze. A practicing Quaker, Hoover felt the slogan "Drink responsibly" to be inferior to "Just don't drink" and if a few laws to keep alcohol away from millions who would abuse themselves and others was the law, it should run its course and by the time it was over perhaps drunkenness would be seen as un-American. Contrary to popular belief, Prohibition had mixed results and actually did bring overall alcohol consumption as well as rates of addiction down. Until the sixties almost half the states and of a large percentage of counties remained dry. To enforce the liquor laws and keep Communists and other criminals, particularly of the so-called organized variety out of the way a permanent government institution was needed and Hoover added to the existing Chicago Crime task force expanding what was then the fledgling FBI and appointing the other famous American who shares his name *J. Edgar Hoover,* to head the post for life or retirement. The fledgling FBI spread its stork wings during The thirties and forties and thanks to Hoover and Hoover, it has tracked down scum and picked up lots of dirt bags for seventy years! Herbert Hoover's legacy as one of our greatest Americans and conservatives is carried on today by The Hoover Institution which he founded at Stanford University where he taught post-Presidentially. It produces biographies and other books and materials dedicated to Constitutional principles and it has launched The careers of luminaries like Dr. Thomas *Sowell and Dinesh D'Souza.*

Always cold to FDR, Hoover found work in Europe helping them during the Depression and in World War II. Ironically both times America had world wars it was Herbert Hoover who helped this country stay in adequate food supply. He did, however, agree to work in a Democratic Administration after the war. He headed up a task force to study the scope of the executive branch for President **Truman,** partially out of a need to reinstate the office to what it was rather than an exercise in virtual dictatorship under FDR. He later endorsed Dwight Eisenhower for President and wrote books and articles throughout his life. He died in 1964 at the time the oldest person ever to have the Oval Office. Herbert Hoover was mourned not as a failed mid-century President but as a great American.

46

Nathan Hale
(1755-1776)

3 of Hearts OF HOPE

*B*orn in Coventry, Connecticut on June 6 a subject of The British Empire Nathan Hale grew up in a world where separation from The British was becoming a very real political and cultural possibility in The immediate future. New England was one of The most enlivened places in the world as political tensions in the making were just starting to stir a pot that in a few years would spill over to ignite a continent. The first series of incidents in this were Samuel Adams' freedom fighters in Boston leading protests against British taxation that culminated in the Boston Tea Party. Weeks later several British soldiers came before an American judge on charges they used unnecessary force in putting down rebellion. At the time Americans still saw themselves as British citizens but the unity of The nation was dissolving fast as American judges sentencing British soldiers proved America could not take a back seat. Hale grew up in this world as the quintessential Eighteenth Century example of a *Connecticut Yankee*.

He was tutored in religion and other educational disciplines particularly The Classics by The Rev. Joseph Huntington. A precocious young man, Nathan entered Harvard in 1769 at the age of fourteen.

He was such a successful student he became a teacher for one year during his nineteenth and twentieth year. While nineteen is an adult, with the process of maturing one wonders how his younger students took to their barely grown teacher. Unfortunately for them, their loss became America's gain the following year when Nathan entered The Army and w weeks became a lieutenant. Shortly after war w declared against The Hale's battalion crossed over to New York to engage in combat. He captured a ship loaded with British spies and earned a special appointment with The Army rangers. A few weeks later he volunteered for a very dangerous mission being sent by His commander behind enemy lines to spy. Dressed as a civilian Dutch schoolmaster he went to find secrets from The British. His mission was almost successful when on September 21, he was caught by British General Howe and sentenced to hang without the benefit of trial or any Americans being part of the process. In less than forty-eight hours he was hanged outside Huntington, New York where he spoke his immortal last words *I regret that I have only one life to lose for my country.*

Nathan Hale was a true hero of hope in The most important and most just revolution the world has ever seen. Volunteering for missions far beyond what was expected, Hale went behind enemy lines and willingly gave his life for His country. Of all The great and famous Founding Fathers, *Washington*, Franklin, *Adams*, *Jefferson*, *Madison*, Hamilton, and the less well-known ones like *John Witherspoon*, John Jay, and George Withe, Henry Knox, only Nathan Hale gave his life for his country. *Patrick Henry* said "Give me liberty or give me death" but he did not personally fight in the war and like most of The Founders he died in his bed at a ripe age. The fight belongs to the men who actually engaged the enemy of all those from our Revolution Nathan Hale stands out as a true man of hope willing to give everything that a nation dedicated as a pure republic with liberty and justice for all, could be born and live in modern times. There is a landmark at Helesite outside Huntington that marks where this Revolutionary hero was captured and Homestead in South Coventary, Connecticut is a Nathan Hale home opened as a landmark.

47

Bob Dole
(1924- Present)

3 of Spades OF HOPE

*B*orn in Russell, Kansas during the roaring twenties but raised mostly during the Depression, the Kansas man came of age in an era where most Americans were poor at least by modern standards but as fellow Kansas man *Dwight D. Eisenhower once said* one of the glories of America is that poor children do not know they are poor, at least not in his age. Sadly today millions who live in poverty from the age of five on recognize their poverty in urine stained small houses, crack dealers and prostitutes in their neighborhoods, used condoms thrown around their houses, and within feet of their homes, and even their churches becoming breeding grounds for the same. It may surprise many of you that this transplanted Utahn from Illinois knows the ghetto firsthand but that is where I lived in my formative adult years in San F and Oakland. If one American who never served as President did more to eradicate poverty or at least bring it back to the benign way to raise children like his parents, and their media benefactors Uncle Henry and Auntie Em, that great hero of hope is Bob Dole.

Born Robert J. Dole *July 22, 1923*, the man worth would go onto be the farmer's senator grew up on a farm. At first wanting to be doctor he curtailed his efforts to get scholarship money to take premed courses after the Japanese bombed Pearl Harbor he joined the Army and went to war. On April 14, 1945 he was shot with shrapnel while dragging a wounded soldier out of the way. Transported to the hospital and saved, he lost The use of his right arm, learning in time to do everything with The left, and live a positive and productive life as an American with a disability. A first marriage to Elizabeth Hanford took place in 1964 but eventually ended in divorce. A U.S. Senator Dole worked his way up to a national presence. At The age of forty-six he began working his way to a national presence coming on board with his good friend President *Nixon, The Disabled veteran* soon became chairman of The Republican National Committee. While The main job is fund raising, it was very difficult at the time, and as the job got more trying, Dole took The offenses of Watergate (of which he was totally innocent) perhaps more personally than anyone in The party, since he was by definition, The man who was supposed to "sell" The GOP even as it was becoming unsellable. He helped the smooth transition of power from the confused and arguably corrupt Ricard Nixon to the squeaky clean Midwesterner Gerald Ford. In 1976 Ford ironically chose another Midwestern to run for Vice-President and in Dole he saw a religious conservative with farming experience who had lived the life of a poor man to balance the challenge of Georgian Jimmy Carter and those of many conservatives in his own party who still felt **Ronald Reagan** was the right man for The job. Ford and Dole lost one of the closest races in national elective history. Dole remained on the floor of the Senate becoming the party's Senate majority leader and when The Democrats lost the Senate he stayed on as minority Leader. In 1980 and 1988 he ran brief campaigns for the Republican nomination for President. In 88 he finished second winning the New Hampshire primary and getting The delegates in Iowa pledging to support him though they favored Pat **Robertson** who was believed to be unelectable. In 1996 he emerged as the front runner to take on incumbent Bill Clinton. Over challenges from Alan **Keyes**, Pat *Buchanan*, and others Dole emerged as Republican standard bearer in 1996 coming clean on two issues. First his name he always signed it Bob and from that point name was "Bob" he always signed his name "Bob" not "Robert J. Dole," although that later became a source of humor for late-night talk show hosts who mocked him occasionally referring to himself in third person.

The other far larger issue was his disability status. Three past Presidents of the United States had disabilities, but in two cases they were hidden and never discussed. The other, American icon Franklin D. Roosevelt occasionally made reference to his polio but it was never discussed in public and in only two pictures does FDR ever show his wheelchair. Ironically despite being a scholar of both Presidents and the Disabled the only time I have ever seen FDR depicted as a wheelchair user was in the movie *Annie and junior* high school plays. Bob Dole on the other hand enthusiastically spoke of being an American with a divisibility someone with only one usable arm, and who takes pride in being the major voice in Senate for the Americans with Disabilities Act, the greatest Civil Rights m since 1965. In 1989-90 he lobbied for the Disabled rights and along with **Orrin Hatch** and Lowell Wicker he was a top champion of the Americans with Disabilities Act which was signed into law on November 11, 1989. When hundreds of Disabled rights protesters, some prominent and others not so hit the streets in Washington D.C. encouraging Congress to pass the Americans with *Disabilities Act*, like other protests the action got a bit out of hand. Some of the rps committed misdemeanors like truancy while two handcuffed themselves to the door of a Congressional staff office and others threw pens and papers telling members of Congress to come and sign them their rights. Bob **Dole faced one of the greatest crises a human being can ever face. On the one hand a member of a community agitating for rights he knows in his heart they should have, on the other hand, a member of the establishment sworn to uphold the laws as they are already written. While I oppose much of the protests like those against war and the 1932 Bonus Army, this is different in the sense that the p were not having basic human rights withheld. Since these rights were being withheld The Disabled had every right to use whatever nonviolent means were possible because what they were asking for was basic human rights.**

Being called out to address his fellow Disabled citizens while in fact being part of The "establishment" they were protesting, Dole stood before The crowd outside Capitol Hill and *said "This* isn't helping *us* any." In one sense it was heartwarming and Bob Dole was 100% sincere in addressing Americans with disabilities as "us", he was clearly one of us and willing to give his all for the cause of equal rights for the Disabled. On the other hand, he was sincerely wrong, this did help us because within eight months of the protest, the *Americans with Disabilities Act* was signed into law. Those who said Dole was of a separate standard had a point, he was a millionaire who could summon all The help he needed, and most Americans with disabilities do not have that, they had to agitate for their rights. Being one of the first open Americans with disabilities to make and enforce national laws, **Bob Dole knew how to keep your friends close and your Enemies closer. For the past forty years or so, Dole had all the rights of those in The top 1% of society by a combination of having worked hard to get there** and being in the right place at the right time.

During the 1996 campaign Bob Dole told millions of Americans about his conditions and got them thinking what i would be like to have an American with a disability as President. Although he lost the election, taking forty-one percent of the vote to a Clinton plurality, Dole made a strong showing in a situation where a few years ago **admitting having a paralyzed arm would have ended his campaign immediately, u**nless of course it was a "Saturday Night Live" skit.

Retiring form active politics at the age of seventy-two never getting to say what could have been the most upbeat words in the English language *I Bob Dole, do solemnly swear to uphold, protect, and defend the Constitution,* he with millions of Americans watched in heartbroken agony as the President from Arkansas disgraced his nation. Clinton had previously given the Kansan the Presidential Medal of Freedom and Dole had been a lukewarm friend of the man who beat him for the Presidency, but after the scandal hit, Dole gave a stirring speech to his cohorts in Washington encouraging them to remove the felon from the White House. The Kansan with the extraordinary Midwestern sense of humor has continued to be one of the greatest spokesmen for conservative principles and the Disabled. In spite of what some of his cohorts have said he was a wonderful Christian man who has led a wonder Christian marriage for four decades and raised his daughter Robin and is probably the greatest American political leader of my lifetime who never served as President. A hero of hope for a number of reasons, Bob Dole **has been an American's American who sees every day as July 4 and f to make all 365 including** April 15 enjoyable to 300 million Americans.

48

Whittaker Chambers
(1901-61)

3 of Clubs OF Hope

§

B orn at the very beginning of the Twentieth Century in Philadelphia, the man who later became America's most noted informant against the Communist Party joined the party that was our sworn enemy in 1925. In both cases Chambers showed rare courage, as the Red Scare of the early '20s was the most bitter time for pro-America verses anti-American sentiment in our history. Not since 1860 did Americans fear for a civil war and anyone with pro-German, pro-Russian, Communist, or ties to organized crime was suspected of being a potential enemy. Interestingly the fear was brief yet profound and for a short time Cincinnati changed their baseball team's name form the *Reds to the Redstockings, to avoid bearing the color that symbolized Communism. Whittaker* Chambers became one of several thousands of Americans who joined the Communist Party to help the man then touted as "the savior of Europe" Nikolai Lenin and after his death in 1924 the movement led by Josef Stalin. **Ronald Reagan** did not even want to talk about Communism at the time, saying it was a menace but largely a quiet one, and other American *icons* like Ernest *Hemingway* and *John Wayne* were happy to see the Russians and even Americans who sympathized with them as good people wanting to do what was best for all people. Many respectable people embraced some of the Communist ideals a the time including Pablo Picasso, Paul Robeson, and (briefly) Charlie Chaplin, and with the Nazi menace and Imperial Japan even staunch Christians had reason to say Communism was no longer public enemy #1. Hemingway was one along with thousands of Americans who went to Spain and fought in the **Abraham Lincoln** Brigade with Communist comrades (though most of the Spanish Republicans were non-Communist anti- Fascists) and both of the living Presidents wanted Franco defeated from Spain. It was also believed by macho Americans like Hemingway and Wayne that the awkward Russian bear could never pose a threat to the great American eagle. Their leader Franklin Roosevelt said in one breath that Communism was a menace but in the next that American Communists posed no threat to the good of the country. This attitude remained largely the same in the mid-forties since Communists bravely fought with Americans in World War II, **Reagan** then still did not want to see them as America's worst enemy.As president of the screen actors guild **Reagan** finally gave his fist speech in 1948 saying that if Communism ever became the menace Fascism was he would fight it just as valiantly. He lived to see that day just months later as did Hemingway. By 1949 John Wayne also committed anti-Communist largely due to Chambers exposing the truth, and Senator *Daniel K. Inouye* in an uncharacteristic but powerful moment said he gave his right arm to fight Fascism and if his country ever needed the left one to fight Communism they could have it too. In fact, Americans were changing swiftly to the hard-line anti-Communist position.

In the thirties Chambers stayed on at this alma mater Columbia University teaching *Daily Worker* a Communist front journal. From 1932-1938 he was a double agent f*or Moscow, though never entering there, he took orders directly from those receiving the orders of Stalin. As a* journalistic editor, he had free reign to go throughout the U.S. and various countries bringing secrets to Stalin and the Communist Party. For six years he stole classified documents from the Americans passing them to the Russians. He also taught Russian troops how to infultrate America. In 1938 he left The underground taking his wife and children and The highly educated scholar who had translated books from other languages and edited other major volumes, took an establishment job at *Time*. He and his wife and children stayed safe, but there was no guarantee he would, as others who similarly left the underground to inform on their former Communist allies, both Americans and Eastern Europeans were murdered. After debate with others who knew about his past, he committed to tell his story to U.S. Congress-VIA HUAC but it would take a decade before he would be given a forum to testify.

Many Americans then and now have asked the question what is wrong with Communism, especially home-grown Communists. Americans are free to be Republicans, Democrats, Socialist, Independents, Constitutionality's, Libertarians and a few even embrace extreme movements. From the Ice People, to the Flat Earth Society, from the Church of Satan to Scientology, the Amalgamated Flying Saucer clubs of America to Holocaust deniers, putting up with unpopular, radical, even nonsensical views has alway been part of the American way. That is why no one in serious positions is seeking to ban the Church of Satan or Holocaust denial, though as individuals and quite likely, even recognizedly as a nation we loathe them. Communism, however is a different brand, unlike Neo-Confederates and most Liberation theologians, the American Communist Party had nothing American about it, in fact it was a front for a foreign power.

Communism, however was a different brand unlike the church of Scientology and dozens of other "un-American" scams and lies, had nothing American about it. In the 20s and early '30s The Soviet Union wanted to take over the world, and what better way to do so than to get large numbers of Americans in high places to spy for them. Due to some intelligent people like Whittaker Chambers that was exactly what they were succeeding in doing in the 1930s. Like those who want to reconquest U.S. territory or the foreign nation Mexico, the American Communist Party was a front for Russia trying got rebuild America as a satellite of the Soviet Union. Others argue that on paper Communism looks good, so why are Americans so jealous for the competition? In the fifties and sixties some argued, and some still argue today, that Communism is just another philosophy, so why not let Communists and capitalists face off in the free market and see who wins. In spite of the obvious fact that the free world has already won the Cold War, the fact remains then and now Communism is not merely a philosophy on paper. *Communism is a system that from Marx to Lenin to Stalin, all the way to the late Twentieth Century, from Mao to Pol Pot, Castro to todays Vietnamese and North Korean governments, Communism has brought mass murder, starvation, loss of human worth, fear and and depravity to millions everywhere it has been practiced. There is no such thing as a Communist government that does not murder, maim, and enslave* large percentages of its people nor can a Communist *government stay in power without doing that to dignified and competitive human beings. Indeed, Communism is the most violent, hateful, and* murderous system the world has ever known and Americans and other Westerners who are sympathetic to Communism cause death and deprivation to millions!

In his later tenure at *Time* Chambers told editor *Henry Luce* he had been a double agent for The Soviet Union. At The time it was not exciting news and was buried in The newspaper, since Fascism not Communism was now our greatest enemy. In 1940 Hitler and Stalin signed the non-aggression pact and the American Communists opposed Britain and the blockade of Nazi Germany, wanting to make sure Hitler and his allies had free reign to carve up Poland and give as much as possible to The Soviet Union. In September of 1941 Hitler invaded the Soviet Union and tried to defeat the great Russian bear before the terrible Russian winter. For the next several years the terribly loud *Cold War* was relatively quiet as the U.S. and the Soviet Union were allies in ending the onslaught of Nazi Germany. The nation led m by Democrats from the FDR years through **Truman** was now completely committed to anti-Communism. The House Un-American Activities Committee was founded by Northeastern liberals wanting to keep those sympathetic with Fascism or Japan in check. By the late 40s the committee was completely committed to discovering Communists and the President agreed that anyone in the public eye be they actors athletes but most importantly government people who were Communists should be disclosed to the rest of the nation. After having been underground for years, and now as a largely private, quiet citizen for a decade, Chambers had his chance to go national.

Beginning on August 25, 1948, he told his story to the House Un-American Activities Committee (HUAC) that Alger Hiss, then assistant secretary of State, was a major member of the Communist underground saying that they had been roommates while both were taking orders from Moscow, and had traveled to Europe with him, in an effort to pass American secrets, that Hiss along with him, under orders from Stalin, was instrumental in infiltrating Eastern European governments for Stalin. During a long series of interviews by U.S. congressmen including *Richard Nixon*, Hiss denied ever having been a part of the Communist Party. He changed his story several times, at first saying he never knew Whittaker Chambers then going back to admit he knew him casually but was never a fellow traveler with him. Through the investigations Nixon proved that Hiss had lied several times about his involvement with Chambers and by extension that he knew Stalin and had been involved with the Soviet Union. Alger Hiss at first had said his workings with them were simply to help the Allies defeat the Nazis, but by the questions Nixon proved Hiss to be a lair and he was indicted for perjury. Indeed that along with other uncovered Communists in the state Department and in U.S military intelligence, especially with Julius and Ethel Rosenberg proved to be the greatest acts of treachery in American history. It was in the words of one anticommunist scholar, "a conspiracy so immense" and though most of the guilt for attempting to expose Communists falls on the reputation of *Joseph McCarthy,* in fact Communists were all over the American government, and McCarthy did not go far enough in exposing them though he worked his last years harder than anyone to expose government corruption. On January 20, 1950 Alger Hiss was proven guilty of perjury and sentenced to eighteen months in jail.

Millions of Americans correctly identified Whittaker Chambers as the greatest hero of his time, this mild-mannered middle-aged converted Catholic who put his life, his freedom, and his reputation on the line. Telling on the third most powerful man in government, exposing him as a liar who had taken orders from America's archenemy, while, he, Chambers himself could have been imprisoned for betraying his country, while that was the last of his worries if Stalin's goons ever caught up with him! Chambers released his memoirs *Witness* in which he spoke of the Communist conspiracy as the greatest tragedy in modern history and would not accept the label hero, maintaining the imprisonment of Alger Hiss was not exciting or payback, in fact it was a tragedy, but was also far too little, too late, as hundreds of other Communist spies were still lurking. The battle would be a losing one unless the U.S.A. and her allies, especially Britain where Communist sympathizers were gaining major government jobs, did not switch gears, rapidly. He claimed the issue of Communism was a crisis for the whole world not just America or The West. He also spoke of American liberals getting closer to Socialism and therefore seeing true Communists as their like-minded counterpart.

The correspondence he kept with *William F. Buckley,* then widely regarded as The "Dean of the American Right" was published by Buckley, after Chambers' death, and many of his articles were featured in *National Review.* Along with Buckley, James Burnham, and others Whittaker Chambers helped revitalize the "right-wing" of American thought. They were the few, unafraid to mention the obvious fact that the Left Wing, now increasingly the mainstream of the Democratic Party, had come to the point of aligning itself with Socialism and even Communism. These unabashed men of The right, not just conservatives, but right-wing activists, while not concerned with holding office themselves, helped secure the nomination of *Barry Goldwater* and later **Ronald Reagan.**

The image **of the great American is often see in the cowboy personification, and our last two heroic Presidents, were both ranchers who regulated the comings and goings of cowboys and animals. In this sense the Pennsylvanian became the quintessential American cowboy. He took on the two most powerful governments of his time, because he knew he was right and would not rest until he brought in his herd.** Chambers died in 1961 a man who had served his country and done The right thing, being awarded The Presidential Medal of Freedom by **Ronald Reagan** posthumously in 1983.

49

Branch Rickey
(1881-1965)

2 of Spades of HOPE

§

*W*estley Branch Rickey was born in The last quarter of The Nineteenth Century in Ohio. Remarkably he was born into a world where a portion of the country had just recently abolished slavery and the nation was divided about whether freed slaves should have the right to vote and serve on juries. While the victorious North was in the final process of retreating their armies from the defeated South. A sport called baseball, a variation of similar games played in England with bats and balls was just becoming a sandlot and neighborhood phenomenon though established teams were already earning money selling tickets to baseball parks.

Rickey grew up a devout Methodist and had was passionate from his youth. A son of the Midwest from perhaps the most versatile state in the Union, he had strong values of faith in God, love of country, love of people, and a desire for integrity justice, and fair play. While he entered adulthood without quite knowing what His unique was, he knew he wanted to do great things and was bound for success. Since he loved baseball he played semi-pro and was a catcher in The Major Leagues for five seasons playing for both The St. Louis Browns and The Yankees. He compiled a modest.239

lifetime batting average. He then became a lawyer after graduating from Ohio Wesleyan University coaching basketball for The school to earn His tuition. His team was integrated but even in Ohio it was not welcome everywhere and just over the river in Northern Kentucky a hotel refused a Black player admittance. While Rickey was arguing with the management and then working on finding his player other accommodations, he returned to see the young man washing his face simulating a change of color. It was then Branch Rickey knew one of the things he wanted to do in life was create a more colorblind society. He had a brief and uneventful legal career and returned to baseball in 1914 managing the St. Louis Browns and from 1925-1942 he managed the St. Louis Cardinals. There he created The Major League farm system preparing professional players with Minor League playing time. This is especially necessary for baseball since unlike other athletes they tend to be fresh out of high school with little education and need some time to prepare for such a public career. In fourteen years with the Cardinals he revolutionized the team and made more changes to baseball than any manager of his day with the possible exception of Casey Stengel. Had he never done anything from that point on he would have already earned himself a place in baseball and American history.

In 1942, the fifty-nine year old began the career for which he would be most established general manager of the Brooklyn Dodgers. For the first three years he did relatively little with them mainly because most of the great players were away fighting in World War II. In 1945 he bought a -part of the team and became team president giving him a main interest in the fate of The most versatile team. In 1945 as the young GIs returned to The States tens of millions of Americans flocked to the ballpark. The war had brought countless changes and the country was now ripe to get back to the ballpark and enjoy the national pastime and nowhere more so than the neighborhoods of New York. Rickey capitalized on this by being the first team builder in over seven decades to integrate his team. He started in 1946 integrating the farm league with three Black players *Jackie Robinson*, Don Newcome, and *Roy Campanella, who* went to play for the farm team, being recruited to play for the Montreal Royals. One spring day he interviewed Robinson about The idea of becoming The first to cross over to play for the Dodgers a decision about which Rickey was clear. He told him that opponents and fans would likely call him every name in the book, some would taunt him, and may even try to injure him. For the sake of integration and changing the game and world with it, Jackie had to be passive and refuse to fight back. He asked Mr. Rickey if he wanted his players to be afraid to fight back and he answered, "No, I want then to be man enough not to." Jackie Robinson was a twenty-nine year old battle tested athlete a husband and father for whom turning the other cheek had never been forte. He chose to oblige and so for the first year, he could say nothing back but only let his playing skills speak for themselves and prove his equality or superiority by hitting harder, running faster, and fielding better than the other players.

Indeed the relationship as well as the team got along famously. Despite major problems throughout the nation, The Dodgers won the pennant in 1947, with Jackie Robinson playing a decisive role and winning Rookie of The year. Largely due to Rickey's stance baseball was successfully integrated and it helped pave pave the way for the rest of the country. In 1962 Robinson was inducted into The Hall of Fame and all barriers in sports broken. Campanella and Newcome also went on to stellar careers. Ironically the Dodgers resisted some of his rebuilding efforts (totally unrelated to integration) and he was persuaded to sell his stock and leave the team in 1950. Less than a decade later, the team moved to LA and Rickey went to back to work for the Cardinals and in his later years the Pittsburgh Pirates. He gave speeches all over the country and on December 9, 1965 he collapsed and was dead within a few hours at eighty-six. Though in his later years he was accomplishing at a shadow rate of His former self, his mind had never weakened and it was very appropriate that he died engaged in activity that had made him a success in life. He is remembered more for his years with the Dodgers, building up a success and making the world a better place in which to live. Even before **Martin Luther King**, Harry Bellafonte, *Lyndon Johnson, and the* current Womens', Native American, and Disabled movements, this Ohio man stepped up to the plate, applying the nonviolent but hard work "truth in action" work and play principles of *Gandhi and Thoreau* to historically successful results.

50

Florence Nightingale (1818-1908)

2 of Hearts of Hope

*B*orn in 1818 in Florence, Italy while her British parents were on a cruise she would go on to have a British mandate to treat British, Turkish and other Allied servicemen in one of the worlds harshest wars to date. Her parents were Unitarians, while it has been called a denomination of "Christianity with working clothes on" or a protestant reaction to Protestants, by rejecting the deity of Jesus Christ, the symbolic Lord's Supper for the Redemption of humanity, the Holy Trinity and the, literal interpretation of Biblical Miracles, Unitarianism has usually been an excuse for Christian secularism. In her later life Nightingale showed she rejected The distinctive doctrines of Unitarianism believing in a literal interpretation of some miracles and the continuing presence of God's Spirit in the ongoing work of the Church. She did, however, retain the Unitarian principle that the key to living a Christian life on earth was in the service of her fellow humans. Ironically if she had been born a Catholic she would have probably become a nun and barely heard from in history and if she were an Episcopal or Methodist she would have been convinced to marry and give up her career early in life.

Florence Nightingale trained in German schools for nursing. Nursing in her day could be called a profession only in the loosest of sense, and its looseness extended to the fact that many nurses were prostitutes, allowed into hospitals for the simple reason that they were the best women to minister to wounded soldiers unsocial needs. Furthermore British soldiers once wounded did not expect to live long so nurses were expected to bandage wounds, write letters, and do such things for dying soldiers. While the hospitals of German battlefields were slightly better, Nightingale expected to rid the world of such practices and even as a teenager she wrote The Queen with the commitment that given the chance she would save soldiers and save the integrity of the British healing units. Eventually she was, with twenty nurses given a mandate to treat British and allied servicemen in the Crimean War. At this time her theories of health and cleanliness were tried on large numbers of sick people in a swift and steady time. When she arrived at Scotari, the British hospital in Istanbul, in 1856 soldiers ewer dying daily of preventable problems like blood infections from bandages that were infected with blood, and scurvy a Vitamin C deficiency caused by too little food in the area. She later admitted that the first seven or so weeks she was there the death toll actually increased due to overzealous bandaging of wounds and the practices of her and other women holding men in her arms while changing bandages. It was also influenced by the fact that many female nurses were transferred out of the hospital to give Nightingale full control over the nursing and eventually allow her to convince the men she was the rightful leader. By the end of 1856, however, the death toll went down but was still far too high and she continually wrote The Queen and other Allied governments with pleas for more money. Nightingale herself got sick with a series of viruses in Turkey and returned home writing about her negative experiences. For almost four years very little was heard from her thigh she wrote in later published coinsurance almost daily. She had broken her own heart by her failings in The Eastern Crimea Front in spite of The fact that she brought deaths down and was the pioneer of nursing in the English-speaking world.

In 1860 Nightingale began writing her volumes that would lead to the pioneer work of nursing as a profession. Within three decade she started her own hospital in Britain and also wrote invaluable instructions to American medical people treating wounded soldiers in The Civil War. Later in the decade she went again as The guest of The Queen to India where she saved thousands of lives by improving the sub-continent's irrigation system. Largely due to her own experiences, she became obsessed with germs and their antidote-cleanliness, and by the late 1870s her rules of cleanliness became established all over the world so that millions from doctors and nurses, to blue collar people and most importantly parents, became daily practitioners of simple rules of clean healthy living. Messages that we take for granted like *wash your hands before you eat, cover you mouth before you cough or sneeze, and clean yourself before touching other people, keep your living space clean, wash your hands after urinating and defecating, and take every precaution of cleanliness when it comes to body fluids especially blood,* go back *to* the writings and practices of Florence Nightingale. Her message of proper health and hygiene influenced Kings, Popes, presidents, parents, and police, and through her no nonsense attitude of enforcing it she created the nursing profession. A woman we may today call *one tough chick* or the toughest SOB in the hospital, she led men by first earning their respect then making them learn in silence convinced that she knew far better than they. While she was a tough and courageous presence, it was all done in love to save lives and make the world a better place in which to live. It also paved the way for English speaking people to become the leading pioneers in health and medicine. She always remained embarrassed about her less than excellent showing in the Crimean War, Florence Nightingale set out as a thirty-one-year old woman to reestablish her reputation. Though mysterious in many ways no one can doubt her success and vowing to make the good outweigh her mistakes almost half a century later she lived up to that goal thousands of times over. In 1907 she became the first woman awarded the British Legion of Merit, a lady of The Round Table, after having been a knight in shining armor, outshining most men. A lifelong bachelorette, Florence saved many men but never let one strap anything permanent around her powerful arms, she was the leader and had to be boss in her relationships. Influencing medical people and medical education, for both men and women, she died in 1908 at the age of eighty-nine a true hero of hope making the world a cleaner, better, safer place to live.

51

Elizabeth Blackwell (1821-1909)

2 of Diamonds

§

E lizabeth Blackwell was born in 1821 in a rural Britain town not far from London At the age of ten she integrated with her family to the U.S. and they eventually settled in New York. Inspired by the story of a friend V. Mary Donaldson who died painfully with uterine cancer, with both women believing it could have been better treated by a woman doctor, she committed herself to becoming a doctor, though no women doctors were known not only in America or Britain but anywhere in recorded history. After being turned down by numerous medical schools, she eventually was accepted to Geneva Medical School in New York. Ironically the students pushed for her admittance as a joke thinking it would be good publicity fort the school, but she graduated at The head of her class in 1849. Blackwell had largely decided to become a doctor because she personally watched her friend bleed to death, she had pragmatic reasons, and now educational and occupational ones. She was a trailblazer, but at The time there was no evidence she intended it as a great victory, to blaze a trail, in fact it would be extremely difficult even after graduating from medical school with highest honors, she had to work hard to show she was worthy. She seemed ordinary in all facets of personality, other than her academic and personal ground she was breaking, she had no great desire to prove her superiority or win a great battle for her sex, she simply wanted to be her best, and take her medical knowledge back to help, those whom she could treat.

She organized the first college for women that largely trained women to be doctors. With a number of courageous women she led a medical team around the front lines during the Civil War. She took similar opportunities to minister to wounded troops in London. Writing many articles and university books, she was instrumental as a pioneer of the sciences of gynecology and antibiotics.

She never married but she raised one adopted child Kathrine Barry whom she raised from age seven and who was her lifelong friend, secretary, and companion. Elizabeth Blackwell was a pioneer in every sense of the word. Few can match her in history, because while most pioneers either begin a new field, or invent a new product or service, she was a pioneer who opened The most vital and lifesaving profession up to at least half the world's population without ever a doubt that women could do it, despite what others said. She was a pioneer in speaking and writing about various areas of medicine. She believed medicine required the personal and spiritual touch. Unlike women of her generation and later ones who would rise to prominence as world leaders, Elizabeth Blackwell was not a "man's woman" or in a classical sense macho or arrogant. Unlike **Florence Nightingale** she rejected the theory that a woman to take a leadership position particularly over men much share their masculinity or even out man the men. While she was strong and courageous, she was clearly a woman, and while not particularly noticeably feminine, she dressed and behaved like a woman and led a whirlwind of change in both workable management and domesticity.

Ironically, like **Nightingale**, she never married and, like other heroes of hope in this series, **Helen Keller** and to date **Condolence Rice** were lifelong bachelorettes. For many women (certainly more so than men) being a strong, independent, and pioneer leader has meant standing alone and proving her worth by not needing a man to lead or support her. While marriage is important to both men and women in securing a helpmate and bringing up children, despite what many believe, history and sociology prove virtually all men and women need The other as a counterpart. More women, however appear capable of being successful and fulfilled without their counterparts and men need women even more, even if they see family life as only one small part of their success. Elizabeth Blackwell lived her latter years in London ironically having become an American citizen, she chose to return to the place of her birth in her older age.

52

Condolezza Rice
(1957-Present)

2of Clubs OF Hope

A woman of many paradoxes all adding up to great success, *Condolezza Rice* was born in the segregated South. Raised on the values of God, family, country, and superior education, Condolezza grew up a great American albeit without the trappings of great success. Both her parents were schoolteachers and though limited in education (and as I will point out even voting rights) in Alabama, they loved the opportunity to teach Black children, they eventually could not pass up greater opportunities in Colorado and the Western states. Her parents became Republicans in the 1950s-because the Democrats would not register them to vote in Alabama and Republicans did. By the age of sixteen she could speak French fluently and, she eventually learned Russian (though not as well) by being a scholar of our old enemy, the Soviet Union. She became an established educator and writer on international issues particularly about East versus West. And by the 1980s she advised Presidents **Reagan** and Bush on the issue. She was the first woman to become a provost (Lecturing dean) at Princeton University. She was also the youngest on staff and The first African-American woman. She also beca*me an advisor to major Republicans, including **Reagan** and Bush. Though*

she knew the 40th AND 41st Presidents relatively casually, it was the father who introduced her to George W. Bush, at the family ranch in Texas, and the two became kindred spirits, probably linked by both ideology as well as personal friendship-almost of a necessary variety (sometimes comparable to David and Jonathon) than any perspective President/advisor since *Richard Nixon and Henry Kissinger. It is next to impossible to see A BUSH-43 Presidency without a Condolezza Rice and it is equally impossible to imagine the national figure Condolezza Rice we know and love without a George W. Bush Presidency.* Though her education work had been her primary contribution in fact she became the first Black, the first Black woman, and the youngest dean ever at Princeton, she eventually stepped down to take her education expertise to Washington to work in issues that were to benefit three hundred million Americans and tens of millions of Arabs, Eastern Europeans, and Sudanese overseas. An avid football fan, she has been talked about as a perspective NFL commissioner.

Th*ough a loyal Republican she is not as conservative as other Black Republicans and she even leans a little to the Left of other women who have served in* **Reagan** *and Bush administrations, albeit to the Right of* **Colin** *Powell,* **she has** *always been her own person and spoken what she thinks to be the truth because she thinks it is the truth, a very important quality in both a security advisor and a secretary of state. In fact she said fellow hero of hope* **George Marshall** *was probably the most distinguished of all secretaries of State. In* 1999 she was part of The exploratory committee to decide if George W. Bush had a realistic chance of being elected President, and appearing with Nancy Reagan was a sort of "laying on of hands" for The next generation. She is pro-Israel but wanted the Israelis to broker a deal with The Palestinians and took Ariel Sharon to task for not wanting to give up more land. She was instrumental in three former Communist countries being processed through NATO and and joining the alliance under American military protection. Though she encouraged the nation's delegate at the U.N. to neither vote for nor veto the use of the term "genocide" for the actions of the Sudanese in Darfur, both because the killing was as much about land as race and ethnicity, as well as the fact that it could slow down the process of independence for South Sudan, the predominantly Christian portion (who heroically achieved nationhood in 2011). *By* emphasizing that the U. N. Tribunal prosecutor was not accountable to anyone outside Europe and therefore unable to provide binding legislation that would punish those Sudanese responsible, she *hastened the process of the Christian South to declare independence and live free (at least politically of control) from the Muslim North in Khartoum.* She also played a role in recognizing independent nations in Kosovo (Eastern Europe) and East Timor (formerly in the "rump" of Indonesia).

More than anyone with the Possible exception of V. P. *Dick Cheney* she was responsible for others being chosen by Bush as staff members and she outshone the far more established members with decades of experience on her, particularly Don Rumsfeld and the nearly universally loved *Colin Powell.* Her dedication won her many supporters even among former enemies or at least people who hate Republicans. While she takes a firm stand for both American and conservative principles she has not been particularly outspoken (except on the job) and has never craved the limelight but had it thrust upon her. Such a respected leader and most likely the most known security liaison in our history, she happily took *the promotion to secretary of State in 2005-for the second Bush Administration,* making her the second woman on that job and the second African-American after her predecessor at State, *Powell.*

In 2005 when a story was reported that American soldiers were spitting on the Koran and desecrating Muslim holy things, she spoke out saying if it true, those responsible will be held accountable, as desecration of the Holy Koran is un-American and undemocratic. I was among those who knew it was bogus from the start, and when reports confirmed it, I just knew what I always knew, that American soldiers would never do what these imbeciles in print media alleged. I will demonstrate why educated observers could only see this as an obvious hoax (though Dr. Rice, who is probably smarter than I, had to react to its possibility, as a holder of high office, she must be ready to react to the worst at all times). Some America-bashing not-too-bright reporter likely heard it and reported it to the international media thinking it would make a good story. Given such media types' anti-Americanism and their desire to stir up trouble between America-the West and the Islamic world the story simply could not have been overshadowed by things like facts and obvious truth.

Most of our troops in Iraq are men (but a good many women) between ages-18-27, most came from Southern, Western, or Midwesterner states, many were middle-class while others grew up poor. A majority were White, a disproportionate number are Black, as are those of Native American, Hispanic, and Americans of Asian, particularly Indochinese heritage. In the South and the West virtually all of them were religious minorities. *While virtually all of them have been in church, many are "lukewarm" Catholics while virtually all of the Mormons who join our military (as with the Boy Scouts an organization that has largely survived in the Twenty-First century due to the participation and leadership of members of the LDS Church) are religious. Most of the Evangelicals have* been in the religious minority except in Georgia, Alabama, and a few counties in the Carolinas. *Most are from middle-class families* with parents in secure but not rich occupations leek teachers, nurses, and business associates. *Many grew up with single mothers. Mormons are in the Midwest and the West and are a religious minority everywhere but Utah and Idaho* where (in part due to their predominance) they are subject to prejudice from non-Mormon residents and new transplants from 15 or 20 states. Blue-collar Catholics were a minority in the West and South, and most grew up with blue collar parents in physical jobs. It should also be said that in the military, Whites are not seen as leaders (like they often are in civi*lian life)* but like everyone *else as men aspiring to become leaders by increasing rank-the leaders are never the Whites or the Protestants or those with the "right religion" but those who advance in rank to sergeant and officer.* Hence they were, Catholics from Ohio, Evangelicals from Tennessee, Mormons from Montana. A band of brothers, all recognized Condolezza Rice as the governmental leader of their Armed Forces. Their soldier brothers and sisters also included Lutherans, Jews, Seventh-day Adventists, Presbyterians, Nazarenes, Greek Orthodox, and even an occasional *Baha'i and the occasional Muslim. Fighting for America together, they* ate together, whites and blacks, showered with Puerto Ricans, slept in the same bunks with

Cubans, and helped Cambodian-Americans lace their boots and strap on their guns. Not a one of these would take another man's book, enemy though he may be and disrespect it in his country. The American soldier may not be prefect, but of such psychotic behavior he cannot justly be accused, it would bring guilt and emotional scars far worse than our U.S. military officers, soldiers, sailors, airmen, and Marines can take. *Killing an enemy is a soldier's job to do, desecrating his book is a crime against nature and humanity!* No red-blooded American disrespects another man's religion in public.

Some will cite the atrocities committed at Abu Ghrab prison which included sexual humiliations. While immoral and despicable, was done with motivations that did not involve degrading anyone's religion. There have been Times when American soldiers do despicable things, even criminal acts, but they do not involve people's' religions. In World War II, for instance Americans interned some Japanese-Americans, both native born and from Japan, so we did unfair things, but even as the war with Japan was in full force, Americans never ridiculed The Japanese Shintoist religion or belittled the role of The Emperor. The other reason the scandal was obviously fabricated and a hoax to educated Americans is that the U.S. is in a strategic relationship with Pakistan, an alliance based on mutual need to fight terror, as with The Soviet Union during World War II. Pakistan is the most Muslim country in the world the home of the capital city of Islamabad, land of Islam. Islam rather than Communism is a religion practiced by a substantial number of both allies and enemies of *the United States*. For all our faults, American soldiers are not stupid brutal or immoral enough to belittle such spiritual belief.

In spite of the pre-scientific (B.S. is the more traditional term-SEE my Matching quiz at the end) Koran scandal and other issues she has had to explain, Condolezza Rice retained her authority, and for the most part her popularity. Sadly, a scandal as bad as the mishandling of the Koran (as if that could ever happen) took place the previous year when reporters caricatured her in political cartoons as "Aunt Jemima" and other cruel names that combined her heritage with subservience (I guess such people think Blacks can make virtually every choice expect following their conservative consciences).

Like *virtually all people and issues involved with the last two years of the Bush Administration* she came under fire even by some conservatives for seeming to give a sense of security to dictators that the USA is unwilling or even unable to stop them. In *fact she stood up to our old enemy Iran, and it helped cause that Islamic dictatorship to back off on designs on Lebanon which (along with the departure of Syria) allowed the country of mixed Christian and Muslim Arabs, to hold their first elections in two decades. She also stood up to the quasi-dictator of Russia, Vladimir Putin, which helped legitimize the democracy of neighboring Georgia. Her action (or more properly well-timed inaction) helped South Sudan declare independence and the longsuffering but God-seeking South-Sudanese were able to declare a republic.*

After serving as the first African-American woman secretary of State, she returned to teaching at Princeton-in part because she can do little to top what she has already done. Her published memoirs are about her eight years in the *Bush Administration, while she* simultaneously worked on a book about her experiences in the segregated South including being an acquaintance of two of the girls who died in the bombing of Sixteenth Street Baptist Church in Birmingham and her parents helping her adjust with love most parents have, but also because of their spirutal and educational backgrounds which many parents lack.

In 2008-I like millions of Americans, especially fellow conservatives pondered whether she would be our next President or assume an equally challenging and rewarding career for our country. Since she easily resumed a teaching career (which must be hard for her students with our celebrity culture-some would either kowtow to any celebrity or act in her presence based on their personal politics-so anyone prone to do either-probably ninety percent of us-should not take her courses), Dr. Rice need not do anything else extraordinary to surprise the nation. That is not to say she cannot and should not, since she may be Vice-President, as well as being a private citizen for life, and *Mitt Romney* or future Republican candidates may make use of her expertise for one of numerous jobs. She may be the first woman President or VP, and to paraphrase one of our lesser known Founding Fathers, *John Witherspoon, America is not only ripe, b*ut rotting for want of a woman President. *She could just as well be a governor, legislator, NFL commissioner, or private citizen. Whatever happens, Condolezza Rice has proven one of our sharpest and most accomplished Americans, like* **Teddy Roosevelt,** *a true Bull Moose (or is it cow-moose???) who set out to do extraordinary things and achieved beyond her wildest dream, not just more than she could imagine, but more than virtually anyone could have imagined of her, because of her faith in God and the abilities He has given her.*

Concluding Remarks

§

ON Heroes and Hope-ikt is well to be said that for the "publisher" who is largely a Christian NET Distributor, some final remarks should be made about what I have written. I think that I should definitely say that to make hero status at this level, according to my rating system, and my committed and highly positive writing style, the heroes all did something conducive to being a hero in the Christian community or at least triumph over adversity in ways Christians can appreciate. While many of these heroes like **C.S. Lewis. King, Peale, Graham, Joan of Arc, Reagan, Boone, Robertson, Falwell, Dobson, Reover, Wilberforce, and Flanagan triumphed with** explicitly Christian messages and an implicit trust and obedience in Jesus Christ; some may criticize or at least dislike other individual entries in the book or say I wanted to put in personal preferences from my own taste, not the Bible or God's Kingdom. I do not purport to be writing anything for God or to be saying anything with which Christians have to agree. It is, however, a Christ-centered work and everything I said is intended to be edifying to people of faith and be consistent with the spirit of the Law and the work of Christ's Kingdom on earth. I used more Biblical references and allusions to the Bible than most books, and specifically *with new references in* **Ben Kinchlow, and Pat Boone** *in his overall framework in becoming a hero,* showed that such heroism is both explicitly Christian and an extension of the Kingdom of God particularly where it comes to use of heroic personality traits to better individuals and institutions. And while some of the heroes, like **Helen**

Keller, Limbaugh, and Hayakawa, rarely argued either their ideology from a religious perspective, or that their goals and careers were intended to further the work of God, what it did require was consistency with the truths and principles that made Christ a hero as well as proved and sustained Biblical literary truth and its ethical and spiritual enablement's for two thousand years. Therefore, while **Richard Simmons** can be a hero of hope without professing any explicit creed or theological goals (though he has held workshops in churches that requested his aerobic expertise), he could not if as part of his career he was seeking to undermine faith in Christ or turn people away from a particular goal in bringing others to the Lord. For that reason, somebody who never goes to church or even one whose lifestyle does not measure up to the principles of the Bible, through countless failures or even a deliberate series of un-Biblical practices can still be a hero of hope, the day he or she practices, in word or deed to undermine the faith of another or turn people or institutions away from Christ-centered practices, he can no longer be a hero of hope and has forfeited any right to claim to sustain an example of a Christian virtue.

Since hope is one of the three "cardinal virtues" of Christianity along with faith and love (FROM I Corinthians 13) it is specifically a virtue people earn and enhance by following the Word of God and obedience to other virtues. Hence, **Churchill** became a hero of hope by expanding the principles of liberty, freedom, equal rights, specifically the right to live, to pursue happiness, and to raise one's' offspring and share life with friends and family in such an environment. **Lewis** won such accolades by specific obedience to God in an attempt to build Christianity by faith and trust, **King and Peale** by similarly promoting hope in love in their people and extending it to the masses. With hope being both intellectual assent and implicit obedience (therefore reminiscent of faith from Hebrews 13) as well as a loving and helpful action, working toward bringing such positive things to our fellowman, people become heroes of hope by many wise beliefs and choices, but therefore must follow them up with strong and confident action. By making sure these principles get through to society at large, **Reagan, Graham, Robertson, Boone, Falwell, O'Connor, McKinley, Rickey, and Rice-**form a sub-division of heroes of hope who spread a combination of confidence and correct principles to make the truth get out. On this point, few would argue that I presented a distinctly Christian, and particularly Evangelical work-with a decidedly Twentieth Century flavor.

Some have told me that although you will see a very conservative perspective in these pages, I included "liberals" in the book. Numerous heroes including **Wilson, Truman, Miller, Bryan, and Marshall** were (for at least a time in their lives) Democrats. Others like **Thomas and Robertson** were Democrats who at one point questioned their practices, and decided later in life to become Republicans; in the latter case, nothing much changed, he simply decided the wisdom of his *conservative and ethical* principles no longer had a home in the Democratic Party, and so, like **Reagan**, nothing much changed when he went from Democrat to Republican. Ann Coulter is right about this, the modern Democratic Party changed from being the party of **Harry Truman** to the party of Rosie O'Donnell. It is my contention that **Helen Keller and Tony Blair** are the only liberals in the book, but I leave you the reader, to make your own judgments about other specific individuals.

Indeed the bulk of my heroes were chosen for a combination of good things they did in such areas as philanthropy, pulpit ministry, government leadership, military service, and individual accomplishment for people on large and small scales. The military leaders and heroes in fact, did what they did out of support for the general public, and specifically the freedom of people like you and me, our parents, and cousins, and neighbors, great and small, educated and uneducated; to be able to walk the streets, throw Frisbees, eat at Fuddruckers, watch *Degrassi,* play miniature golf, read novels and joke books, cheer for the Cubs and the Jazz, walk home with our fried chicken and Coke in hand, and attend the church of our choice; without fear of harassment from enemies. For that reason, **Joan of Arc, George Marshall, Douglas Macarthur, and Condolezza Rice,** were special for things far more than swords and bullets, but because those swords and bullets brought freedom and improved quality of life. In a few cases, **Winston Churchill, Theodore Roosevelt, Ronald Reagan, Harry Truman, WM McKinley, Marshall, and Rice;** they added a special dimension of being men of leadership in both war and peace *in all but one case-they became three dimensional heroes-men of letters, man of leadership, and man of war. In **Reagan's** case we can add man of God*-making him a four-dimensional hero. As such men and women changed civilization by improving our freedom and right to enjoy the good things we have in life, they made peace and freedom more accessible and even laid the groundwork for it to become (and still be in the process of becoming) the norm in places where it has never been. In America and other democracies they reinforced a true concept of tolerance, the fact *as I alluded to but did not explicitly say* in the text, that only in a "liberal" democracy are things like homosexuality and the practice of religions that differ from the Judeo-Christian truth, can be practiced by members of our fellow democracies who desire. Unlike the kind of liberal tolerance that says we cannot force liberals to a debate about ethics *or even express such preferences, save in the most explicitly religious context,* traditional tolerance says we can allow people to do things we dislike or even consider immoral without saying we have to endorse them. Just as neo-liberals (as opposed to classical liberals) can "tolerate" our practice of conservative religious principles I articulated in this book, we allow our fellow Americans, to live as homosexuals or Muslims, or Scientologists, without embracing it. Heroes of Hope like *Schlesinger, Limbaugh, and Kinchlow,* have pointed out that homosexuals and those of minority faiths, have such protection in America because of our Judeo-Christian principles, while countries that are not democracies do not allow homosexuals and members of religious minorities to peacefully co-exist in large part because they do not expose Christian values that include tolerating what they believe to be detestable and loving those who gave them no tangible reason to love them.

Another legitimate question is why heroes became heroes of hope and by what rating and in what order. I deliberately emphasized this as a work and therefore rated them on how they brought hope into the world or improved hope at times and in places it was lacking or nonexistent. I was asked which of the heroes I like most, and though he is not # 1 in the book I have to say **Ronald Reagan,** since after Jesus Christ, after I strive to pattern my entire life, he is the hero who has most touched me and made me believe that I can be my best and even accomplish things previously denied me. He is not rated number one because I rated all the heroes relative to how much hope they had and how much they gave, relevant to what advantages or disadvantages they had and how well they used it. He was a great hero, and his life exemplified hope with about a **96.7% accolade making him rate a little lower than Churchill, Thatcher, and even Wilson. M**any of the heroes have disabilities, like me, so I rated either sustaining a privileged life with one-**Keller and Tada, or building one previously absent by people including Wilson, Reover, and Dole-**as very important factors to live with hope and bring it to others. For that reason, one of my greatest heroes George W. Bush did not make the list; though I admire almost everything he did before and during his Presidency, because he had many advantages to start, and also his "assistant" **Condolezza Rice** overcame many of the obstacles he never faced. Some of this is reflected in the bonus feature of "junior varsity heroes of hope," since many of these overcame in numerous ways, but less dramatically or excitingly, than the fifty-two. **Churchill and Lewis** are two of my TOP 5-favorites-but are rated even higher because of the specific fact that hope factored more into their lives.

Since faith and love in addition to hope are cardinal virtues, I do intend to write the books "Heroes of Love" and "heroes of Faith" but it will depend on good writers like you insuring the books sell. I also indicate in another bonus feature, that an overwhelming number of people were rated for this book and roughly ten or twelve others got *92% accolades* or a superior rating, enough to make the list, but not to be featured, since I wanted exactly fifty-two heroes.

While I did not talk about myself very much in the text, I try to make myself a positive example, drawing on the fact that hope starts out with creation and the theological and temporal realities in the Bible, but it continues and is sustained in the hearts and minds of you and me. Only by believing in it ourselves and exercising that hope and faith daily can we do the things that are needed to achieve what God has put us on earth for, and to reflect on improving our lives and those of others suffering from a lack of hope and faith. Since hope is less often discussed in church, I wanted to lead off-my career with a book about hope to encourage the reader on this theological virtue. I also usually write far more about disabilities and the Disabled, so this "series" is perhaps the least "Disabled literature" I will write. I also have written and will continue to write large offerings of fiction so I hope both the factual historian as well as the entertaining and innovative novelist came through in this book.

I hope you have experienced this book not merely as a work of history, though history *particular that of hope,* is the primary topic. It is more importantly about why the forty-one men and eleven women became heroes of hope, and for that, I hope you are inspired as well as informed. Finally I hope those of my reader who are not great fans of history, or "politics" have come away with a different perspective that *history* is not names and dates and who killed whom when and where; but that it is all about people, their feelings, their choices, their relationships, and *we faithfully and prayerfully expect* how right prevails over wrong and truth over falsehood. While my heroes are treated with accolades, in fact that is the perspective I used, from the initial ratings all the way through the process of writing this book through two printings and dozens of proofreadings, I did not make them faultless. I saw no need to cover up **Lewis' original wavering, Limbaugh's** drug addiction, the struggle to live the Christian life, or the struggle many met in early years and some continue to meet in their day-to-day lives.

Finally, I will say these brief words about heroes. Since the word seems so specifically Western, English-speaking, and primarily American, this definitely played a role in the writing, that said, the use of the term goes back to ancient times, and every culture and every tradition, in addition to virtually all honest people have had their share of heroes. The Bible uses heroes throughout the text and Paul Johnson has even said the book of Judges (one most people, including educated Christians rarely read) can be termed *the Book of Heroes.* THE heroes in that book shine for overcoming both adversity and faults and the major ones, Ehud, Jeptah, Jepthah, Gideon, and Samson all overcame what would be insurmountable factors in other cultures to lead their people to vicotry. Other Biblical heroes include Abraham, Joseph, Moses, Joshua, Caleb, Samuel, King David, king Solomon, Isaiah, Daniel, John the Baptist, Paul, Peter, James, and John. Biblical women of hero status include Hannah,

Huldah, Deborah, Jael, Mary, Mary Magdalene, Rahab, and Pirsilla. Such heroes demonstrated a willingness to use the faith and other gifts with which God allotted them to win victories and do the best for their people Many of them are similar to the heroes of faith in this book. Another factor these heroes possessed is that all of their lives tended to be ordinary until the point where God chose to use them to be extraordinary. All their lives, years and perhaps decades of preparation were saved up in their minds, until that moment of ultimate triumph came. Many of my heroes, particularly some of the lesser-known ones, like **Keyes, Wilberforce, Fiske, Chambers, and Blackwell** claim that distinction. It may have been a long process of years and decades such heroes prepared for to get them to the place, but when it finally came they were ready to use the gifts God had given them to make the heroic decisions that changed the world. The other irony about lesser known heroes is that they are often reluctant heroes. **Norman Vincent Peale** took a church of a different denomination in a part of the country where he had lived, because he needed to answer a challenge to prove his call to himself and God, not to become rich or famous. Dan Quayle did not seek higher office for its own sake and was as surprised as anyone when he was named to the second highest office. **Dave Reover** did not seek to become the greatest Pentecostal evangelist of his day, and has born the office with quiet dignity. **Ben Kinchlow** did not seek to become cohost on the third highest rated TV show and then begin a controversial ministry in radio and WEB print saying controversial things no one else had the guts to say. **Tony Blair** sought higher office for the sake of its party and specifically recent forebears, not to lead the country into new places where it had never been. **Alan Keyes** spoke the truth to a generation who had known too few highly educated Black leaders and did not set out to be both the most respected of a new generation by the right, and the most loathed of the left. **Elizabeth Blackwell** sought to use medical principles that had worked for men on her generation of women and men and did not really care whether many people knew about it or not. **Whittaker Chambers** told the truth to people who needed to hear it, confronting a generation stagnant after having fought a world war and not really having any desire to hear truths that could send them back to war or at least the imperative to rearm. Even the two crowned heads of state in this book became heroes for doing the very unroayal thing of standing up to oppressors to fight for the poor and the marginalized. Paul Johnson in writing the book *Heroes (COPYRIGHT 2007-HarperCollins publishers,* 10 East, 53rd Street, New York, NY) divides the categories as God's heroes, Earthshakers, War Heroes (IN THE ROAR OF THE Canon's mouth-*Washington, Wellington, and Horatio Nelson), taunted heroes in a man's' world, THE Heroism of the hostess, and heroes of nobility **Lincoln** and* Robert E. Lee. Two other specialized sub-categories are THE TRINITY who tamed the Bear-**Reagan, Thatcher, and** Pope John *Paul, II* and as I did he put **Churchill** in a category all by himself-*a generous hero.* While the two books I have read that are most like this one are the Johnson one and the H. Paul Jeffers, which I cite, the irony was they wrote about the same time I did, and I did not read either one (at least in entirety) before I finished writing my first book, so I can honestly say my inspiration was the Bible and the heroes themselves, other great books by two great men are just coincidentally like mine. As I have been implying; if heroes like **Joan of Arc, Roosevelt, Marshall, and Macarthur** and by extension **Churchill, Reagan, Wilson, McKinley, and Rice** can be a sub-category, heroes of the sword, and Dr. **Laura, Limbaugh, Dobson, and Nightingale can be heroes of the pen** (or in some cases the broadcast booth); a new sub-category including **Keyes, Wilberforce, Fiske, Peale, Reover, Kinchlow, Blair, Blackwell, and Chambers** may be said to give the Twentieth and Twenty-First Century a new dynamic, the *reluctant hero*.

As Paul Johnson asks about the future of heroes since it seems such a past concept both from the reality of Biblical and other ancient heroes as well as the fact that most of our undisputed heroes, including the few modern figures who made all three works mentioned-**Joan of Arc, Lincoln, Churchill, Reagan, and Thatcher** seem so amazingly dated-is there such a thing as heroism for our age for heroes of the future. I hope the other fourteen living heroes in the book-their stories and inspiration-including those of **Schlesinger, Limbaugh, Robertson, Boone, Simmons,** prove the answer is a resounding "yes.!" While many new heroes including explicitly Twenty-First Century ones are popping up and dozens, even thousands are seeking a spot in books, television, radio, the battlefield, and public office, I hope everyone has the great experience of knowing some we call parents, teachers, clergy, neighbors, and friends.

This Was The First Feature
After The Entries-

§

S tudy Questions ABOUT Heroes of Hope: For these study questions T Here are no right or wrong answers, though some will obviously be credited far more than others. The reader is encouraged to think about what he has read and form answers on his ideas and opinions regarding The facts he read in the text. This is especially encouraged if The material is being used for a homeschooling lesson, church discussion groups, or another study such as can be encouraged for college history preparation or entrance exam.

Discussion Questions

1 *How* did Churchill encourage his people during their dark days?
2 In what ways was Winston Churchill an eclectic?
3 In what ways did Churchill's career IS Similar to that of C.S. Lewis? IN what ways do they differ?
4 How did C.S. Lewis become a Christian?
5 How did Martin Luther King become a symbol of the American dream?
6 In what ways was Martin Luther King's life a Christ-centered one?
7 *In* what way did Norman Vincent Peale engage in religion-bating during the 1960 Presidential election?

8 How can it be said that Norman Vincent Peale saw America at her best and worst?

9 To what factors did Norman Vincent Peale attribute his ability to enjoy so much of life?

10 How can it be said that Margaret Thatcher's career was running above the Twentieth Century?

11 Why did Thatcher take her people to war against Argentina?

12 Why did the President of the U.S. support Britain in a war against an American hemisphere country?

13 In what ways did Helen Keller in spite of her disabilities have advantages over others in the situation?

14 How did Lincoln's early life prepare him for his ultimate mission?

15 Why did some people think Lincoln's Senate loss in 1858 was Providential?

16 Why is the Republican Party today called the Party of Lincoln? In what ways shads it remained faithfuls to the objectives of Abraham Lincoln? In what ways has it failed? Explain your answers.

17 *Why did* Lincoln request the White House band play *Dixie* when Robert E. Lee came to the White House? Why does this request bring tears to many eyes but a desire to punch (hopefully a bag) to some fists? Explain what emotions it congers in you.

18 How did Clarence Thomas make the EEOC relevant to peoples' lives?

19 *In what ways is Joni Earaskon Tada's life an example of* mere Christianity?

20 In what ways has Joni differed from other people with disabilities?

21 In what ways has she shared the plight of individuals with disabilities and our community?

22 What are some of the accomplishments of the Reagan Administration?

23 If Ronald Reagan did as I *and millions of other say, save the entire concept of Western civilization,* why have church leaders of every denomination, specifically Evangelical Protestants been

so reluctant to regard him the hero of the Church and acknowledge him as the hero of faith he is?

24 Why is it significant that Dan Quayle was the first Baby Boomer to run on a national ticket?

25 How does Theodore Roosevelt compare to other Presidents?

26 How did Roosevelt come to be compared to people like Hemingway and John Wayne?

27 Why was Lincoln able to win by such a larger margin in 1864 than 1860?

28 Why was Reagan hesitant to become a political candidate in the sixties?

29 Why did four people at the White House refuse to applaud Mother Teresa's speech? What is your reaction to this refusal and its philosophical undertones?

30 Why did many people object to Pat Boone dressing in punk style? How did it affect his relationship with the Christian community? What is your opinion of the event?

31 In what ways did the South lag behind the rest of the country for decades fate the Civil War? Is it still behind the rest of the country in most areas? Explain your answer?

32 In what ways has the party of **Lincoln** formed a big tent while the other party has not? Why do you think that is and what are the ramifications for the country? Why did many lifelong Democrats change after 911?

33 How has American treated Israel since she became a nation in 1948? How has that decision affected us?

34 Why do many people believe living under Communism is a fate worse than death?

35 Why did President Eisenhower not immediately support our Israeli allies when they moved into Egyptian territory? Why did the Soviet Union not immediately supports its client state? IF both superpowers had reacted differently how would it have affected history? Why is Jerusalem an international Holy City?

37 What was unique about the Empire America acquired in 1898?

38 If you could live your life for just one thing what would it be?

39 Who would you call a hero of hope? What qualities or achievements would you expect them to have?

40 In what ways did Tony Blair say his generation is different from all others?

41 How has Rush Limbaugh's career affected America?

42 Why did this writer say even after Limbaugh's addiction, and the proof he took measures to cover it up, he still holds the moral high ground?

43 How did Queen Wilhelmina become a hero of hope to her people from exile in England?

44 Why has the issue of homeschooling been dealt with more reasonably on talk radon than in the mainstream media?

45 *Why did* Dr. Dobson refuse to run for President in 2000? IF he had how would it have affected the overall process in your opinion?

46 *How* does the statement that heterosexual men rarely form close meal friendships relate to day-to-day reality?

47 *How would you define male friendship?* DO married men define it differently from single men? Do Christians define it differently from non-Christians?

48 How did Harry Truman's life from 1948 on become an example of the American dream?

49 *Besides World* War II how did Truman's career affect America?

50 *What* set Tony Blair apart from other European leaders of his time?

51 *In* what ways was Blair's work with Bush an example of globalism? In what ways was it an example of exclusivity?

52 How did Jerry Falwell change his career and his ministry in the late 1970s?

53 *Why* did Jerry Falwell become the leader of the organization that became Moral Majority? Were these good reasons? Why or why not? For other reasons should Falwell have still been the man with that leadership?

54 *In* what ways is electing godly candidates to public office similar to building the Kingdom of God? In what ways are they different? Can both be done effectively at the same time?

55 Why was Bob Dole chosen to run for Vice-President in 1976? Why was the election so close?

56 How did James Dobson's career change from a Christian journalist to a national pacesetter?

57 *In* what ways can a layman who stands out for Jesus lose privileges or opportunities in the secular world?

58 Why was it impressive for Dole to discuss his Disability status in 1996?

59 <u>Why</u> did Cardinal O'Connor way it is always wrong to protest religious meetings? Do you agree? Why or why not?

60 In what ways did George Marshall choose to come down on the side of forgiveness?

61 *How would the world be different today* if the separation of Korea issue had dealt with successfully in the 1950s?

62 How would the world have been different if similar issues could have ended the tension between Taiwan and mainland China?

63 How did Japan make such a swift transition from militant dictatorship to democracy?

64 Why was Macarthur removed from command in the Far East? Was that the correct decision in your opinion? Explain your answer.

65 If William Jennings Bryan did not agree with fighting World War I why did he volunteer for service? 66 In what ways can joking about a disability be beneficial for the listeners?

67 In what ways is such joking different from mild or routine humor?

68 In what ways did Florence Nightingale help shape the modern world?

69 In what ways is the world better today because there are women doctors?

70 Why did this writer say without reservations, he always knew the allegations about American soldiers desecrating the Koran were not true?

71 What jobs are in Condolezza Rice's future? Explain your answer.

72 Since Poland has been on the receiving end of much of the worst of the Twentieth Century, why have they been so quick to break out of the victim mode and became a Twenty-First Century democracy?

73 Is Richard Simmons an entertainer, a serious writer, and scholar or somewhere in between?

74 In what ways was Whittaker Chambers the quintessential American cowboy?

75 Why is Communism an evil system? Why do conservatives object to the frequent statement that Communism looks good on paper?

76 How did Branch Rickey become the first Civil Rights heroes of the Twentieth Century?

77 Why do sports figures sometimes have influence that other professionals and public digress do not?

78 In what way was Christian X's leadership and his work for his country of importance comparable with all other leaders of World War II Including **Churchill?**

Trivia Questions

1 How many Times did Winston Churchill escape from The Boers at Pretoria?
2 Who succeeded Churchill as Prime minister The first time?
3 Who was President of The United States when Churchill died?
4 Who was President of USA when C S Lewis was born?
5 What fictional land did The Penvise children visit?
6 What was The name of The typical figure of Christ in that land?
7 What is The land of Lewis' science fiction series?
8 Martin Luther King attended colleges in what two cities of The United States?
9 Norman Vincent Peale was born and raised in what U.S. city?
10 In what Year was Dr. King assassinated?
11 Norman Vincent Peale knew every President of the United States starting with whom?
12 What did Peale say was The greatest invention of his lifetime?
13 What was Margaret Thatcher's husband's name?
14 Prime minister Thatcher launched a war to protect what island of the British Empire?
15 How many years did Mrs. Thatcher serve as Prime minister?
16 Clarence Thomas is a native of what state?
17 How old was Judge Thomas when he made it to The Supreme Court?
18 C.S. Lewis' wife was a native of what state?
19 How old was Ronald Reagan when he became President?

20 Who was The first Republican Jerry Falwell endorsed for President?

21 Jerry Falwell was almost shouted down on The steps of The capitol building in what state?

22 What was The name of The musical The Moral Majority took across The nation?

23 How many kids did Billy and Ruth Graham have?

24 The only church Billy Graham ever pastored is in what state?

25 Pat Robertson finished third in The GOP nominations for President in what year?

26 Billy Fiske was a champion of what sport?

27 What was Pat Robertson's large media station called over the years he owned it?

28 Name one new word or phrase Rush Limbaugh has added to The English language?

29 Harry Truman's rivals had a song they were ready to sing to congratulate what Presidential contender?

30 Pat Boone starred in The *Cross and The Switchblade* as a minister of what denomination?

31 Ben, Corrine, and Tucker are the children of what hero of hope?

32 Dr. Laura's flagship radio station is in what city?

33 S.I. Hayakawa transformed himself from mild-mannered educator to conservative icon during his teaching at what college?

34 Herbert Hoover is a native and only President from what state?

35 Besides Orrin Hatch, what two senators spooked against Bill Clinton's behavior before it became politically correct to do so?

36 Who was the chief prosecutor for The U.S. at the war crimes Tribunal in Nuremberg?*

37 Who was The first president of Israel?

38 Who was governor of Georgia before Zell Miller?

39 What is the name of Jerry Falwell's autobiography?

40 What is James Dobson's wife's name?

41 Richard Simmons was born in what state?

42 How many years did Tony Blair serve as Prime minister?

43 Whittaker Chambers became famous in part for "outing" what government figure?

44 Herbert Hoover was known for all The following except: a he could speak Chinese fluently b an avid fisherman c friend of his political rival Franklin D. Roosevelt d strict Constitutioanlist

45 Who did Harry Truman prefer to have as his successor for President?

46 What city did Douglas MacArthur visit his first time back in America in twelve years?

47 Why did Cincinnati change The name of their baseball team?

48 Branch Rickey previously managed what team, before The Dodgers?

49 Anticommunism was a major theme of all The following except a. John Wayne b. Ernest Hemingway c Scoop Jackson d Pablo Picasso

50 Florence Nightingale was named in honor of what?

51 How old was Condolezzza Rice when she became a Princeton provost?

52 What major position was Dr. Rice first given in the Bush Administration?

Answers to Trivia 1. two 2. Clement Attlee 3 LBJ 4 William McKinley 5 Narnia 6 Aslan7Perelanda 8 Boston and Philadelphia 9 Cincinnati 10 1968 11 Theodore Roosevelt 12 air conditioning 13 Denis (spelling not required though it seems to be the preferred British spelling) 14 Falkland Islands 15 almost twelve years (accept 11 or 12)16 Georgia 17 forty-four 18 New York 19 sixty-nine 20 Eisenhower (not intended to be a trick question, but putting up a sign or bumper sticker is an endorsement, we all have that power) 21 Wisconsin 22 *I Love America* 23 five 24 Illinois 25 1988 26 bobsledding 27 The Family Channel 28 may have harmless little fuzzball bundle of mush, maggot infested FM-crowd, Yutt, bleeding-heart liberal, drive-by media. Advanced conservative studies, illustrating absurdity by being absurd, and with half my brain tied behind my back (no one should miss this question with all The possible answers) 29 Tom Dewey 30 Assemblies of God 31 Dan Quayle 32 Los Angeles 33 San Francisco State (OR University) 34 Iowa 35 John Ashcroft and Ben Nighthorse Campbell 36 *Francis Biddle (this question like The following one is very hard since I only mentioned it in passing,* *if you are scoring in some way give yourself extra if you get this and the next one) 37 Chiam Weitzman* 38 Jimmy Carter 39 *Strength for The Journey 40.* Shirley 41 Louisiana 42a little less than twelve years and just a few weeks shy of Thatcher's record 43 Alger Hiss 44 c 45 Adlai Stevenson 46 San Francisco 47 to avoid being called "Reds" as in Communists 48 St. Louis Cardinals 49 d. 50 The town in which she was born-Geneva, Italy 51 36 52 chief security advisor/liaison

Matching Quiz

M atch the Hero of Hope with The following Clues:(Aces and Face cards)

1 Winston Churchill

2 C.S. Lewis

3 Martin Luther King

4 Norman Vincent Peale

5 Margaret Thacher

6 Clarence Thomas

7 Dan Quayle `

8 Billy Graham

9 Helen Keller

10 Woodrow Wilson

11 Joan of Arc

12 Abraham Lincoln

13 Mother Teresa

14 Ronald Reagan

15 Theodore Roosevelt

16 Pat Boone

a launched a preventive war with Argentina

b served on term in Congress from a Whig district

c served on D.C. Court of Appeals

d succeeded by William Howard Taft

e peasant girl from a small village

y. *April Love*

z. Just as I AM

aa This Incredible Century

bb *That Hideous Strength*

cc held Florida campaign with Billy Graham,

f started institute for health with a man named Smiley

g encouraged people to forget their age

h father pastored Presbyterian churches

j. presented oral arguments in *Clark v. Vinson*

j. appointed Clarence Thomas head of EEOC

k grew up in North Carolina

l pastor of Marble Hill Collegiate Church

m only illiterate in The series

n *the Business of Heaven*

o. called America The last best hope

p said Reagan won The Cold War

q. penetrated The Iron Curtain and North Korea

r buried IN Washington D C

s performed wedding of President Eisenhower's grandson

t *Cross and The Switchblade*

u. raised by grandparents, taught by nuns

v. helped destroy apartheid in South Africa

dd Pax Americana

ee serious basketball fan

ff spoke a timeless message to all nations

gg Bedtime for Bonzo

hh refused to perform sex scenes

ii spoke out against abortion at White House dinner

jj humiliated by Lloyd Bentzen but threw it back in face

kk Indian citizen

ll married an abrasive New Yorker

mm believed to be learning disabled

nn sang "Paradise City" in all black attire

oo. Reassured occupied nations of Europe

pp helped save Christmas by saving eggnog

qq was a Post Millennialist

rr knew 16 Presidents

ss.son of Jennie Jerome

tt. Let every vile insult no matter how unfair roll off back

w. mentioned in theme song of *Maude*

x. Could be The oldest and first Pentecostal President

WW served in The Army Reserves in World War I

XX refused to play dominoes with Russians

YY born in Kentucky

ZZ worked for John Danforth

aaa supported by Strom Thrumond and Arlen Specter

bbb asthma attacks in both youth and adulthood

ccc launched The most overlooked crucial war in U.S. history

ddd Modesto Manifesto

eee *A New Song*

fff jailed for violations of minor traffic laws

ggg lived ninety-five years

hhh died right after his ninety-third birthday

iii youngest American to serve as President

jjj JN Roberts got job some say he deserved

uu New Yorker on Mount Rushmore

vv took fledgling republic to leader of The world

lll announcer for The Cubs

mmm spent three hours in prayer every morning

nnn used a bully pulpit to rake The mud

ooo *Letters to Children*

ppp laid ten thousand bricks

qqq ran first highly charged campaign at age-73

rrr football coach

sss. Friends with Booker T. Washington

ttt. New York City police commissioner

uuu sang Michigan song in a Fascist's movie

vvv born in Alabama

www preached to integrated audiences in land of apartheid

xxx in his youth he told overly curious reporters what The President said

yyy both praised and condemned Lenin

Matching answers to the first 16 heroes of Hope

a. Thatcher	aa Peale	aaa Thomas
b Lincoln	bb Lewis	bbb Roosevelt
c Thomas	cc King	ccc Reagan
d Wilson	dd Wilson	ddd Graham
E Joan of Arc	ee Boone	eee Boone
f Peale	ff Graham	fff King
g Peale	gg Reagan	ggg Peale
h Wilson	hh Boone	hhh Reagan
i Thomas	ii Mother Teresa	iii Roosevelt
j Reagan	jj Quayle	jjj Thomas
k Graham	kk Mother Teresa	kkk Graham
l Peale	ll Lewis	lll Reagan
m Joan of Arc	mm Wilson	mmm Mother Teresa
n Lewis	nn Boone	nnn Roosevelt
o Lincoln	oo Churchill	ooo Lewis
p Thatcher	pp Reagan	ppp Churchill
q Graham	qq Wilson	qqq Reagan
r Wilson	rr Peale	rrr Wilson
s Peale	ss-Churchill	sss Roosevelt
t Boone	tt-Quayle	ttt Roosevelt
U Thomas	uu Roosevelt	uuu Boone
V Reagan	vv Roosevelt	vvv Keller
W Joan of Arc	ww Peale	www Graham
X Boone	yy Lincoln	yyy Keller
Y Boone	zz Thomas	
Z Graham		

Match The hero of Hope with The following clues-And note 1stThe term "pre-scientific" was from a General Psychology book whose author I do not know said-"B.S." stands for "Before Science" and I have been saying it ever since-a pre-scientific is something that is B.S.

1 Pat Robertson	13 Rush Limbaugh (29)	25 William McKinley (41)
2 Alan Keynes (18)	14 WM Jennings Bryan (30)	26 Christian X (42)
3 Dr. Laura Schlessinger (19)	15 John J O'Connor (31)	27 Fanny J. Crosby (43)
4 Billy Fiske (20)	16 WM Wilberforce (32)	28 Douglas MacArthur (44)
5 Joni Earakson Tada (21)	17 Queen Wilhelmina (33)	29 Herbert Hoover (45)
6 S I Hayakawa (22)	18 Jerry Falwell (34)	30 Nathan Hale (46)
7 Orrin Hatch (23)	19 James Dobson (35)	31 Bob Dole (47)
8 Zell Miller (24)	20 Ben Kinchlow (36)	32 Whittaker Chambers
9 Dave Reover (25)	21 George Marshall	33 Branch Rickey
10 Harry S Truman (26)	22 Edward Flanagan (38)	34 Florence Nightingale
11 Tony Blair (27)	23 Lech Walesa	35 Elizabeth Blackwell
12 Ben Gurion (28)	24 Richard Simmons (40)	36 Condolezza Rice (52)

a. worked with Catholics, Baptists, Mormons and Jews believers and unbelievers to circle precincts and establish huge computer mailing list

b righted wrong after friend simulated color change

c wanted a sword to make North Korea and China act like Japan

d converted to Judaism in part after seeing TV documentary

e Bring It on

f Language in Thought and Action

g divided world into good VS Evil countries

h went to battle against two most powerful countries at The time

i no more Jewish than Mickey Mouse

j went horseback riding almost daily

k colonel in The Civil War

l helped smuggle Bibles behind The Iron Curtain m lived and did Christian service in Nebraska

n helped wounded servicemen in Turkey

o started a fitness revolution

p took 100% pay cut when he became President

1 fifty-eight Year military career

r pastor of Thomas Road Baptist Church

s born in Western Canada

t hosted 2nd most popular radio talk show

u From Cape Guirdeau, Missouri

v hosted "Pat Sajak Show"

w The Great Lakes Mission

x plays piano by ear y revitalized talk radio

z would do his part in Vietnam if asked

aa chose a Native American Vice-President

bb stood up to proteseters at Mass

cc *His Eminence and Hizzoner*

dd born in Ireland

ee owned a hat shop

ff "African-American Ed McMahon"

gg wrote a foreword for Tammy Bruce

hh named after both grandfathers

ii removed jungle brush

jj Rushmore Coffee Company

kk disguised as Dutch schoolmaster

ll denied being homosexual

mm spiritual leader of 3 million Catholics

nn pronounces The word "youth" like its an Indian tribe

oo relocated ministry to Colorado

pp Proper Care and Feeding of Husbands

qq led a military that includes Pentecostals, Presbyterians, Cubans, and Muslims

rr Remington Rand Corporation

ss national award from Food for The Hungry

tt-sued mayor in a dispute between friends

uu took over Praise The Lord Ministries

vv supported Parents and Friends of Lesbians and Gays

ww worked as a janitor in college

xx held newspaper that gave false election results

yy never been to Idaho or Nevada but always wanted to go*

zz brought Hawaii into USA

aaa mother of Julianne

bbb helped establish Scottish parliament

ccc jumped on mobile sound truck and pulled out all the cords

ddd his brother ran for Vice-President

eee sweats to the oldies

fff mentioned by Archie Bunker in theme song

ggg Methodist deacon

hhh only woman at the medical school

iii could as easily be NFL commissioner or Vice-President

kkk the New Britain

mmm offered to pay opponent's fine

ooo Catholic layman who preached in terms associated with pulpit pounding Evangelical ministers

qqq liberal lion helped raise cubs from Poland to Guatemala

sss toughest "grandma dog" in the hospital

uuu *When God Doesn't Make Sense*

www Pennsylvanian married to an Arkansan

yyy *founder of Moral Majority*

AAAA *went to Washington with Orrin Hatch and* Paul Laxalt

CCCC would not congratulate pro-abortion senator

eeee in better health in sixties and seventies than before

GGGG helped revitalize Georgia and other Southern states

jjj A National Party no More

lll liberal praised mainly by conservatives since 911

nnn called television the "electronic babysitter"

ppp answered pre-scientific charges against U S soldiers

rrr youngest provost at Princeton

ttt pioneer of sexual healing

vvv *Father of British Christian Parliamentary wing*

xxx *disagreed with The President about troops in Korea*

zzz *broke neck on a Maryland beach*

BBBB "my life has been a series of miracles"

dddd founder of a modern nation

FFFF Gary Bauer ran for President in part because he declined running

hhhh carried torch in 2002 Olympics

JJJJ Paul Weyerich was his "part-time mentor"

LLLLL first "big boy" to take small states' concerns national mmmm *Amazing Grace*

OOOO Last President to take The oath in The Twentieth Century

qqqq answered a birthday card from Hitler

ssss featured in The *Hiding Place* film

kkkk hosted The 1996 Olympics

nnnn prayed for guidance to help Christianize a "semi-civilized" people

PPPP lost to our first four-term President

rrrr spoke to people in exile from England

tttt only modern politician to speak at both Republican and Democratic national conventions

Answers

a Falwell	aa Hoover	yy Blair	xxx MacArthur
b Rickey	bb O'Connor	cc O'Connor	yyy Falwell
c MacArthur	dd Flanagan	ee Truman	zzz Tada
d Schlessinger	ff Kinchlow	gg Schlessinger	AAAA Hayakawa
e Robertson	hh Truman	ii Rice	BBBB Hatch
f Hayakawa	jj Miller	kk Blair	CCCC Keyes
g Truman	ll Simmons	mm O'Connor	DDDD Gurion
h Chambers	nn Limbaugh	oo Dobson	EEEE Robertson
i Christian X	pp Schlessinger	qq Rice	FFFF Dobson

j Christian X	rr MacArthur	ss Falwell	GGGG Falwell
k McKinley	tt O'Connor	uu Falwell	HHHH Walesa
L Kinchlow	vv Schlessinger	ww Hatch	IIII Miller
m Flanagan	xx Truman	yy Blair	JJJJ Miller
n Nightingale	zz McKinley	aaa Wilhelmina	KKKK Walesa
o Simmons	bbb Blair	ccc Hayakawa	LLLL Hatch
p Hoover	ddd Bryan	eee Simmons	MMMM Wilberforce
q MacArthur	fff Hoover	ggg Miller	NNNN McKinley
R Falwell	hhh Blackwell	iii Rice	OOOO McKinley
s Hayakawa	jjj Miller	kkk Blair	PPPP Hoover
t Schlessinger	lll Blair	mmm Bryan	QQQQ Christian, X
u Limbaugh	nnn Hayakawa	ooo Rice	RRRR Wilhelmina
v Limbaugh	ppp Rice	qqq Blair	SSSS Wilhelmina
w Hatch	rrr Rice	sss Nightingale	TTTT Miller
x Reover	ttt Blackwell	uuu Dobson	
y Limbaugh	vvv Wilberforce	www Marshall	
z Simmons			

• *And as a brief message to Tony Blair now that your active service as head of Her Majesty's government is over, next time you are in The States I would love for you to look me up and we can see some wonderful places I know in Nevada and Idaho together.*

Second Bonus Feature:

§

*T*hese are heroes whose heroism is undisputed, but who did not merit entries in The text. A special group of heroes is recognized here for what they did in three very important circumstances that did not get more than a cursory mention in The text. I make note here that three of The greatest Presidents, in our history, each a hero of hope, was The target of an assassination attempt. Though each was a hero before and after The attempt, as well as in part for survival. As they came dangerously close to losing their lives, The men who saved them are heroes in their own right, if it were not for them, many of the achievements of the heroes of hope may not have been possible.

In 1912 **Theodore Roosevelt was** running for a third term, when a mentally deranged gunman named James F. Schrank shot him in Milwaukee. Since he had fifty pages of his speech ready to be delivered, it may be said The paper or even his longwindedness, was the first thing that saved him that day, since the bullet hit the papers. He gave the speech as planned, and a doctor in the audience, *Dr. John B. Murphy* gave him first aid. Presidents did not have full-time security detail at the time, and Dr. Murphy could not pinpoint the exact location of the bullet, in relation to the heart, and he did not want to make the mistake that was made on President Garfield, in which probing of internal organs, led him to eventually bleed to death, from his wounds, he suggested the Rough Rider see his friend, *Dr. Joseph Bloodgood in* Chicago. The appropriately named Chicago surgeon graduated from Johns Hopkins University, quite possibly the only one at the time that equipped doctors to operate on such injuries, but he refused to operate on the twenty-sixth President's heart, and his wise decision may have helped prolong **TR's** life, but leaving The bullet in him, may have made him more susceptible to a stroke and The technology of The time was inadequate to treat both.

In March, 1950 members of a minority Puerto Rican separatist group opened fire around the White House when President **Harry Truman was** expecting to be commuting from the rose garden to give a speech a few miles away. After an unusually long lunch, the thirty-third President was taking a nap ironically if he had not been in his room, he would have much sooner been prepared and therefore walked into gunfire. Again, The irony was his being saved partly by circumstances he could not predict or control. Two Secret Service agents were shot as were the two terrorists who recovered in prison- *excuse me, but are we the only country who cures men who try to shoot the President and kill officers of the law! Donald Birdzell and Joseph Downs* were shot but eventually made full recoveries. When the President realized that men in his service were taking bullets intended for him, he (with The Secret Service behind him) ran down from his room to the scene of the crime. He saw Agent Leslie Coffelt fighting for his life and he encouraged the doctors to take him to the emergency room immediately. *Special Agent Coffelt* became the only American Secret serviceman to die in the duty of protecting the President of the United States. A hero, almost too good to serve his country and his President, one of the few consolations to his family may be the name he earned from this distinction.

On March 30, 1981, a mentally deranged man obsessed with actress Jodie Foster, and the movie *Taxi Driver,* took a gun to the White House. As the fortieth President, **Ronald Reagan** was leaving The stage after giving a speech, the man rushed toward The President and fired approximately eight bullets. One hit "Rawhide" making him the only sitting President to survive a bullet wound. *Jerry Parr,* a Secret Service agent who pushed **Dutch** into the vehicle, became the first to save the President's life that day. T*im McCarthy, a* Secret Service agent got in front of the President to deflect the bullet, and was shot in the arm but made a full recovery. White House press secretary *Jim Brady (1930-)* a career public servant from Central Illinois was shot in the back and remains paralyzed on the right side from the neck down. Washington D.C. Officer *Tim Delahanty was shot* on the left arm but recovered. Washington University surgeon, *Dr. Joseph Giordano* saved the President's life by operating on him, as heroic as his recovery, it could just as easily have gone the other way, few people then knew how close we came to losing the *Gipper* and he was restored to health under the authority of university department head *Dr. Benjamin Aaron.*

The Third Set Of Extra Features -Also-Rans And Near Misses

§

*P*eople *who did not make Heroes of Hope-but just as well could have: Lafayette, J. Edgar Hoover, Joseph McCarthy, Nicky Cruz, Spiro Agnew, J.C. Watts, Dwight D. Eisenhower, Thomas Jefferson, Paul Laxalt,* David Limbaugh, Steve Largent,

The following are *Near Misses: They did not make The Heroes of Hope entries in spite of a superior rating: SEE The Glossary-LIKE THOSE I identify there I will almost certainly write about them in future works:* Susan B. Anthony, Shimon Peres, Moshe Dyan, Carrie Chattman Catt, Haley Barbour, Chaim Weitzman, and Chaing-Kai-shek.

As noted before, four heroes of hope won The Nobel Peace Prize (one won a Nobel Prize for literature) though the two men who most deserve prizes for making peace, **Winston Churchill and Ronald Reagan** were not awarded by The European committee, and people like *George W. Bush, **Tony Blair, and Condolezza Rice** also deserve* to be nominees if not Nobel Prize winners but probably never will with the committee's general liberalism. We never know who promotes peace, or even good literature anymore since often not being nominated for an award says something more impressive about you than being nominated-*especially when silly geese like Jimmy Carter and Barak Obama can win it.*

Lech Walesa is the fifth hero of hope to be a Nobel Prize winner. *Heroes of Hope who won The Presidential Medal of Freedom: Churchill, Billy Graham, Margaret Thatcher, Reagan,* **Blair-5th non-American** *Whittaker Chambers, and Bob Dole.*

Mother Teresa is The sixth Nobel Prize winner in this book, but at least four other Americans won the award in between **George Marshall and Mother Teresa.**

Theodore Roosevelt won a Congressional Medal of honor for The Spanish-American War, but it was not recognized until over a hundred years after his exploits.

NOTE-Twenty-seven people are in both this book and my next work-"American All-Stars" **Martin Luther King, Norman Vincent Peale, Clarence Thomas, Dan Quayle, Ronald Reagan, Abraham Lincoln, Harry Truman, Bob Dole, Herbert Hoover, Orrin Hatch, Pat Robertson, Billy Fiske, Rush Limbaugh, Alan Keyes, Woodrow Wilson, John Cardinal O'Connor, George Marshall, Douglas Macarthur, William Jennings Bryan, William McKinley, Fanny J. Crosby, Whittaker Chambers, Nathan Hale, Branch Rickey, Condolezza Rice, DR Laura Schlesinger, and Helen Keller.**

Places of Heroes of Hope: 2 heroes of Hope came from Alabama, 4 from Virgina, 2 from Connecticut, and 2 from Georgia. Four are Texans

6 came from New York

3 from Pennsylvania 3 from Ohio 2 from *Illinois* 2 from Missouri 2 from Nebraska

1 EACH FROM Massachusetts Arkansas, Iowa, Kansas, Louisiana, North Carolina, New Jersey, Florida, *Utah* California

Countries with one or more: ***6 from The United Kingdom***

1 each from Albania, India, Canada, Denmark, France,Israel,The Netherlands Poland, Ireland

Notice that several heroes of hope are counted as being from more than one state or country. That is perfectly legitimate as I count myself as being from Illinois and Utah, **President Ronald Reagan** never stopped being a Midwesterner from Illinois, but he was in every sense a man of The West, namely California. Lyndon Jonson was from Texas, but he was more a man of Washington D.C. George H. W. Bush was from Massachusetts and Texas, *George W.* is as much a Texan as one can be, but he was born in Connecticut. I only counted **Churchill** *once* though he is American with Dutch and Iroquois ancestry and spent some of his middle years in Dundee, Scotland (he also lived two-and-a-half years in India). When we think about **Churchill**, we can only see him as an Englishman (and even he commented on his overall identity) that he must be thoroughly an Englishman just as *bacon* and *eggs* can be lunch or dinner, but we primarily think of them as breakfast. **Douglas MacArthur** is counted as Arkansas and Texas, as with many military people he never felt at home until his teenage years in Texas, but he also lived in Washington D.C., The Philippines, Australia, and Japan, and many would say he was as good an Asian as a lot of Asians, just as **Churchill** was a better American than most Americans, but I counted him once and MAC twice. I also counted **James Dobson** as being from Texas since he graduated from high school there and considers it his home. **S.I. Hayakawa, as American as apple pie and Californians,** to many can never stop being Canadian.

A question for me might be what hero of hope is mentioned the most times in the book *As you may have guessed, it is Ronald* **Reagan** *mentioned seventy-eight times in addition to his entry. His closest competitor,* **Churchill was** *mentioned thirty-two times in addition to his entry,* **Theodore Roosevelt** *takes the bronze medal for twenty-five mentions outside his entry,* **Truman was mentioned** *twenty-four times outside his entry, and* **Lincoln nineteen** *times. The "booby prize" for least mentions, one outside their entries was tied by,* **Billy Fiske, Dr. Laura Schlesinger, Zell Miller, Dave Reover, David ben Gurion, and Elizabeth Blackwell.**

Definitions

terms defined and a glossary of people identified

abilities blindness-to my knowledge this series is The first use of The term, but like colorblindness means a person can be familiar with individuals Within a group without and (in the one case is not conscious of the person's color or ethnicity) in the case of abilities blindness a person can be friends (or in another sense can compete-in such things as a political election) with people who are different from themselves and and you can be very intellectually cognizant without bearing conscious of The fact that your friends, dates, or potential mates; or those of your friends and family, have one of various disabilities. You can like such people not because of their disabilities nor in spite of them, but simply know them and their disabilities separately. As with colorblindness it has its heroes, Bill Cosby, **Martin Luther King**, and **Clarence Thomas** became champions of colorblindness-as an aside President Barak Obama could have been an example of colorblindness, instead he became one of the worst examples of color consciousness, though he was not an evil man like Bill Clinton nor an antisemitic Fascist like some of his supporters, *heroes of abilities blindness can be said to include **Joni Earakson Tada, Helen Keller, and Bob Dole.***

ADA-The Americans with Disabilities Act-signed into law by George Herbert Walker Bush, in 1990 mandating that no person can be discriminated against do to a disability, mental or "physical" "real or perceived" for any institution that receives government funds or any business that employs at least fifteen people the Act guarantees the Disabled equal access to hiring and equality under The law largely to level The playing field that throughout history has not been equal It mandates that no person may be discriminated against for otherwise qualifying work, so applicants must demonstrate an ability to perform tasks while a disability is not to be broguth up or considered as a factor for employment. The Act also requires that the Disabled have access to legally qualifying amenities like such as buses, telephones, and medical insurance.

altar call-the part of a Christian service in many denominations particularly Baptists and Pentecostals also called the "invitation" where participants are asked to "come forward" and make a decision for Christ. While altar calls are largely geared toward the unconverted to get them saved through Jesus Christ, other times altar calls are used to encourage the congregants to pray about certain matters especially in settings where all or virtually all of The congregants is already saved such as a Christian school. While there is nothing in the Bible about giving an altar call, neither is there anything forbidding it, so it can be Biblical, while a direct invitation to come to Christ is always pertinent to your audience. **Billy Graham** has made The altar call an indispensable part of Evangelical services, while others taking an older cue from the Puritans who helped establish this country, take the opposite view later championed by Karl Barth that The preacher should simply proclaim The Gospel and let each person decide on his own reaction amendment-a change and in terms of written constitutions it is something written in and made to change laws or otherwise improve on a document Since written constitutions are by their very nature intended to be based on ironclad laws they are fundamentally hard to change The U.S. constitution can only be amended by a vote of two-thirds of The states or two thirds of both houses of Congress. The first series of amendments was passed in 1789 with The vote of eleven states and signed into law by two men George Washington and Fredrick Muhlenberg the first speaker of The U.S. House of Representatives. So controversial was changing The Constitution then, as now that two of the original thirteen states refused to vote for something so basic, because it could put federal restrictions on state legislatures. Since then not one of those basic rights has been changed, though congresses and courts have occasionally altered laws to make it apply to states. Since then, the seventeen Times The Constitution has been amended in two hundred and twenty-one years have included to outlaw slavery, guarantee voting rights to women and to all citizens, extend citizenship rights to all born and naturalized Americans, and lower The voting age. The point is very clear, The federal Constitution is such a sacred document, it can be amended only in extreme measures with a mandate from both legislating branches of government apartheid-bizarre and evil system in South Africa from 1948-1994 in which race was The deciding factor in which rights a person had, basically white versus non-white South Africans It was instituted by The Nationalist Party and despite worldwide opposition it was defended by South African governments as a necessary bulwark against Communism or centuries-old tribal fighting, and The Communists used it as a propaganda technique, one of The West's darlings has such a cruel system-(Jan C. Smuts the first president under the apartheid system was actually a founding member of The U.N. who served in **Churchill's** wartime cabinet). After worldwide opposition and sanctions they gradually gave rights to non-Blacks until 1994 when Fredrick W. DeKlerk dismantled The apartheid system and held The first national election, one-person-one-vote.

Axis Powers-originally from The Rome/Berlin Axis, expected to shape Europe, it became the name of the countries opposed to The Allies in World War II, Germany, Japan, Italy, and a few satellites and supporters backlash-a reaction to an undesired act often in a political context backslide-to fall away, turn from one's faith, or to digress on issues of morality. *Christians tradition frequently uses The term but it divides us, people who believe in Arminian theology, especially from Wesley on to his offshoots, believe that a backslidden person is one who has (voluntarily) walked out of God's gracious arms and therefore is no longer a born-again believer, unless he comes back, he is he is outside The grace of God and must get saved and "rededicate" his life to Jesus or be outside God's grace. People who follow The Calvinistic tradition (see below)* typically believe in "eternal security" that once a person is saved, he is always saved and cannot get out of The grace of God, even by personal choice. Since this is not a theology work I did not deal with The issue in The main text, but I believe some backslidden people have fallen away from The grace of God, and while my (especially Baptist) brothers will tell me God has adopted us, and no matter what their sons do, they are still their sons, I counter to say that some sons ought to be disowned by their father, if Charles Manson were a relative of mine, I would have no contact with him and would even support his execution.

Baby Boom-time period between 1945-1964 after The GIs returned from The war and had many children quickly in a short period of time In 1946 it had The second highest number of births of any Year in American history. While The Baby Boomers eventually became the leaders, their generation spanned The first culture to grow up with TV and mass media marketing, and gave them a distinctive culture unknown to previous generations bishop-though an office of prestige in many churches, among The Latter-day Saints, he is a lay officer in The Church for a neighborhood ward, chosen by a vote and called to serve for a limited time.

Boer-the Afrikaans word for farmers so called all European (primarily Dutch) immigrants to South Africa, though when The Boer War was fought in The 1890s, less than 4% were farmers The name has been retained for historical significance and is synonymous with "Africans speaking South African" bully pulpit-first applied to **Theodore Roosevelt,** *a symbol of power, allowing* The user, usually The President of the United States to loudly proclaim matters of morality important to him, a form of moral authority especially recognized to have his moral judgments in the public eye, always being preached to The people.

Calvinistic-a branch of Christian theology that deals with salvation and God's predestination, with The motto *Salvation is of The Lord.* While non-Calvinistic Christians usually believe that to, and non-Calvinists sometimes take a position for "free will" The key doctrine of their Arminian counterparts, Calvinistic Christians tend to emphasize the sovereignty of God over The free will of man. There are *not necessarily any churches or schools of thought that can always be deemed Calvinistic or non-Calvinistic, though The Presbyterian and Reformed fellowships were founded on Calvinism, while the Roman Catholic Church strongly rejects it as a system of theology, since it was of course a new theory of Protestants.* Most Episcopals, Pentecostals, Quakers, Mennonites, and Lutherans see little use or positive improvement from the Calvinistic school of theory, while The Seventh-day Adventist church as well as Wesleyans and the Salvation Army have made its repudiation part of their theology. Many Baptists believed a modified view of Calvinism which emphasizes salvation *is of The Lord, but also rejects irresistible grace and The idea that Jesus died only for some sinners. There are five point Calvinists* often expressed with The TULIP acronym- for-*total depravity, unconditional* election, *limited* atonement, *irresistible* grace, and the *perseverance* of the saints with The impossibility of apostasy. While most Baptists and Methodists adamantly deny being Calvinistic, and follow an Arminian school of theology after Dutch theologian Jacobus Arminius, the Calvinistic branch of theology has gained great influence and influenced all The Church in four centuries.

Canonize-literally means "to make one a saint" and in the strictest sense of the word only Catholics and the Eastern branch of orthodoxy believe in and practice it, with a lower case "C" it can be used more generically to mean make saintly, or glorify, or venerate a hero, who may or may not be deceased.

Civil Rights-basic rights, from birth granted to all citizens. Meant to guarantee equal opportunity; The U S Constitution was intended to apply Civil Rights to everybody but in reality until recently only white men and in some places only white Protestants, had them granted. The Civil War was fought in part to give Civil Rights, but it required nine subsequent decades of things like marches, and demonstrations to secure Civil Rights for all Black Americans. Until 1934 The senior race on this continent generally did not have them (although thousands made it through assimilation), and until the last decades of the Twentieth Century, women, the Disabled, and some other groups were still agitating for equal rights. *Today all Americans and groups should be grateful for the contributions to Civil Rights, starting with the Founding Father, and* **Lincoln** *and those on his side in the Civil War, to the Black, Native American, immigrants' rights, religious freedom, Disabilities rights, and womens' movements that have made Civil Rights the law and the rule* rather than the exception in this country.

Commonwealth-areas or places that work together and are known for having economic and other resources in common When used with a capital "C" it usually refers to The British Commonwealth, the U.K. and nations that are in trade association with The U.K. and recognize The British monarch as the head of the organization. While There is much difference between Canada, New Zealand, India, and Zimbabwe, they all share cultural ties to Britain and for The good of their people, regard themselves within The Commonwealth. The word with a small "C" is often used to mean a collection of resources, and four U.S. states prefer the word to "state" because the latter term can merely denote a line on a map.

Constitutionalist-a party that believes There should be no federal authority except the military and for some extreme needs like protecting children They tend to run to the right of the Republican Party and therefore win few elections except in some local communities. With a Lower case "C" The word can also mean one who strictly believes in the Constitution regardless of party, and many patriotic Americans prefer to be identified with it while shunning the formal term as a name for an unpopular relatively new party.

cowboy-symbol of The Old West, and by extension much of America. Since as a rule, it can be an image from New York to Kansas, and Massachusetts to South Carolina, because of its identity as The quintessential American figure, it is often used both positively and negatively, as one who pays much attention to detail, or one who takes risks with little regard for consequences. The reality is somewhere in between since as opposed to ranchers, The cowboy was a hired hand who did not regulate his comings and goings but took orders from the boss of the bunkhouse.

dominoes-from the game and particularly the manifestation thereof knocking down a rival players, or taking them away, it became The Cold War image of both major players having a domino effect, as in the case of the Soviet Union, they really were trying to line up all the dominoes, whereas until **Reagan,** U S Presidents were merely trying to prevent them, **Reagan was The first** to begin taking The Communists dominoes from them, starting with Grenada, then Nicaragua, and eventually Poland, until The other countries of The Warsaw Pact broke with the Soviet Union, and all the country's including Ukraine, often considered part of Russia, voted to separate and vote in their own non-Communist governments, and in 1991 Russia itself disbanded the Communist government and The Soviet Union ceased to exist. The term is similar to stronghold but much stronger since one can live in a Republican or Democratic stronghold without being taken by force the way one is when he becomes someone else's domino.

EEOC-Equal Employment Opportunities Commission a government bureau that seeks to eliminate discrimination based on race, gender, age, ethnic or religious background, and since 1990, disability status.

entrepreneurial-a process with spiritual and intellectual overtones, when it involves a true businessman, an entrepreneur is distinct from a businessman or an owner, or even a capitalist, in that the entrepreneur puts up his own money, labor, sweat, and human potential, investing his all in the company, hence the use of the phrase "entrepreneurial spirit"

Euro-centric-a practice or philosophy that prefers Europe, the Western world, and often the Caucasian race.

Evangelical-members of Christian denominations including The Assemblies of God, Christian and Missionary Alliance, Seventh-day Adventist, and most Baptist united by the public proclamation of basic and essential doctrines of Christianity, the virgin birth, the authority of the Bible as God's Word, the deity of Jesus Christ, His atoning death on the cross, Resurrection, salvation by repentance and faith in Him, and in the Second Coming of Jesus Christ. Evangelicals are united in the belief in these essentials and in addition to theology their aim is to tell others about these truths, often setting themselves aside from other Christians by the belief that it is the individual responsibility of every believer to witness to the truth of Jesus Christ.

exegesis-from a Greek term it means to explain a text, especially the Bible and sometimes can mean giving a similar explanation of a person or institution.

ex officio-Latin for "by office" an ex officio member or leader is one who holds a position of authority over his peers who are generally elected or appointed two people who tend to be ex officio members are pastors and the presidents of organizations including colleges, who tend to sit on boards by their office, with others who were elected or appointed.

Gracey Mansion-home to The mayor of New York and seat of power in the city.

Great War-what World War I was called the latter name being given after World WAR II began,

hat trick-three of something, used in hockey, soccer, and occasionally basketball, in politics it means election to a third term.

hippie-one who practices the lifestyle counterculture popularized in The sixties, marked by rebellion against established culture and the belief that the values of their culture are wrong and only this generation knows the truth, and must therefore protect society from the dated values of the "old folks." Hippies engaged in behavior that was called dropping out and included things like extreme hairstyles, tattooing and body piercing, psychedelic drugs, and "free love" or promiscuous sex. Not all hippies fit all the generalizations of this definition some liked it only for the music and free association, as the Jesus Movement of the 70s showed. Some continued in Hippie into the late 70s and 80s though many like former President Bill Clinton became the leaders of the establishment.

Hostile environment-legal term for a situation at work in which where the working atmosphere is so difficult that either by events of a sexual nature or other things with tendency to harass or make employees feel uncomfortable, the employer has brought on himself, justification for lawsuits, even if no physical damages can be assessed-it can also be paraphrased by saying that even if one did not get fired, commit suicide, or become physically or mentally incapacitated, the behavior is so extreme either by the employer or people under his control whom he failed to regulate, where a **reasonable person, may have, under the same circumstances, been rendered unable, to live, to work, or to keep a physical or mental capacity intact.**

Hyperbole-an obvious and sometimes humorous exaggeration, like "its raining cats and dogs" the point of using hyperboles as figures of speech is that other than not needing to be taken literally, they are taken very seriously to mean what they say, but it is obvious from the context that what is meant to be said is something true but it simply had to be stated in words stronger than usual to communicate the point effectively.

Icon-one who has become the exemplary embodiment of something to the point of being its greatest symbol.

Industrial Revolution-time period especially of The Eighteenth and Nineteenth Centuries where materials like ink, paper, and machinery became The norm in Western particularly English-speaking countries.

Iron Curtain-invisible wall that separated the free world from the enslavement from Moscow, The Russians imposed a dictatorship on the Soviet Union and other nations, and all the nations East of Berlin eventually became literally enclosed in an Iron Curtain in 1961 when Khrushchev built The Berlin Wall to keep people out of West Berlin and free Europe Other Communist walls keep people in political bondage as the Bamboo Curtain is still a reality today for over a billion Chinese who cannot leave, and similar governments in North Korea, Vietnam, and Cuba keep their citizens in perpetual slavery to Communism.

Joshua-from The name of the Biblical figure who succeeded Moses, one who succeeds another in leadership of a great cause.

lexicon-there are three definitions it can be the language of a person, a brand, OR a body of knowledge, which is how it is usually used as in "THE American lexicon" or the "Christian lexicon" from an older term for a Greek dictionary.

junta-a military government often self-imposed or at least taken by force without popular vote or will of The people, especially prevalent in Latin America from The Latin word for "to join"

kibbutz(im-plural)-a communal farm especially for those in Israel who helped build The new nation.

mere Christianity-"Cliffs notes" Version of Christianity which prefers no particular denomination a concept coined by **C.S. Lewis** as a simplistic explanation of Christianity] *it is too crucial to become a cloche, and we must remember that Anglicans, Baptists, Methodists, Nazarenes, Pentecostals, and Roman Catholics, all practice mere Christianity like in The Hymn Onward Christian Soldiers, which states we are one in hope and doctrine,* denoting those truths that unite rather than divide Christians. The JUST The Facts-version are the essentials of the Virgin birth, death and Resurrection of Christ, His Second Coming, atonement, and living in Heaven, both ad Divine Master of The saved, and coming King as just of The lost; the reliability of The Bible as Christian Scripture and the belief that God created as Intelligent Creator. A simple synopsis is that mere Christianity is the belief in Jesus Christ, The Eternal Son of God, Crucified, buried, risen, ascended, and coming again with life and liberty for all who believe.

Modesto Manifesto-terms of agreement signed by **Billy Graham and** his staff in Modesto, California promising to adhere to behavior like sexual purity and financial integrity, worth reemphasizing mainly because over the years Billy and his team have adhered to the rules to the letter.

monolithic-having one set of values or standards, like the Catholic Church. And other churches, in their case the Pope, sets down those doctrines that are not disputable or debated. Monolithic doctrine is such that it is settled and therefore not debated. While most churches and other organizations that promote absolutes, like Boy Scouts have monolithic issues, ironically people who believe e in monolithic values tend to be some of The most interesting and best debates where disputable issues matters are involved.

Muckrakers-term first applied to Ida Tarbell and used by **Theodore Roosevelt** in paraphrasing John Bunyan's Pilgrim's *Progress* from a character who would not work for Heaven because she was too busy raking The muck below. While used negatively, like bully for you, **T.R.** Eventually became a muckraker himself, and worked to make irrevocable challenges to the meatpacking industry that affect our lives today. Then as now The term is sometimes used with mild insult, as one who will do all he can to write a wrong, similar to "crusade" the visual illustration being, this person is taking a rake against a whole advanced system.

Muslim-one who practices the world's largest non-Christian religion and rejects the title "Muhammadan" since they do not worship Mohammad nor does he occupy the same role as Christ in Christianity Believers in The five pillars of Islam: fasting, alms giving, prayer five times a day, The pilgrimage to Mecca, and that there is one God and Mohammad as his prophet-some add The sixth pillar *Jihad, which literally means struggle,* in the emphasis of one's world view, many Muslims see Jihad as struggle to get right with God and live by His precepts daily, while others, truer to the teaching of Muhammad prefer the violent means of converting people or at least bringing revolution that can be won by Muslims, and while many Muslims strongly reject any violence to propagate their faith, many more believe The Holy war is the preferred method of practicing their faith, for some, if not for them.

Napoleon-leader of France and much of modern Europe at The turn of The Nineteenth Century, he instituted a system of government by which The republican and secular became "enlightened" while it was modeled after the U.S. Constitution it bore similar resemblance and that is part of why the *American republic* has retained one system for two hundred years and Europe has gone through scores of revisions and wars and misunderstandings (France alone is on their Sixth republic) and with the exception of Britain and a few small countries, Europe is always going through democratic and republican reforms-while Napoleonic extremes including his anti-monarchical concepts were rejected by much of Europe after his defeat, it influenced every Western culture to The point where something after 1815 is The post-Napoleonic era or age.

NASA-National Aeronautics and Space Administration

NATO-the *North Atlantic Treaty Organization that was formed in 1947-in response to The Soviet Union and their satellites forming an alliance under The Warsaw Pact-*(Another clear evidence that one side won The Cold War-NATO still exists-the Warsaw Pact doesn't and Warsaw is in our camp) The Warsaw Pact was an alliance of dictators while The organization led by The United States was designed to aggressively oppose dictatorship from Moscow and prevent other countries from being taken over by The Soviet Union. The charter members of NATO were *The USA, United Kingdom, France, the Netherlands, Belgium, Luxembourg, and Lichtenstein. The following Year The Washington/North charter was invoked to directly include Canada and in 1949 West Germany and Italy became a full member of NATO. At various* times, as countries became republics, and new military bases were needed, The members of NATO Grew to fifteen, with *Greece, Iceland, Portugal, Spain, and Turkey capping off the Western Alliance members. After The Soviet Union came down and The Warsaw Pact dissolved, NATO was still needed as a pan-European pro-Western* alliance, and In 1997 it was expanded under Bill Clinton to include three former Communist countries, *Poland, the Czech Republic, and Hungary.* That brought The membership to eighteen, under President Bush, seven other countries were added, *Bulgaria, Estonia, Latvia, Lithuania, Romania, Slovakia, and Slovenia* bringing the number of NATO nations to twenty-five. NATO fought as allies in Korea and the Persian Gulf but the charter itself was not invoked until 1999, to take out a criminal government in Serbia, which led to the creation of the nation of Kosovo *After 911-NATO* first invoked the charter in defensive action, *all The NATO Countries agreed unanimously about the need to remove the government of Afghanistan, and then fighting in the area in and around Kandahar after first* stabilizing Kabul. For the first time in its history, NATO Later split on a military action, when several members, primarily France and Canada disagreed about the 2002 war in Iraq, although NATO used troops after the regime was defeated. In 2002, in the midst of The War on Terror President Bush opened NATO talks with Russia, after the number of her former satellites in NATO had grown to five, the Russian and Western leaders met in a goodwill gesture, vowing never to be Enemies again. Still *the military alliance exists mainly for two reasons, to prevent Russian resurgence in the region and to prevent (and when need be defend against) attacks on any member.*

Nisei-a Japanese-American specifically one born before the Baby Boom

OAS- Organization of American States an alliance between the countries of North and South America and as usual *dominated* from Washington, though it originally began in Bolivia and the original charter signatories had their second (and first voting) meeting in Tobago, Colombia in 1950. The nations involved there or joining later are *Argentina, Bahamas, Barbados, Belize, Bolivia, Brazil, Chile, Colombia, Costa Rica, Cuba, Dominica, Dominican Republic, Ecuador, El Salvador, Grenada, Guyana, Haiti, Honduras, Jamaica, Mexico, Nicaragua, Panama, Paraguay, Peru, Suriname, Trinidad and Tobago, USA, Uruguay, and Venezuela. The alliance* brings together various countries of the Western hemisphere in an effort to defend those countries in need. While it's in line with the Monroe Doctrine, they opposed all imperialistic attacks on hemisphere countries, the Monroe Doctrine was in force a hundred twenty six-years before there was an OAS, and Presidents **Roosevelt,** Taft, and **Wilson** all used it to intervene in affairs of this hemisphere. THE Organization was officially founded in Colombia in 1950 largely so that each country *would have one vote, so say, if the USA wanted to change a criminal regime in Nicaragua or wanted to encourage Ecuador to align more closely with the West rather than the oil producing nations of the East, it could be outvoted,* but with the stipulation, only by democratic governments. *The nations of the OAS unanimously voted to expel the Cuban Castro government from participation, Cuba is still a member but no representative of the Castro government can participate.* The Organization was later expanded to include Canada and Caribbean nations who won their independence from England, France, or the Netherlands (ST Kitts and Nevis, St. Vincent and Grenadines, and St. Lucia). While each of these and also the U.S., Chile, and a few other countries control islands and dependencies throughout the hemisphere, only Puerto Rico has at least 100,-000 people. *IN 1983 it was the smaller, newer nations of the OAS especially Dominica and Jamaica the former under Eugenia Charles, the president who stood with the U.S. on grounds of liberating a nation instigating violence in the hemisphere that helped convince* **Reagan** *to liberate Grenada. It was remarkable for being a war against the government of a tiny country, all but a U.S. satellite for reasons of geography, as well as a member of the British Commonwealth, where our closest ally was not thrilled about us meddling while we also had qualms about Britain's war with Argentina, which we came to support.* The Grenada Offensive was the first war of its kind that could rightly be called a disciplinary police measure even predating Operation Desert Storm, which broke new historic ground as an international peace mission for order and righteousness.

Operation Blessing-nonprofit organization set up by **Pat Robertson** to feed and minister The Gospel to people around The world.

Paradigm-a model for both new inventions was well as philosophical ideas. Keynesian economics was a paradigm that was accepted until it was largely disproved and replaced by the economic philosophy of Milton Friedman and and other economists at the University of Chicago, while New Testament Christianity brought in a paradigm shift whereby true grace shifted from faith in God sending a Messiah in the future, to the personal acceptance of the Modern Messiah, namely Jesus Christ.

Paul-the man who literally became The first Christian writer as The great apostle to the Gentiles, he was responsible for Christianity going from East to West, literally from India to Spain, either through himself or those missionaries he personally sent within a generation; he also wrote two-thirds of The New Testament and is more personally responsible for Christianity than anyone but Jesus Himself.

Pentecostal-members of Evangelical denominations who believe that the gifts of the Holy Spirit remain in operation and hence part of the Christian experience is seeking and exasperating in the gifts of the Spirit which include speaking in tongues and divine healing and sometimes specialized gifts, like praying for miracles, distinguishing between good and evil spirits, and speaking words of wisdom, which can involve interpreting the will of God. While Pentecostals and their cousins Charismatics are found in all denominations. Charismatics are usually in non-denominational churches or their smaller equivalents, while or as charismatic members of virtually every major denomination. The distinction is that Charismatics believe that tongues and other spiritual gifts are sometimes present with the work of the Holy Spirit while Pentecostals believe that *language speaking (speaking in tongues or glossolalia) is the initial physical evidence that one has received the baptism in the Holy Spirit. The Major denominations that were built on the Pentecostal distinctiveness are the* Assemblies of God, Foursquare Gospel Alliance, Church of God (OF Cleveland, Tennessee), and the Vineyard Fellowship. Other Charismatics prefer to have fellowship with Pentecostals while remaining within the orbit of the older denominations. "Oneness" churches which deny the Trinity doctrine (the United Pentecostal Church-UPC is the largest) are within the *Pentecostal orbit-but largely "dis-fellow-*

shipped" from larger Pentecostal gatherings by mutual separation based largely on the others' belief in the diversity of the Godhead. Other Charismatics are believers in the Spirit-filled distinctives within almost every denomination, Catholic, Methodist, Presbyterian, Baptist, Nazarene, Seventh-day Adventist, Episcopal, using Pentecostal distinctives they can call themselves Pentecostal. When such people of faith call themselves "Charismatic" it is usually to distinguish themselves as self-contained functioning within the denomination, to differentiate from both independent charismatics and Pentecostal denominations. Though non-denominational Charismatics usually call themselves that, it is a newer trend, and until the 1960s the term was always "Spirit-filled Catholic" (OR Methodist, Presbyterian), etc. *Note this Disclaimer:While Pentecostal and Charismatic Christians believe in the gift of prophesy, the Bible is always the final word and the only source of eternal doctrine. Pentecostals are first and foremost Evangelical and believe the Bible to be the final authority on all matters of faith and therefore every word must be subject to Biblical authority and no one ever adds words or concepts t other Cannon of Scripture. Furthermore* the word "prophesy" literally means "speaking for God" and non-Pentecostal Christians sometimes speak of "hearing God's voice" or "being the voice of God" so there is ultimately no difference in practice from these two forms of speaking for God.

PFLAG-Parents and Friends of Lesbians and Gays-a group that seeks to affirm The dignity of friends and relatives who "come out"

plurality-the highest number of votes cast in an election where there is no majority; in the 1992 election, Bill Clinton won with 43% of The popular vote, with George H.W. Bush getting 39%, and Ross Perot 19%.

progressive-wanting to improve and experience better dynamics in life for our fellow human beings, while The term can be used in several contexts and was briefly the name of a political party championed by **Theodore Roosevelt,** today the term is usually synonymous for "liberal." This has been the case as liberals control the media and they say they have made use of The term to combat The use of "liberal" as a negative label. That way the liberal media can say they are really progressive. This fails for two reasons, while I'm in full agreement with the right of every group to define itself, the almost exclusive use of the term for liberals unjustly implies that conservatives are regressive or stagnant. The other reason is The same media does not give conservatives The luxury or defining ourselves, while many conservatives are visionary, *they would never call us that and if we started telling the media, we are not conservative, we are visionary, they would never make that switch the way they have to progressive. This is consistent with many in the mainstream media taking words apart to define groups positively or negatively, as how they have so negatively labeled "Fundamentalists."*

Reaganomics-media label sometimes used with pride by **Ronald Reagan** and his many enthusiasts basically just good-old-fashioned capitalism, letting businesses and private earners keep their money and encouraging more entrepreneurship, more purchasing power, and generating more money from the top, to the middle, to the bottom, and back up.

Reconstruction-time period immediately after The Civil War in which the victorious Union sought to readmit and where possible rehabilitate the defeated South. Starting with former slaves, they sought first to readmit them, and for the most part initiate them into their American citizenship, and then when possible, forgive the Southern states, and take them back into the Union on an equal footing.

Renaissance-time period in The Fifteenth And Sixteenth Centuries with revival and intellectual emphasis on music, art, literature, culture, and sometimes an overt rejection of God and supernaturalism.

rhetoric-often used negatively as a rhetorical question is one that does not need an answer and "rhetoric" sounds similar to rigmarole and other negative terms; in fact from an educational perspective it is an art, being able to speak well, and a rhetorician is one who has mastered the liberal art of rhetoric, an artist, like a scientist, mathematician, or historian, a master of a Nineteenth and Twentieth Century art, that relatively few people really master, it is quite likely the most rare version of greatness in a liberal artist (Liberal in the sense of "taught inclusively in the schools to liberate" an educational not political use of the word), a rhetorician is also called a semanticist, linguist, or a liberal rhetorical psychologist.

rigorous-accurate, rigidly strict, severe, and exact.

Salvation Army-a Christian denomination founded in the Nineteenth Century by General William Booth that seeks to preach the Gospel of Jesus Christ while also meeting spokespeople' needs for food, clothing, shelter, and comfort. A nonprofit organization since 1881, the former Methodist minister wisely established the organization in England believing that to do great works., the Biblical standard requiems first and foremost that we preach the Gospel, but that it can fail if we do nothing to take care or the peoples' physical needs. He wisely established that all such care for temporal as well as eternal needs should be based out of a local church, so the individuals could continence to get minstrelsy By ht end of the century his daughter Evangeline came to America where the organization became a force and she became its top general. Many people think it is merely a service organization but it is a full-fledged church with about 1.2 million members worldwide and while it is struggling today as it has not in decades, it is a major force, dewing 9-11 it was the number one contributor of blood and other relief efforts.

SDI-Strategic Defense Initiative the policy of the **Reagan** Administration to get a nuclear shield to defend America and the Western world from a nuclear attack the media immediately degraded it by calling it The Star Wars program, but it was actually meant to prevent wars and their cataclysmic consequences and whatever else one may think of it it is far superior to MAD-Mutually Assured destruction implied in the fact that is one country attacked the other, they would respond with a nuclear attack, at least in **Reagan's** vision there would be no destruction.

Silent Majority the greatness number of people in a community or country as opposed to those who make the most noise-i. e. the vocal majority. Such people go to work and manage their families often without any need to discussion their beliefs or tell people (and are therefore rarely cognizant) "WE ARE part of the Silent majority and everyone who disagrees with us is not." The expression was first used by President *Nixon and Vice-President Agnew* who said the few who shout them down at gatherings may be a vocal majority but a silent majority still support their President, the government, and the need for law and order While *Agnew applied it to the Vietnam War in contrast to its then many protesters the* fact remains, about any issue a vocal minority often gets heard at the expense of the silent majority. Stu ides shew win the middle of the Civil Rights era over 80% OF white Southerners supported Blacks' unfettered right to vote, but the loud protesters were a vocal minority often taken to be the majority. Similarly in the South and Midwest many antagonists against the Vietnam War were taken to be the majority, while those who opposed the protests were for the most part not anti-Civil Rights, but merely had views against a philosophy that allowed a vocal minority to drown out the voices of the Silent Majority. Similarly in 2002, polls showed 76% OF Americans supported using force to change the criminal regime in Iraq, but in spite of that Silent Majority, the news media and some government institutions repeated the words of a vocal minority as though it were the majority. Whatever the issue, the Silent Majority of Americans tend to share and to favor a few basic clues, like respect for human rights, public safety, equality in education, the desire for a common language, the need to keep drugs illegal, punishing criminals severally as their crimes merit and for both punitive and deterrent reasons, and the desire to protect the flag. While the term is euphemistic and can never be used as an absolute because no one person ever speaks for the view of a whole country, group or for a majority of institutions Presidents and other leaders often use it to garner support from a majority of Americans who generally share their commitments (after all a majority of voters usually elect them) and they like to remind us that the majority want strong defense, equality of opportunity, and less national government. More than anyone in recent times **Rush Limbaugh** almost singlehandedly appealed to the Silent Majority and in similar times **Ronald Reagan** became the most effective President while appealing to the SILENT Majority. Other heroes of hope who have appealed to the Silent Majority include **Churchill, Hayakawa, and Walesa.**

Special revelation-that taught by God in His revealed Word, the Bible, as opposed to simply evident from creation.

theology-literally The study of God, it is the study of man's relationship to God and whether he can have a personal relationship with God, His attributes, and if he can know him personally.

Truman Doctrine-concept annunciated by The thirty-third President after World War II that The world should be divided in half between Communist and anticommunist; originally to raise money for The nations directly opposing Communism. Its first beneficiaries were Greece, Turkey, and Persia (Iran), it later led to military intervention in Korea and Vietnam. The fact that The world was divided into Communist countries and their Enemies made many immoral or mildly dictatorial countries like Argentina, South Africa, and Spain in our camp, while it *opened a first world mentality for all those who were opposing Communism, opposing The Second world,* The unaligned were generally regarded as "Third World" meaning neighbor right nor "damnably wrong" and not Left in the sense of endorsing Communism, though Marshall Tito, the dictator of Yugoslavia prided himself on being a benign leader who was good for his country (he wasn't!) but his supporters saw in him a perspective first-world alternative to both capitalism and Stalinist while his Enemies saw him as just an alternative Soviet-style dictator.

Utahn-the preferred spelling for a native or resident of the Beehive State, There is *not a second-"A" in Utahn no matter what my computer says!*

War of Northern Aggression-the obviously editorial and accusatory name for the "Civil War" used by many Southerners Like usual,there is some truth to the label but even less than "Civil War" which is also a misnomer since The South was concerned with independence not taking over anything from Washington. "The War for Southern Independence" has been used as another editorial label, while "The War Between the States" will probably remain the most historically fair to all sides.

worldview-what a person believes about life, but rarely states except when it is challenged, popular worldviews include Christianity, secular Humanism, and Communism.

World Vision-ministry that includes the departments of Samaritan's Purse and Operation Angle Tree at Christmastime, a philanthropy for many years under the leadership of Bob Pierce and now taken over by William Franklin Graham, IV

Zionism-belief in The Holy Land, particularly putting Israel-the historic land of the Bible also known as Palestine and parts of Jordan, Egypt, and Lebanon under control of Jews-today Israelis;to be the Biblical, political, and spiritual home of the Jewish people, in The Nineteenth and early Twentieth Century it was a philosophical concept, a dream from the Bible and a possible likelihood due to political realities and the strong struggles of Jews, primarily European, but others from North America, South America, Australia, South Africa, The Middle East, and Northern Africa, it became a reality in 1948 and since is the standard of all who love and accept the Jews.

Glossary

This is a list of people identified who have been singled out for positive mentions. This is not a general index of people, it is a list of positive commendations, names of those who made the glossary are those who did not make the book, but are singled out for positive mention, and I may write about them in future books (some are already in the works) they may even be termed-*junior varsity* heroes of hope.

123 names of people identified

Abernathy, Ralph Baptist minister and successor to **King** at Southern Christian Leadership Council

Adams, John second president of The United States (1797-1801)

Adams, John Quincy-sixth President of The United States (1825-9)

Adenauer, Konrad (1876-1967)-West German chancellor first elected leader of post-Nazi era, he led The country from 1949-1963

Agnew, Spiro T-Vice President under Nixon and the.first Greek-American in a national election;.resigned in disgrace and forgotten by many though he was elected on two landslide tickets, and may someday be revised for consideration especially as a conservative icon

Ali, Muhammad (1946-present) boxer known for his greatness in the ring as well as his charismatic personality that thrilled the fans, did many great things for his country, *in saying this you know from the rest of the document I'm not endorsing everything he has said or done in his public career, but in his more recent years after the diagnosis of Parkinson's disease* became a spokesman for some positive American values and has helped build bridges between the Western world and Muslims especially about kinder treatment of Jews-while the best we can say about that is that his heart is in the right place, he apologized for some hateful things he said in the sixties, and *has built bridges to conservatives nominally supporting Ronald* **Reagan's** *reelection (1984) and actively campaigning for GHW Bush in 1988- and especially by his close friendship with* **Orrin Hatch** he is also friends with George W Bush who gave him the Presidential Medal of Freedom in 2005 and with **Billy Graham** the boxer who used to call himself the greatest has said God has given me this condition to remind me He is the Greatest

Aquinas, Thomas-Greek theologian canonized by The Catholic Church, with Augustine a pioneer in theology and educational philosophy

Ataturk, Kemal Mustafa-1881-1938 Turkish leader so much a nationalist that to this day Turks who believe in his philosophy of government are called "Kemalists" the way American democracy is Jeffersonian, again not an endorsement of everything he ever said or did but he set a tremendous example of leadership for a large and potentially homogeneous country to be a secular democracy emphasizing human rights and anti-Communism and cooperation with the rest of the Western world-which is still the predominant philosophy in Turkey in the early Twenty-First Century

Attlee, Clement-Prime minister of Great Britain between **Churchill's** two terms (1945-1951) led to nationalization of much of Britain's resources

Baker, Howard (1925-) U.S. senator from Tennessee and Presidential candidate

Beck, Glenn-(born 1964) American radio-talk show host in the tradition of **Rush Limbaugh** mostly known for his ability to take unpopular viewpoints to their logical conclusions to insure American exceptionalism in every generation, championing the indispensable works of the Founding era and their relevance today in his brief ride across the national spotlight he has already become the writer of twelve bestselling books and he is also known for his committmeent to the LDS Church

Begin, Menahem-1913-1992 Prime minister of Israel-1978-85 famous and infamous for the way in Lebanon, but he also established further ties with Evangelical Christians in North America as the greatest foreign asset to his country

Benedict 480-543 monk and founder of the Benedictine order-an industrious order of praying monks

Bennett, William J. (1941-present) conservative Catholic formerly secretary of Education under **Reagan he became** noted as an advocate for classical scholarship and his conservative books and like **Limbaugh** came under fire for being exposed, in his case as a heavy gambler

Blanton, Smiley (1926-1990) psychiatrist and speech pathologist, who, with **Peale** founded The Institute for Christian Living which helped millions come to a better understanding of themselves and their relationship with God, along with *Guideposts* newsletter, it helped to teach that Christianity and psychology and other mental health fields are not at odds, they can be each other's best ally

Blume, Judy(1936-) author especially known for coming of age novels that explore the sexual, geographic, religious, and aesthetic journeys of children and teenagers (especially middle-class ones) in formative years, so recognized not so much for such ideas, with the possible exception of *Tiger Eyes,* she rarely broke new ground, but because she writes so well, she always entertains, teaches, and inspires millions of readers

Bright, Bill (1921-2003) Founder Campus Crusade for Christ preacher and Evangelical writer-established the Four Spiritual Laws

Bruce, Tammy (1961-) commentator, writer, and writer of The *New Thought Police*

Bryant, Anita-former Miss Oklahoma and runner-up for Miss America known both for her singing and her outspoken Christian commitments which included controversial anti-gay rights (borderline anti-gay) rhetoric, some of which she recanted later in life

Buchanan, Patrick J. (born 1936) Journalist political commentator and Republican candidate for President, served in Republican administrations and ran for President twice, but after failing to get the GOP nomination, he ran on the Reform Party ticket, taking the leadership away from its founder, Ross Perot but failing to get 1% of the vote in national election

Buckley, William F. (1925-2008) dean of American conservative scholar, writer founder *National Review*

Burke, Edmund (1729-1797) conservative British Parliamentarian known for his belief in "Natural law" The laws of God and nature being intertwined

Bush, George (1924-present) Forty-first President of the United States

Bush, George W. (1946-) 43rd President of the United States known mostly for the War on Terror, he also passed groundbreaking laws to punish corporate criminals

Cain, Herman 1945-Georgia based businessman restaurateur and and conservative whom I mentioned in my first public writing before *he became a celebrity in 2012 he started off strong as an outsider running for the Presidency*

Campanella, Roy (1921-1993)baseball player one of the first Blacks to play in the Major Leagues, after a disabling neck injury went on to a career as a coach

Campbell, Ben Nighthorse-1936-present Colorado senator the first Native American to win elections at that level in sixty years, he crossed over to The Republican Party in 1994 and in 1998 won his seat as a Republican by the biggest margin in Colorado history

Carnegie, Dale (1885-1955) author How *to Win Rinds and Influence People a runaway bestseller as well as HOW TO Stop Worrying and Start Living*

Carson, Johnny-1925-2005 pioneer late-night talk show host television comedy

Casey, Bob (1933-2000)-prolife Democratic Pennsylvania governor, known for the case that allowed abortion in his state, challenged to The Supreme Court, by Planned Parenthood, the High Court gave concessions to both sides, letting states outlaw abortion at certain stages while by a 5-4 majority, the Court still upheld the national legality of abortion

Chavez, Linda (1947-) conservative activist and sometimes advocate for Republican administrations she served in the **Reagan Administration** and later was a failed nominee for higher cabinet office when her philanthropy to illegal immigrants was disclosed

Cheney, Dick (1941-) forty-seventh Vice-President of the United States, known among other things for making the Vice Presidency an equal partnership conservative who for thirty years as a statesman and businessman made major contributions to the nation, he actually ran Gerald Ford's reelection campaign in 1976, and as congressman at large for the great state of Wyoming, he became minority whip, an obvious feat for a representative with relatively few constituents

Cleland, Max (1956-) moderate Democrat, lost three limbs in Vietnam and went on to a stellar career as a senator from Georgia, served on the Senate Finance Committee and held moderate to liberal economic views but heroically went to bat for his fellow patriots to protect the U.S. flag

Cleveland, Grover-(1837-1908) Democratic President, became pour first and to date only non-successive President, (1885-1889-and 1893-1897) known for his integrity and courage

Clifford, Clark M. (1906-1998) Longtime Presidential advisor and man Friday to **Truman** some say he was an apprentice, others say he was the President's mentor, he spoke and wrote extensively for Democratic politics especially coming out against alleged corruption in the Nixon and **Reagan** administrations, but he he almost singlehandedly insured recognition of the Zionist republic, Israel

Coolidge, Calvin-1872-1933 thirtieth President of The USA-1924-29 known for promoting business and presiding over peacetime prosperity arguably our most underrated peacetime President, also known for his quick witticisms

Cosby, Bill-(1934-) comedian and educator known for his realistic portrayal of Black men as good husbands and good fathers, and productive members of the establishment, his advocacy of Black education, the Black family, individualism, self-sufficiency, and the need to shun crime and drugs

Coulter, Ann-1961-conservative pundit and writer of hugely successful books

Danforth, Jack-(1926-present) Missouri lawyer and longtime senator, he is also an ordained Episcopal minister

DeKlerk, Fredrick W. (1936-)South African politician and Nobel Peace Prize winner known for dismantling The apartheid system, giving Blacks their voting rights and representation one-man-one-vote ending fifty years of racial policies

Dempsey, Jack-1895-1983 heavyweight boxing champion probably the first most popular boxer in the United States also known for his conservative speeches and philanthropy especially outspoken about adoption

Disraeli, Benjamin-(1804-1881) writer, English statesman, advocate of Christianity as *Completed Judaism,* Prime minister 1870-76, he further taught the glories of the British Empire as the moral leaders of the world and the need for a Jewish homeland, Zionism

D'Souza, Dinesh-(1961) research fellow at the Hoover Institution conservative writer known for questioning orthodoxy on race and immigration issues, was reconverted to Evangelicalism and became president of a Christian college

Dewey, Tom (1904-1970) former New York DA and governor lost close races for President in 1944 and 1948, like Jimmy Brooks and to date Mitt Romney-famous for coming in second lost close races

Ditka, Mike 1940-football coach best known for The 1985-86 Bears

Douglass, Fredrick (1818-1895) American hero, author, and Christian spokesman The first to document life as both a slave and a fugitive first as a teenager he became successful at escaping slavery and throughout his life as a writer and journalist he became The nation's most outspoken abolitionist and after The war a major spokesman for Black equality and the Republican Party, held various offices in at least three administrations +8-

Eisenhower, Dwight D. (1890-1968) general who became thirty-fifth President 1953-1960

Elizabeth, II-1926-present reigning monarch, possibly the most revered in the history of the United Kingdom, she became the greatest asset to the monarchy after the death of her father King George and has reigned since 1953

Finny, Charles G. (1802-1875) American lawyer, scholar, revivalist, and later Christian educator

Francis of Assisi (1181?-1226) one of The most renowned Catholic saints of all time specifically known for his philanthropy and founding The order based on his name

Ford, Gerald (1913-2007)thirty-eighth President, The only one (1974-77) to serve as both VP and President without being elected either he was a wise and moral leader who helped protect American interests in the Pacific and Guthry to bring down inflation

Franklin, Benjamin-(1706-1791) statesman, inventor, and scientist known for So many thins as The modern stove, the pioneering of American libraries, and bifocal lenses

Franks, Tommy (1945-) general known for consolidating US AND Allied troops in Iraq

Gandhi, Mohandas K (1869-1948) Indian religious and anti-colonial leader revered for The "Truth in Action" policy that brought an end to British rule helped to form The world's largest democracy

Garn, Jake (1927-present) Utah senator known both for his conservative views and his work on the Space program which included a stint in space himself

Goldwater, Barry-1909-1998 conservative Arizona senator lost The '64 Presidential race to LBJ

GEO VI-1895-1952 reigning U.K. monarch during World War II, known for his valor under pressure

Grant, U.S. (1818-1885) known largely as **Lincoln's** most competent general, he became the eighteenth President and became the only President to outlaw The Ku Klux Klan as a terrorist organization and he stood stalwartly for Southern states giving Blacks their rights and under his leadership tens of thousands voted, owned property, and worked ion the legal system, most for the first time. Though plagued by a weak second term, with his secretary of State Hamilton Fish he almost salvaged some bad policies, and he is justly memorialized on The $50, every time we see a $50 we should look up and thank God he was such a great man, especially when they put an evil one on the $20

Gresham, Joy (1907-1960) American poet and prize winning writer-married **C.S. Lewis**

Gray, John 1764-1845 British leader and emancipator of the slaves living in Britain

Guliani, Rudolph W.-(1940-present) he had previously been a Democrat councilman and prosecutor but changed parties to become **Reagan's** deputy attorney general known for cleaning up New York and became one of The staunchest fighters of terrorism since the eighties After the 911 attacks he stood shoulder-to-shoulder with Bush and became a leader of solidarity even a father figure in New York, got point with The Right for saying politically incorrect things about the Saudi monarchy the President cannot say, ran for President in 2008

Hamlin, Hannibal-(1809-1886) lawyer, senator from Maine, and Vice-President during the first term of **Abraham Lincoln**

Harvey, Paul (1918-2009) Chicago-based radio talk show pioneer

Havel, Vaclav 1936-present longtime playwrite and dissident he became the first democratically elected President of post-Soviet Czechoslovakia, resigned after the dissolution of the country and became the first president of the Czech Republic (1993-2002)

Hawking, Stephen 1942-English physicist best known for *A Brief History of Time, and his theories* of radiation

Hefflin, Howard (1921-2005) Alabama senator Democratic with mixed liberal and conservative views but also a staunch advocate for protecting the U.S. flag

Hemingway, Ernest (1898-1961)American writer best known for writing about people who dealt with grace under pressure and defeating it or fighting to the death against enemies and other elements that war against them physically, mentally, or spiritually

Hughes, Charles Evans (1859-1941) statesman, Presidential candidate, and chief justice 1930-1940 instrumental in passing the first movie codes and blocking some of the more unconstitutional New Deal measures

Humphrey, Hubert H. (1901-78) Democrat from Minnesota, U.S. senator and Vice-President (1965-69) lost the race for the Presidency in 1968

Jackson, Henry "Scoop" Washington senator known for being the last mainstream Democrat to stake his career on the fight against Communism

Inouye, Daniel K. (1924-present) U.S. senator from Hawaii-today the second longest serving senator in U.S. history; he went on to a stellar career after losing his right arm to enemy gunfire in World War II

John Paul, II-1920-2005 Catholic pontiff (79-2005) known for his staunch stances on religious freedom worldwide and opposing Communism

Jefferson, Thomas-third President of the USA most known for writing the Declaration of Independence and orchestrating the Louisiana Purchase for him his bigger accomplishments are the University of Virginia and writing its statute for religious Freedom

Johnson, Lyndon Baines-(1908-1972) known as LBJ-36th President of The United States (1963-1969)

Johnson, Paul (1927-present) British historian known for conservative and monumental treatments of large issues, most notably with *Modern Times (1988-several revised editions)*

Kemp, Jack-(1933-2009) conservative political figure from Buffalo best known for work in supply side economics as a U.S. congressman he was director of Housing and Urban Development (1989-1993) and a Presidential candidate who ran on the ticket with **Bob Dole** for Vice-President in 1996

Koch, Ed-(1924-present) mayor of New York, known as a conservative Democrat who did a realistic job cleaning up The city and later supported the war time policies of George W. Bush

Kissinger, Henry (1924-) genius German-born American security liaison and Presidential advisor much like **Condolezza Rice he became** the kindred spirit to Nixon and his Jewish heritage especially as he was open about being expelled with his family from Nazi Germany (before most of his relatives had any chance, and remained during the war) winner of the Nobel Peace Prize for negotiating what was ultimately an incomplete peace with North Vietnam but it ended twenty years of war

Kohl, Helmut (1930-present) chancellor of Germany and major contributor to victory in the Cold War he presided over West Germany when the Berlin Wall was in place helped preside over its downfall (1989-1990) and then was first chancellor of The reunified Germany (1990-1997)

Laxalt 1927-governor of Nevada and U S senator best known for being the closest male friend of **Ronald Reagan**

Lincoln, Mary Todd-1812-1885 wife of **Abraham Lincoln** who in spite of stereotypes was one of The greatest first ladies and female leaders America ever had

Linkletter, Art (1912-2010) humorist radio and later television personality and social commentator

Little Richard-1932-present very talented American singer and Seventh-day Adventist minister ironically for years he shunned one or the other, he was alienated from rock-n-roll by Gospel musicians then for years shunned the Gospel due to his desire to perform for rock audiences returned to rock music and shunned the Gospel until about 1986, since then he has been a Gospel singer and speaks at churches around the country, while still performing rock music as long as it is not inconsistent, he has spoken publicly about keeping the seventh day Sabbath

Lloyd, David George-Liberal prime minister of The U.K. during World War I and reasonable mediator between America and France in 1919

Luce, Henry(1898-1967) longtime publisher and founder of *Time*

Lugar, Richard (1932-) Indiana Republican senator

Major, John-(1939-present) Conservative leader of Britain who succeeded **Thatcher** as Prime minister

Marlborough, DUKE OF THE Original was John Churchill (1650-1732)

Marti, Jose (1853-1895) Cuban nationalist icon of resistance he gave his life to free his country from Spanish rule

McCarthy, Joseph- 1901-1956 U S Senator from Wisconsin most known for the "witch hunts" against Communists, in fact he sacrificially devoted his life to expose those on a government payroll who may be traitors, corrupt, or possible security risks, and some of them actually turned out to be double-agents for Moscow

McCain, John 1936-present Arizona senator and two-time candidate for President famous as a war hero and Vietnam POW-he ran a poor campaign in 2000 which virtually ended when he attacked some of the GOP's greatest stars and what they stood for, but in 2008 his campaign did much better he won a hard Guthrie victory in the primary and chose Sarah Palin as a running mate, they finished second, taking twenty-three states

McGraw, Dr. Phil (1950) TV psychologist, writer, and speaker famous for his association with Oprah Winfrey, and helped lead accountability moral health of the early Twenty-First Century

McPherson, Aimee Semple-1890-1944 Canadian-born founder of the Foursquare Gospel Alliance known for her flamboyant life-style, she was also the first woman and one of the first preachers anywhere to generate a large audience for Christian broadcasting

Miller, Dennis (1954-)actor, comedian, and shockingly now conservative talk-show host, formerly like other Hollywood "talking heads" a Yes-man for the Democrats, he became, after 911, a staunchly pro-America spokesman for conservative values and candidates

Miller, Larry H. (1944-2009) businessman and philanthropist first known for his car dealerships, the first in Utah to reach a larger market, he also helped build up The Jazz NBA team

Moody, D.L. (1837-1899)American pastor and revivalist

Neave Airey-1913-1980 British war hero and government official who escaped the Nazis and helped the prosecution at Nuremberg murdered by Northern Irish terrorists while serving there as home secretary

Nixon Richard (1912-1994) thirty seventh President of the USA (1969-1974) the first President to resign the office but what is not often remembered is before that he was the first to blow the lid on American Communism, a "Crime " for which the Left never forgave him, he also banned biological weapons, an indispensable measure to America's safety, and changed U.S./China relations. Working with both our allies and enemies in Vietnam, and best of all starting the War on Cancer-research which has helped millions live longer, healthier more productive lives

Norquist, Grover (1956-) conservative activist Leader American Revolution spokesman for lower taxes, entrepreneurialism, and freedom of conscience

Pascal, Blaise (1623-1662)French theologian, apologist, and mathematician

Peary, Robert (1856-1920) American admiral best noted for the Spanish-American War associated with *William McKinley* and the mission to liberate the Philippines the most monumental Naval undertaking to that time

Phillips, Howard-1941-Jewish-American with lifelong interests in various religious movements, he helped put **Ronald Reagan** in The White House and **Jerry Falwell** found The Moral Majority, but later felt the Republican Party was inadequate and founded The American Taxpayer Party, running for President, and later changing The name to the Constitution Party,

Pitt, William (1759-1806) British prime minister during the American Revolution instrumental in losing the war but also helped secure Ireland and India for the BRITISH Empire

Player, Gary (1925-present) South African golfer acknowledged for his rigor and sometimes a Christian spokesman

Powell, Colin (1938-) secretary of State in The first term of George W. Bush, he had previously been a general largely responsible for Desert Strom and acknowledged as a dream candidate for President, but his main achievement as secretary was The movement to overthrow The Iraqi regime

Presley, Elvis-1935-1977 singer and entertainer who pioneered rock-n-roll became The most influential white musician in recorded history since Beethoven

Reagan, Michael (1945-present) keeper of the **Reagan** legacy, one of the first late-night talk-show hosts to command a nationwide audience **like Limbaugh to daytime though he is Ronald Reagan's** son he is his own man, one of the first people to use the Internet worldwide as radio's equal or superior, also outspoken in favor of adoption and pursuing anyone guilty of child abuse, neglect or molestation

Reed, Ralph (1963) former leader Young Republicans and the Christian Coalition, he led a largely conservative Christian movement and with his experience made it competitive very professionally eventually becoming the #1 lobby group in America, in 1999 he left to become an advisor to the Bush campaign and later lost a very close election for lieutenant governor of Georgia

Rehnquist, William H.(1930-2004) fourteenth chief justice of the US Supreme Court first appointed by Nixon and then elevated by **Reagan**

Roberts, John 1945-became The fifteenth chief justice of U.S. Supreme Court after appointment by George W. Bush

Robinson, Jackie-1917-68 baseball player best known for breaking The color barrier, he was one of The greatest players of his time setting records for stolen bases and runs scored

Rogers, Will (1874-1935) Pioneer radio-talk show host, actor and visual entertainer, also known for his speeches on Native American assimilation; he was the first radio celebrity and as such he had opportunists to change the country for positive values-though at times he also showed mere pragmatism, his reputation was elevated because he was the first great American to die in a plane crash

Romney, Mitt (1947) governor Of Massachusetts and Salt Lake Olympic commission boss-in 2008 he finished second in the Republican nomination for President, becoming the first Mormon to run a credible campaign for the highest office in the land, but in 2012 he came out of the wilderness to become the inheritor of the mantle, and must be able to stop Obama *and became the forty-fifth President to the United States, wad if he does, political correctness would dictate he put some boring* veterans on the Supreme Court, I say political correctness, be trend by a screwdriver, just as before Romney was on the ticket they talked about it, make the Supreme Court justice a native of Utah, or a member of the L.D.S. Church, or both in one. I say come on Mitt, be a Bull-Moose, and since about 38% of Americans practice some very conservative religion which has never had a high justice, Pentecostals, mainstream Baptists, and Mormons, put not only one of these kinds of man or woman on the Supreme Court, but put one on every time you have a chance to fill a vacancy-especially when Clinton and Obama put Secularists on the Court every time they had a chance.

Roosevelt, Franklin D.-known as FDR longest serving President (1933-1945) presided over the Depression and World War II

Roosevelt, Ted (1887-1994) American icon, son of The twenty-sixth President, as soon as Nazi Germany *advanced he did all he could to oppose it, served in The British Army, even giving up his American citizenship for a time so he could command British troops. He eventually commanded American troops as well, leading in Normandy, and dying of a heart attack a few weeks later, ALSO one other son-Quentin (1899-1918) makes The JV list for giving his life in World War I*

Schuller, Robert 1926-present longtime pastor Crystal Cathedral known for positive messages and pioneer in Christian self-help with uplifting books

Shcharansky, Nathan (1927-) Russian born dissident Israeli citizen and cabinet member

Smith, Gordon (1952-) Oregon senator known for his conservative views

Sowell, Thomas (1930-present) senior research fellow at the Hoover Institution

Starr, Kenneth-1946-federal judge best known as special prosecutor in Bill Clinton scandals

Steele, Shelby (1946-present) author and scholar of mixed Black and White heritage a brilliant writer who tries to encourage his fellow Americans to act as 100% American

Stewart, Potter (1915-1986) mayor of Cleveland and supreme Court justice

Straw, Jack (1946-)British foreign minister Labor-served as **Blair's foreign** policy minister, takes liberal views on most issues, but heroically dealt with The War on Terror and Operation Iraqi Freedom

Taft, Bob-U.S. Senator from Ohio, conservative known as "Mr. Republican" went for the GOP nomination several times but never got it

Thompson, Jim-Republican governor of Illinois-1976-1992

Thurmond, Strom 1904-2004 US Senator former segregationist Democrat, he became a Republican and fought for many of The positions he previously opposed-served in Senate from 1965-2002 which you would think would be a record but since my first writing, it became the third highest (Robert Byrd of West Virginia is now longest serving senator ever)

Tolkien, J.R.R.-1889-1972 Christian scholar, professor, writer "Lord of The Rings" books

Twain, Mark (1826-1910) American writer, one of the first purely so, for being the first to deal honesty with purely American issues like life on the frontier, race relations, and the struggle between youth and manhood.

Washington, Booker T. 1856-1915 American former slave, founder Tuskegee University educator in on every great revolution of America in The late Nineteenth and early Twentieth Centuries from the revitalization of Southern agriculture, to race relations, to training military men for two world wars

Washington, George-(1732-1799) first President of the United States leader of forces in the Revolutionary Army and one of two Presidents to sing The Constitution only one needed to sing the later installment of the Bill of Rights, The first President in world history, and the only man to lead The installation of law and republican democracy in that era, still in place today

Watts, J.C. (1955-present) Oklahoma Congressman and ranking Republican eventually floor manager of the House, first Black American since Reconstruction elected to Congress as a Republican to represent a Southern constituency, one of the best GOP leaders of his tenure and now shines as a talk-show host and businessman

Wayne, John-(1912-1980)American actor known for his patriotic films and his conservative views, helped fight Communism in Hollywood and testified about it before U.S. Senate, he was a photogenic picture of the American icon image

Wesley, John1703-91 founder of Methodism one of the most effective and honored clergymen of all time

Weyerich, Paul (1942-2008) American Catholic activist and co-founder of the Religious Round-table and the Heritage Foundation and with **Jerry Falwell** Moral Majority, in later years he belonged to a group of Proto-Catholics who kept the Mass in Latin and held to more conservative practices and he was ordained a deacon (not a priest since he was married)

Witherspoon, John-1723-1794 only minister to sign The Declaration of Independence he helped establish a progressive outlook on education and institute religious freedom especially among various Christian denominations

Wonder, Stevie (1950-) real name Steveland Morris singer, song-writer, and actor, one of the most talented people alive, very important among other reasons because of all people born with a disability still alive today, he is probably the most accomplished

Yankovich, Weird Al (1959) singer, songwriter, accordion player, parodist, comedian, one of the funniest men alive, also known for getting established talent and new people in videos with them aw such he has reached huge audiences with his audio-visual material

Yeltsin, Boris-(1935-2007) first democratic leader of Russia though a former Communist he was president under Mikhail Gorbachev and fought for independence, led his country 1991-99

Select Bibliography Books Recommended For Further Study

§

*W*herever possible I try to cite work using MLA guidelines but I take full responsibility for anything not properly cited. Other lists of indispensable books or less important but still recommended books can be made available and of course I will write about many of these other people I mentioned and cite specific works as my writing becomes more widely read, so if you The reader want to see better material you have to read my current work and get others to read it.

The Bible of course is always The most indispensable book throughout this book all cited quotes are from The New International Version (NIV) though most all translations are good as long as they were made to translate The Word of God and get men and women understanding The revealed Word as God wrote it. All growing Christians should have at least two translations handy at all times, and more is better.

The Great Republic: A History of America by Winston Churchill *updated with expanded text and commentary from great speeches by Winston S. Churchill, III Copyright, 2000, introduction and notes 1999, Winston S. Churchill. III*

The History of The English-Speaking People, re-released by Barnes and Noble Press, 1995

The Gathering Storm, Winston Churchill, Winston Churchill Foundation, Riverside Press, Cambridge, 1946

the Grand Alliance, Winston Churchill Cambridge, 1946

Forty Ways to Look at Winston Churchill, ny Gretchen Rubon, a Ballentine Book published by Random House, New York, 2003

Franklin and Winston: The Intimate Story of an Epic Friendship by Jon Mecham Published by Random House, Publishing Group, New York, 2003

Mere Christianity by C.S. Lewis published in The USA, by Touchtone Books, Simon & Schuster, 1943

Other Indispensable books by C S Lewis: *Miracles, first published in The USA In 1947; The Problem of Pain; A Mind Awake.* Harper Collins 1962, a compilation of quotes by C.S. Lewis, edited with an Introduction by Walter Hooper, 1968 *surprised by Joy, re-released, 1986, copyright by Owen Barfield; The Abolition of Man originally written in 1944* copyright C.S. Lewis, copyright renewed, 1972 by Alfred Cecil Hardwood and Owen Barfield. *Letters to Malcolm Chiefly on Prayer* published in the USA, Harcourt Brace, and company, Copyright to The C.S. Lewis estate; the Four Loves, copyright to C.S. Lewis and Joy Lewis. The Business of Heaven, Copyright C.S. Lewis, PTC LTD 1984; the Lion, the Witch, and The Wardrobe (with all other Narnia books, unless specified, available from Touchstone) *Screwtape Letters,* by C.S. Lewis, Touchstone Books edition, division of Rockefeller Center, New York, New York, 1982 CSL copyright 1962

Jack, a Life of C.S. Lewis by George Sayer, Harper and Roe, published in the USA Crossway, a division of Good News Publishers, Wheaton, Illinois

King Came Preaching, Dr. Merwyn A. Warren InterVarsity Press, Downers Grove, Illinois Copyright 2001

Why We Can't Wait, Martin Luther King Signet, 1964

This Incredible Century, Norman Vincent Peale, published by the Peale Center for Christian Living, 1991

The Power of Positive Thinking, Fawcett Crest Publishers, 1956

The Downing Street Years, Margaret Thatcher published in The USA BY Harper Collins, 1997

The Story of my Life, Helen Keller, Bantum Books, 1902

Standing Firm, Dan Quayle, Harper, San Fransisco in association with Zondervan, 1993

Worth fighting For Dan Quayle Harper, San Francisco/Zondervan

Just As I Am: The Autobiography of Billy Graham, Copyright Harper Collins in Association with Zondervan, 1997

Peace with God by Billy Graham, originally written in 1953, re-released, W Publishing Group, Copyright, 1994

Angels by Billy Graham, Doubleday and Company, Inc Garden City, New York, 1975

Reagan: AN American Life by Ronald Reagan, Simon and Schuster, 1990

A New Song, Pat Boone, Creation House Publishers, 1976

Bring it On, by Pat Robertson, W. Publishing Group, a division of Thomas Nelson, Inc, Nashville, Tennessee, 2003

Beyond Reason, Pat Robertson and William Proctor W. Morrow and Company, Madison Avenue, New York, New York Copyright 1985

the Ten Commandments: Significance of God's Law in Everyday Life, Dr. Laura Schlessinger with Rabbi Stewart Vogel, Harper Collins, 1998

The New Thought Police, Inside The Left's assault on Freedom, Tammy Bruce *Three Rivers Press New York,* New York, 2001

Joni, By Joni Earaksan (Tada) published by Zondervan, 1970

Language in Thought and Action, by Samuel I. Hayakawa, Harcourt, Brace, Janovich, New York, New York, updated-1978

A National Party, no More, Zell Miller, Story and Hall Publishers, Macon, Georgia, 2003

Truman:1945, Year of Decisions by Harry Truman, published by Time Books, 1955

The New Britain, my Vision for a Young Country, by Tony Blair, Westhaven Press, Boulder, Colorado, 1994

Allies, by William Shawcross, Public Affairs, New York, New York, 2004

the Way Things ought to Be, by Rush Limbaugh, Simon &Schuster, 1993

His Eminence and Hizzoner, John Cardinal O'Connor with Ed Koch, William Murrow and Company, New York, 1989, with funds provided by The Catholic Charities for The Archdiocese of New York Aging services

God's Politician, by Garth Lean, Holmes and Howard, 1987 *Amazing Grace in The Life of William Wilberforce by John Price, Crossway Books, Wheaton, Illinois, 2004*

Strength for The Journey, by Jerry Falwell, Simon & Schuster, 1987

The hiding Place, Corrie ten Boom, with John and Elizabeth Sherill, originally published in London, current editor, Chosen Books, 1971

The New Dare to Discipline, by James Dobson, Tyndale Publishers Wheaton, Illinois, originally published in 1970, re-released in 1992 \

Straight Answers-ibid, 1998 Family Man:A Life of Dr. *James Dobson, by Dale Buss,* Wheaton Tyndale Publishers, 2005

Still Hungry (after all these years) MY Story, Richard Simmons The Richard Simmons Living Trust, GT Publishers Group, New York, 1999

Unlimited Partners, Bob and Elizabeth Dole, Simon &Schuster, published at Rockefeller Center 1988, new edition, 1996

Witness by Whittaker Chambers published, Regenery, Gateway, re-released in 1987

Opening Day: Jackie Robinson;'s first season, Jonathon Eng 2007

Florence Nightingale:Avenging angel-Hugh Sable Press, 1998

My Grandfather's Son, Clarence Thomas, Copyright, 2007, Harper-Collins, publishers

Some Miscellaneous Books

Understanding Bible Doctrines, by P.C. Nelson published by The Assemblies of God Publishing House, Springfield, Missouri, in 27th printing, 1998

A Brief History of Time, Bantum Books Stephen Hawking, re-released 1996 (through many printings)

The Complete Idiot's Guide to World War II By Mitchell G. Brand, Alpha Books, 2004

Modern Times, Harper Collins: AN American Classics Book, by Paul Johnson, 1991

The Book Of Virtues:BY William J. Bennett Simon and Schuster, New York, New York, 1993

The Case for Israel, by Alan Dershowitz, published in Hoboken, New Jersey, by John Wiley Press, 203

Politically Incorrect, by Ralph Reed, published by Word, Dallas Texas 1994

Fighting for Life;by Pennsylvania Governor Robert Casey, Word Publishing Dallas, Texas, copyright 1996

Lend Me Your Ears:Great Speeches from History, selected and introduced by William Safire, originally published in 1992, by The Cobbler Corporation from the WW Company of New York and London, re-released in The USA

The Princess Bride (see also novel by William Goldman) Act Three Communications, films, a Rob Reiner film, 1986

A *History of the English-Speaking People Since 1900, Andrew Roberts, Harper Perennial, first published in Great Britain in 2006, by Weidenfeld & Nicolson first hardcover edition in USA-2007 by HarperCollins Publishers*

The 100 Greatest Heroes-Inspiring Profiles of one Hundred Men and Women who Changed The World-H. Paul Jeffers Copyright 2003,with The Kensington Publishing Corp. 850 Third Avenue New York, NY 10022

Memoirs, Douglas Macarthur-Released 1964-a very important book, but more recent things and good sources about MacArthur will be updated in future books

Corps Values BY Zell Miller

Rush Limbaugh:AN Army of One-by Zev Chafits, 2008

The Iron Lady:John Campbell Penguin Books, LTD 2009

No Higher Honor by Condolezza Rice, 2011

CPSIA information can be obtained
at www.ICGtesting.com
Printed in the USA
FSOW04n0405131117
40943FS